CONDITIONS OF PEACE:
AN INQUIRY

ALSO BY EXPRO PRESS

Building a Peace System   *Robert A. Irwin*
Beyond the Bomb   *Mark Sommer*

Conditions of Peace: An Inquiry

Security
Democracy
Ecology
Economics
Community

Grace Boggs   Robert Borosage   W.H. Ferry
Dietrich Fischer   Sharon Howell   David Orr
Arjun Makhijani   Michael Shuman   Julia Sweig

Edited by Michael Shuman and Julia Sweig

The Exploratory Project on the Conditions of Peace
Washington, DC

Published 1991 by: EXPRO Press
Exploratory Project on the Conditions of Peace
1601 Connecticut Avenue, NW, 5th floor
Washington, DC 20009
U.S.A.

For more information about the Exploratory Project on the
Conditions of Peace (EXPRO), write to the address above.

Distributed by The Talman Company
150 Fifth Avenue, New York, NY 10011

Library of Congress Cataloging-in-Publication Data

Conditions of Peace: An Inquiry/edited by Michael Shuman and Julia Sweig.
    Includes references.
    Library of Congress Catalog Card Number: 91-77041
    ISBN 0-936391-40-5 (paperback)

Printed by Wickersham Printing, Lancaster, Pennsylvania
Book design and production by Rachel Faulise

Dedication

In memory of our colleague, Archie Singham (1932 - 1991), who said shortly before his death that this book would be a testament to the beginning of the end of the Cold War.

EDITORS' NOTE

Conditions of Peace: An Inquiry is the culmination of nearly eight years of work by a group of scholars and activists collectively known as the Exploratory Project on the Conditions of Peace (EXPRO). As Robert Borosage explains in the opening essay, this book grew out of an EXPRO project called "The Citizens' Peace Treaty," which attempted to define how the average person could create a global peace system to replace the war system that has been operating since the beginning of recorded history. Five "tracks" were created — security, democracy, ecology, economics, and community — each representing a different approach to peace. The essays that follow summarize the principal findings of each track.

We are grateful to five people who conceptualized, researched, and wrote up the preliminary conclusions of each track: Dietrich Fischer (Security); Deanne Butterfield (Democracy); David Orr (Ecology); Arjun Makhijani (Economics); and Colleen Roach (Community). In most cases, these individuals endured more than three years of spirited debate and continual rewriting.

EXPRO owes significant intellectual debts to Robert Irwin and Mark Sommer, whose earlier books — *Building a Peace System* and *Beyond the Bomb*, respectively — were the first products of EXPRO and deeply influenced everyone's thinking.

EXPRO board members Elise Boulding, Randy Kehler, Liane Norman, and especially Andrea Ayvazian provided invaluable guidance as we transformed two thousand pages of prose into six short essays. Carol Ferry shared her expertise at copy editing, as well as her unmistakable candor and wit.

We are thankful for many individual donors and foundations who lent their faith and generously provided financial support: Aaron Diamond Foundation, Rockefeller Family Associates, General Services Foundation, New Land Foundation, Streisand Foundation, HKH Foundation, Winston Foundation for World Peace, Tides Foundation, Corliss Lamont, Michael Seinhardt, Kenneth and Harle Montgomery, and a long-time anonymous donor. Ruth Adams of the John D. and Catherine T. McArthur Foundation deserves special thanks for giving a seed grant to EXPRO in 1984.

Among the friends of EXPRO who provided comments and other forms of assistance were Richard Barnet, John Cavanagh, Colin Danby, Paul Ekins, Richard Healey, Saul Landau, Sasha Natapoff, Jim O'Connor, and Marcus Raskin.

Full-time graduate school for one of us and a full-time job directing an organization for the other begat the need for a creative, hard-working deputy. Those shoes were filled admirably by Patrick Steel.

Finally, we wish to thank one another for the necessary humor and patience to get us through what seemed like two of the longest years of our lives.

Michael Shuman & Julia Sweig, Editors
October 1991

CONTENTS

INTRODUCTION

STONY POINT AND THE NEW WORLD ORDER: A REFLECTION

Robert L. Borosage

We can "fulfill the long-held promise of a new world order," President Bush told the nation in his 1991 State of the Union address, "where diverse nations are drawn together in common cause, to achieve the universal aspirations of mankind: peace and security, freedom and the rule of law." The President spoke as war raged in the Persian Gulf, a conflict he described as the "defining hour" of the new world order, a struggle for "a just and lasting peace."[1] The ancient roman adage — *si vis pacem, para bellum* (if you seek peace, prepare for war) — once again was given its ultimate Orwellian twist: if you seek peace, make war. President Bush is not the first American leader to justify war with the promise of peace, but the President's invocation of a new world order struck a deeper chord. It came in the wake of the sudden and unexpected events that brought an end to the Cold War, shattering assumptions that had framed global politics for over forty years. A new order was struggling to be born. Could it in fact yield progress towards a "lasting peace?"

There could be no more fitting backdrop for a review of the inquiry of the Exploratory Project on the Conditions for Peace (EXPRO). EXPRO was founded at the height of the Cold War on the heretical presumption that if we seek peace, we must prepare for peace. At a time when conventional opinion dismissed discussion of peace as silly if not subversive, when peace activity itself was too often limited to opposition to specific wars or weapons systems, EXPRO addressed the question that was given sudden urgency by the end of the Cold War: What are the conditions for a durable peace?

Stony Point

The birth of the Exploratory Project on the Conditions of Peace can be traced to an irritated outburst that disrupted the 1982 Minneapolis Exchange on Disarmament between peace activists from the United States and scholars from the Soviet

Union. After two days of contentious debates on arms control, nuclear and conventional force deployments, and Third World interventions, a long wrangle about NATO and the Warsaw Pact was cut short by a loud, impertinent question: "What is this all about? You are talking about weapons that can destroy the planet? To what end?" No answer was received. The background conference chatter stilled for a brief moment; a speaker mumbled a stock evasion; the proceedings continued.

For the questioner — writer, activist, and philanthropist W. H. Ferry — this moment reflected his increasing dismay with arms makers and arms controllers alike. Concluding that both were devoting too much thought to weapons and warfare, Ferry insisted that it was time to start thinking about peace.

What we need, one acolyte suggested, is a Manhattan Project on Peace. What could be afforded, however, was far more modest. With funds scraped together from small, adventurous foundations and a few idiosyncratic persons of wealth, a small, changing band of scholars, peace activists, and former government officials was brought together to form the Exploratory Project.

Beginning in the fall of 1984, EXPRO's participants met quarterly for two to three days in an austere, Methodist retreat center near the Hudson River known as Stony Point. Their discussions struggled to break through the strictures that the Cold War had placed upon political imagination. Representing a growing number of international scholars and activists probing similar questions, they were able to mine a rich vein of research on peace in Europe and the United States. They plumbed both current policies and fundamental questions: How could the accelerating arms race between the superpowers be reversed? Was violence inherent in human beings? Was war integral to the economic health of the state? The group decided early on that its role was to sow many seeds, and not to germinate just one crop. Different approaches and different perspectives were engaged; no agreement was forced. Participants were encouraged to publish their thoughts independently, and over time an extraordinary array of books, articles, and organizing projects was generated directly or indirectly.[2] To invite concerned citizens into the search, EXPRO devoted scarce funds to publish a study guide on "building a peace system."[3]

In its last stage EXPRO sought to develop a Citizen's Peace Treaty, envisioned as an integrated set of agreements that might enlist citizen and governmental support. The Project created "tracks" on security, democracy, ecology, economics, and community. And each track was asked to inquire into the challenges that would have to be addressed to build a durable peace and to suggest long-term goals and short-term transition strategies. Excerpts from papers written on each track make up the bulk of this reader. The effort to integrate the five tracks into a single peace treaty or proposal was put aside in the end. Differences in focus and approach, time constraints, and resource limitations made integration impossible. Yet taken together, EXPRO's deliberations provide valuable guideposts for thinking about peace as we enter the "new world order" invoked by the President.

THE WAR SYSTEM

War dates in recognizably modern form — that is, with large armies clashing on the battlefield — to the very beginnings of what we call civilization. History is largely a catalogue of wars and conflicts in which peace is seldom more than a brief interlude. Indeed, the concept of peace, as we think of it, probably did not come into prominence until the emergence of nation-states in the sixteenth century. As states began to create internal law and order, military power was increasingly directed outward towards other nations in an emerging nation-state system. As the state system evolved, wars became more destructive but less continuous. Peaceful methods of regulating interstate relations — treaties, congresses, commerce, and mediation — were developed, though never perfected.[4]

The traditional analysts that dominate Western scholarship in international relations, self-described as "realists," view war as inherent in the state system. States are said to compete naturally for power, and they inevitably resort to war in pursuit of their objectives or fantasies. Realists such as Henry Kissinger, schooled in the "lessons" of Munich and the events leading up to World War II, dismiss plans for international peace as utopian, if not dangerous. Democratic countries are said to be susceptible to the mirage of a peaceful world free of the sacrifice demanded by war and military readiness. If, in an anarchic world of competitive states, peaceful countries let down their guard, the door is opened for aggression; "appeasement" only leads to war.[5] "It is essential," writes Yale historian Paul Kennedy, "to conduct peace with constant regard to the war (or wars) that you may be called upon to fight."[6] At best, great powers and shifting coalitions might produce a balance of power that deters aggression and makes war less frequent. But great powers rise and wane, others aspire to global influence, and the resulting struggles invariably take military form.

A competing perspective, the idealist tradition, can be traced back to the liberal political philosophers of the seventeenth and eighteenth centuries — Locke, Rousseau, and Kant. Since civil society and legitimate authority can create a domestic order based upon consent and peaceful modes of settling disputes, idealists argue that a similar order is possible internationally. Achieving international order, according to the idealists, requires the development of international law, democratic processes, global commerce, and special peace projects.

Often dismissed as utopian, the idealist conception is based not on naiveté but on a differing perception of reality. It sees war as an institution constructed by human beings that can be altered or abolished by human beings. The constant preparation for war only ensures that war will inevitably be fought. Focus instead must be placed upon the creation of legitimate authority and peaceful means of settling disputes. Thus, the idealists envision an international civic culture that might transcend the competition of states and might be capable of resolving conflicts without resort to violence.

In taking as its charge the exploration of the conditions of a durable peace, the EXPRO inquiry clearly placed itself in the idealist tradition. But if wars have been fought since the development of the modern state, and if the causes of individual conflicts are truly infinite in variety, how can one seriously think about peace? EXPRO authors found it best to begin by considering the nature of the system that produces war.

In *The Parable of the Tribes,* Andrew Bard Schmookler suggests that wars result from a form of natural selection. In simplified terms, he argues that throughout history militaristic societies routinely preyed on societies that were more pacific. A threatening warrior tribe or nation makes its neighbors feel insecure and causes them to build up arms; those that fail to respond are enslaved or slaughtered. Successive generations learn to meet the perceived threats of the day without regard for the cumulative effect of such responses over history's course. In the process societies become transformed into war systems, geared socially, politically, and economically to the maintenance and glorification of their capacity for organized violence.[7]

EXPRO analysts found exploration of the "war system" a useful starting point for thinking about peace, even as they rejected the notion that it was an inescapable result of natural selection. By "war system," they meant the interactive world of belligerent states deeply committed to war as the ultimate means of settling disputes, a system comprising a wide range of interlocking, reinforcing institutions, policies, and habits of mind that insured constant preparation for war and recurrent spates of fighting.

The Cold War provides a modern example of the war system. At its center were the great powers, the United States and the Soviet Union, each professing an ideology with global aspirations, each demonizing the other as aggressive and malevolent. For the United States, the Soviet Union was, as President Reagan phrased it, "the focus of evil in the modern world."[8] For the Soviet Union, capitalism was inherently aggressive and militarist, and global peace could only transpire through the triumph of socialism.

Each power drew complementary "lessons" from World War II. For the United States, Stalin was equated with Hitler, communism with fascism. Munich had proved that totalitarian societies were inherently expansionist and had to be confronted militarily. To negotiate from a position of military weakness only encouraged further aggression. For the Soviet Union, the United States was the leader of aggressive capitalism. Hitler had proven that capitalist countries evolve toward a fascism whose storm troopers would inevitably invade the Soviet Union. Thus, both countries defined security primarily in military terms.

Nuclear weapons and the threat of nuclear war were central to the rationale and dynamics of the war system. The threat of nuclear destruction, initially more mythical than real, was clear and present by the mid-1960s. There was no defense. Since nuclear weapons could not be disinvented, an enemy attack had to be deterred — a word derived from the latin *terrere*, literally to terrorize. Deterrence was said to be a matter, not of military capability, but of perception. It was not sufficient to be able to destroy the other country several times over; one also had to display a credible intent. Since no one could be certain what was essential for that psychological task — particularly to frighten leaders assumed to be innately evil — the arms race had a dynamic with no natural limit.

The combination of global rivalry, modern technology, and clear-and-present danger resulted in continuous preparation for warfare on an unprecedented scale. The great powers and their allies and clients maintained huge standing armies, an elaborate base structure, and a steady arms build-up. The United States spent over 8 trillion dollars on the military (in constant 1982 dollars) over the four decades of the Cold War. The Soviet Union, a far less developed country, probably spent less but sacrificed more, devoting a far greater proportion of its gross national product to defense.

Both great powers sustained permanent wartime institutions to manage the conflict. In the Soviet Union, with its highly centralized economy, the military and supporting industries were able to command resources and manpower over civilian needs. In the United States, with a market economy and no tradition of maintaining large standing armies in peacetime, the military and a number of private enterprises created what many have dubbed the "national security state." Within the framework of a republican constitution, powerful institutions for permanent mobilization were created: a large military force on constant alert; an active covert and overt intelligence apparatus; and an executive structure dedicated to managing commitments and subventions across the globe. A military-industrial-scientific complex grew up with significant political and economic power. Routine secrecy veiled security policies and institutions, weakening the normal checks and balances of a constitutional government. As Commander in Chief, the President managed crises through executive fiat.

Both great powers sought to mobilize public support for their war efforts. In the Soviet Union, the controlled press and media painted a lurid portrait of the threat from the West. In the United States, citizens were assumed to be isolationist and insensitive to global "responsibilities," and public opinion was seen as an obstacle to be managed. In the early years of the Cold War, McCarthyite purges enforced a social consensus. But even after McCarthy's reign of fear ended, only a narrow spectrum of views was acceptable among those given responsibility for making foreign policy. What the Reagan Administration termed "public diplomacy" — propaganda, fear campaigns, and making the case "clearer than truth," in the classic phrase of Dean Acheson, President Truman's Secretary of State — was regularly employed to sustain popular support for costly weapon systems and periodic wars.[9]

A novel feature of the Cold War was the creation of two opposing alliances — NATO and the Warsaw Pact. Both blocs were institutionalized through joint command systems, common strategy, and ongoing maneuvers and exercises. Their face-off across the center of Europe arrayed the most destructive arsenals and military forces ever assembled.

Over time, more and more of the world was drafted into the Cold War rivalry. Various regions became "theaters" of struggle, from Southeast Asia to Central America. Local, regional, and ethnic rivalries were elevated to crucial symbols of a global war of maneuver. A socialist revolution could transform small, impoverished Nicaragua with its three million people into what Reagan's United Nations Ambassador called "the most important place in the world," once it was denoted a symbol of the Cold War struggle. Both the Soviet Union and the United States sought to reproduce their economic model, or at least to gain clients and allies, in what became known as the Third World. One result was the proliferation of weaponry across the globe.

The war system was strong enough to survive occasional interludes of peace. After the U.S. defeat in Vietnam, conservative administrations led by Richard Nixon and Gerald Ford dramatically altered the thrust of U.S. foreign policy. The military budget was cut by almost a third over five years. A period of détente with the Soviet Union was ushered in after the signing of several strategic arms-limitation treaties. China was recognized. But the war system was sustained. Covert interventions were launched in Chile, Angola, and Cambodia. Arms control only pared excesses from a continuing arms race. And ultimately the war system reasserted itself with a vengeance. Retired generals, hawkish security analysts, and military industry executives began a furious campaign for "rearmament," warning of a mythical "window of vulnerability" caused by theoretical Soviet advantages in nuclear-weapons capabilities. A series of revolutions in the Third World followed by the Soviet invasion of Afghanistan brought détente to an end. By the end of the 1970s the Carter Administration was leading the country into a new arms buildup.[10]

In the realist conception of politics, a conflict between the great powers was inevitable. The United States and the Soviet Union emerged from World War II as the only two nations willing and able to assert themselves on the global scene. That they represented two different ideologies only added fervor to what would have been a conflict in any case. While some realists deplored the excessive militarization of the Cold War, they could see no alternative to the balance-of-power system, which they credited with preventing a major war in Europe for over forty years. Historian John Lewis Gaddis, for example, concluded that we might look back on "our era, not as 'the Cold War' at all, but rather, like those ages of Metternich and Bismarck, as a rare and fondly remembered 'Long Peace.'"[11]

For EXPRO authors, the war system was neither peaceful nor inevitable. Portrayed as a means of protecting "national security," it generated and exacerbated wars across the world. Europe itself was not free of war, as the Soviet Union enforced its order in East Germany (1953), Hungary (1956), and Czechoslovakia (1968). The United States was directly or indirectly involved in combat virtually every year of the Cold War. An estimated 125 wars were fought in developing nations. Even if the origins of many of these had little to do with the Cold War, a remarkable number were nevertheless intensified by the rivalry. By 1987, 27 wars of various sizes were being waged around the world, more than any other time in recorded history, and these resulted in roughly 477,000 deaths. Ruth Leger Sivard has estimated that by 1988 close to one trillion dollars was being spent on military establishments worldwide each year. The great powers and their allies accounted for 82 percent of global military expenditures over the past thirty years, 92 percent of all arms exports, and 99 percent of the world's nuclear warheads.[12]

EXPRO participants, held a perspective that could be found in the American and European peace movements and in the non-aligned movement in the Third World — that the entire Cold War rivalry was a cover story. The elaborate military strategies and exercises in Europe were preposterous charades in a world of 50,000 nuclear warheads. The elevation of small, poor countries like Nicaragua and Mozambique into global contests was irrational. European scholars began to argue that the Cold War was really a joint project of the two Great Powers, an "imaginary war" in Mary Kaldor's term, that served primarily the interests of the armed forces, the defense and intelligence bureaucracies, and the weapons industries within the two rivals.[13]

For the Soviet Union, the Cold War helped to enforce its hold on restive East European peoples and to justify the failures of a repressive and increasingly unpopular system. For the West, the communist threat excused brutal suppression of challenges to an inequitable economic order in the Third World, while putting a limit on political imagination in the First World. Popular revolts were blamed on communists "taking advantage" of poverty and misery. Military dictatorships were justified as necessary bulwarks against revolution.

For thirty years the United States has boycotted and isolated Cuba, an island ninety miles off the Florida coast. For the Cubans, the continuing enmity of the

Yankees provided a constant impetus for popular mobilization and a permanent excuse for the failures of a bureaucratized and stagnant system. For the United States, the enmity provided a clear warning to other countries in Latin America that it would not forgive nationalization of property, revocation of debts, or excessive assertions of independence. The punishments meted out to Cuba also helped inoculate the region from daring to replicate a system able to provide health care, education, and basic necessities for its entire population. By the end of the 1980s, when the continued confrontation lost any semblance of a strategic rationale, both countries seemed to prefer a stable enmity to the uncertainties of a normal relationship.

By the 1980s, the Cold War system, once central to the economic growth of the Soviet Union and the United States, had become an increasing economic burden to both. Mikhail Gorbachev recognized that the Soviet economy was collapsing under the weight of military spending, repression, and bureaucratic suffocation. As he moved to reform the Soviet Union internally, he also adopted "new thinking" in foreign policy: the new goal was to reduce external threats so that attention could be placed on internal transformation.

For the United States and its European allies, the Cold War initially had many economic benefits. Military intervention enforced an otherwise unsustainable export of cheap oil, minerals, and other resources from South to North. Military spending provided a constant fiscal stimulus, with war being an effective antidote to the stagnation that periodically plagues capitalism. The Great Depression ended only with the help of World War II; Korea provided a boost against recession in the 1950s; Vietnam did the same in the 1960s (though it also fueled a destructive inflation). By the 1980s, however, the rise of Germany and Japan as trading states meant that military spending was an ever more costly tax on the U.S. economy. Soviet disintegration was mirrored in the relative decline of the United States in the global economy.

Most importantly, the Cold War began to lose its capacity to persuade. The gulf between its professed ends, security and peace, and its constant product, insecurity and war, became increasingly evident. If the proverbial visitor from another galaxy were told that the only way to gain the blessings of peace was for people to pour their wealth into the production of weapons of mass destruction, to issue regular threats of nuclear annihilation, to sustain vast military bureaucracies and forces, to train their young to kill, and to send them off now and then to slaughter and be slaughtered, he or she would surely consider us mad. When Gorbachev finally set out, in the words of Gyorgy Arbatov, to "deprive you of an enemy," the Cold War system began to unravel. But even Gorbachev could not anticipate the extraordinary democratic uprisings that swept through Eastern Europe, bringing down four regimes and ending the European divide with less violence than Central Park witnesses on a good night.

The end of the Cold War has opened new opportunities to build a system of peace, but for EXPRO participants a fundamental question is whether the institutions of the war system can ever be dismantled. The reinforcing elements of the system — demonizing enemies, defining security in military terms, maintaining large standing armies, shrouding decision-making in secrecy, mobilizing popular acquiescence through propaganda, and celebrating violence through cultural glorification of war — must all be supplanted by the elements of a new system dedicated to peace.

AFTER THE COLD WAR: THE CONDITIONS OF PEACE

For over forty years, events in a disorderly world had to be viewed through the fog of the Cold War. Dramatic global transformations were obscured by the clash of East against West, Soviet communism versus American capitalism. But once the Cold War mists began to lift, old and new realities suddenly came into sharper focus. By 1990, a number of works were published suggesting that the post-Cold War world could be an era in which war might become, if not obsolete, of far less importance and frequency.

Among conservative cold warriors, the collapse of the communist nemesis meant that there was not much left that was worth fighting for. A State Department official, Francis Fukuyama, argued that the twentieth century was ending with the "unabashed victory of economic and political liberalism." Invoking Hegel, Fukuyama argued that history was effectively over because of the widespread embrace of a "universal homogeneous state," which he defined as "liberal democracy in the political sphere combined with easy access to VCRs and stereos in the economic."[14] Although many parts of the impoverished world remained mired in conflicts of historical proportions, large-scale warfare had become obsolete as the inexorable spread of democratic capitalism integrated more and more of the globe into a peaceful world order.

Fukuyama's celebratory essay, while extreme, articulated a growing realization that beneath the Cold War divide, dramatic changes had begun to create the conditions for peace. One such change was the increasing integration of the global economy. As early as Aristotle, philosophers have suggested that the spread of commerce would make war less likely. Nations that trade with one another have good reasons, and strong lobbies, against going to war. Surely this is even more true in the modern, global economy, where giant corporations and banks have constructed complex production and distribution networks that transcend national boundaries. It is virtually impossible for any nation, from South Africa to China, to wall itself off. The prosperity enjoyed by any one people is increasingly related to the prosperity enjoyed by others. National economic plans are now vulnerable to decisions made by distant corporations or cartels. At the same time, formal and informal transnational public arrangements have had to be created to regulate global corporations. In Western Europe twelve countries have gradually relinquished elements of national sovereignty to the institutions of the European Economic Community. The International Monetary Fund, the World Bank, and various informal cooperative arrangements have evolved to create a rudimentary regulatory structure for the global economy. In this kind of environment, wars, even regional wars, are increasingly viewed as disruptive and unprofitable.

Nations seeking to prosper in the new global marketplace must educate their citizens and open their borders to new information technologies at the base of the new global economy. Computers, faxes, and xerox machines are not inherently subversive, but as more citizens acquire these technologies, and as ideas flow across borders, authoritarian structures will be harder and harder to maintain. The democratic currents in recent years that swept the world from South Africa to Tiananmen Square, from Argentina to Eastern Europe, were spurred on by the example of struggles elsewhere. A new global civic awareness is emerging. At the very least, atrocities in even the most distant countries can no longer pass without notice. What had long been a tenet of liberal philosophy — that the spread of commerce and ideas will make war less imaginable — seems no longer merely an article of faith, but an immediate prospect.

If the global economy has rendered war less profitable, modern military technology has made it more irrational. Both superpowers concede that a nuclear war between them is unthinkable. A nuclear war would create such untold catastrophes — economic ruin, plagues, whole regions unfit for human habitation, even a "nuclear winter" — that the victor could not be distinguished from the vanquished. After four years of fueling the largest peacetime military buildup in history, even Ronald Reagan, the most conservative president in modern times, began repeating the mantra that "nuclear war can never be won and must never be fought." Given the growing destructiveness of non-nuclear weaponry and the risk that their use could escalate into a nuclear war, large-scale conventional war also seemed increasingly counterproductive.[15] In Vietnam, Afghanistan, and even little Nicaragua, both superpowers learned the limits of their technological military prowess when faced with determined nationalist movements in otherwise impoverished nations.

With the end of the Cold War, both conservative and progressive thinkers began to change their ideas about what constituted security. We are moving from a "geostrategic to a geoeconomic era," wrote the hawkish pundit Edward Luttwak, in which "methods of commerce are displacing military methods."[16] Dovish scholars like Richard Barnet have called attention to pressing "real security" concerns that had been slighted in the ideological passions of the Cold War — environmental degradation, growing economic inequality, and the uncontrolled flow of drugs and guns.[17]

The crisis of ecological sustainability is a dramatic testiment to the real security threats we all have in common. Writing for EXPRO, ecologist and educator David Orr argues that both environmental hazards and nuclear weapons "threaten the survival of human kind. They differ primarily in the speed with which they might render the planet uninhabitable, but not in their finality. We may have only a few years — perhaps a decade or two — to reverse some trends such as ozone depletion and global warming."[18] No national boundary line or known defense system can deflect pollution, acid rain, solar radiation, or climate change. Nor can these challenges be solved by the West without the East or the South. Chernobyl was a Soviet disaster until the wind blew over Western Europe. The Grande Carajas iron ore project in Brazil, which has entailed the removal of forests from an area larger than France and Britain put together, threatens the entire world's biological diversity and carbon cycle.

The pressing, interrelated threats of environmental degradation and poverty can only be adequately addressed outside the assumptions of the war system. Indeed, military power not only provides no answer to these threats but also exacerbates them. The war in the Persian Gulf, for example, like recent wars in Southeast Asia and Central America, created several eco-disasters of unprecedented scope: the fouling of the Persian Gulf with the largest oil spill in history; the poisoning of the region's air with plumes of toxic smoke from burning oil wells; and the outbreak of epidemics in Iraq from the devastation of allied bombing.[19]

The spread of democracy throughout Eastern Europe, Latin America, and parts of Africa provides a further element in the obsolescence of war theories. "[T]he unprecedented fact about the present day," summarized *Los Angeles Times* columnist William Pfaff, is that "the leading powers are democracies and history suggests that democracies do not go to war with one another."[20] If democracy takes root in the Soviet Union, Eastern Europe, and Latin America, large areas of the world might look forward to a more peaceful order.

Added to this is the remarkable commitment to disarmament by three of the four major global powers. The rising economic powers, Germany and Japan, retain constitutional limitations on their military forces, and in both countries popular majorities strongly oppose a more active military posture. The outcome of the political upheaval occurring in the Soviet Union is unpredictable, but the current leadership has resolutely wedded the process of internal reform to an active peace policy abroad. No matter what happens to Gorbachev's reforms, even conservative commentators admit that it is hard to envision the Soviet Union becoming a major threat to the United States and its allies in the near future.

Could it be that an interdependent, democratic, and peaceful world order is coming into being? Realists, of course, dismiss what Henry Kissinger called the "false dreams of a new world order." The world is changing from a clear, bipolar conflict to an "infinitely more complex" era "of turmoil," Kissinger argues. Economic rivalries with Japan and Europe, nationalist conflicts, fanatical fundamentalist forces all pose profound security challenges.[21]

Ironically, EXPRO participants tend to have a similarly skeptical assessment of the current moment. They view the obsolescence-of-war theoreticians as offering a strange melange of insightful analysis and blindered naiveté. True, broad areas of the world — in Europe, and in North and South America — enjoy what Kenneth Boulding has called a "stable peace." And true, the spread of weapons of mass destruction, the evolution of an integrated global economy, and the spread of democracy all serve to make war more costly and more irrational than before. But however irrational, war seems no less prevalent. Nuclear weapons have not prevented nuclear or non-nuclear powers from waging full-scale wars. The proliferation of conventional weaponry across the world has fueled wars of escalating violence and destructiveness. The first post-Cold War years witnessed the U.S. invasion of Panama, the Iraqi occupation of Kuwait followed by the Gulf War, increased tensions between India and Pakistan and between Israel and its Arab neighbors, Syrian control of Lebanon, violent civil wars in Liberia and Ethiopia, coup attempts in the Soviet Union, the Philippines, and elsewhere, and continuing "low intensity" conflicts in Cambodia, Afghanistan, Angola, and El Salvador.

The new global economy is also not an unmixed blessing for peace. As EXPRO author Arjun Makhijani argues, nations and peoples are not integrated into the new global marketplace in similar or equitable ways. Nothing is more disruptive of traditional cultures or economic arrangements than the encroachment of the modern capitalist economy. In poorer countries, for example, export agriculture has driven millions of peasants off subsistence farms and into squalid urban slums. There they provide a reserve of unemployed labor, becoming a source of turmoil and migration, a spore of disease and desperation. The World Bank estimates that almost one in six of the world's people are chronically malnourished. The gap in per capita income between developed and developing countries is now over twice as large as it was thirty years ago. Every minute, it is estimated, 15 children in the world die for want of essential food and inexpensive vaccines. While advertising a material life of unimaginable splendor available only for a few, the new global economy exacerbates this inequality, foments national and ethnic resentments, and causes economic dislocations that are often the breeding grounds for violence. The spread of fundamentalist and separatist movements, for instance, may be directly related to the encroachment of a global materialist economy, beyond the control of the national governments.

The growing threat to the global environment may divide as easily as it unifies. The struggle for scarce resources is a traditional source of war, and if the Western consumerist culture cannot be sustained on a global level, the conflict over who will bear the cost of change is likely to be fierce. Pressure might build for what David Orr calls a "global eco-mangerialism," enforcing adjustments on the weak by the strong. Already some mainstream environmentalists envision "an IMF of ecology," which would condition Third World debt relief on population controls, wilderness preservation, and energy consumption ceilings. One could even imagine that someday the United States, the most indebted nation in the world and the largest per capita consumer of energy, might be subjected to similar conditions. Any global consensus on what to do is likely to break down as the sacrifices needed become significant. "Ecological scarcity," William Ophuls has argued, could create "overwhelming pressures toward political systems that are frankly authoritarian" — and toward a global system with more war and strife.[22]

Nor does the spread of newborn democracy necessarily offer an antidote to war. Democracies do not tend to wage war on one another, but over the last few decades Western democracies have fought or funded many of the wars in Asia, Africa, and Latin America. As is evident in Central America, military interventions generally make evolution toward democracy more rather than less difficult. In point of fact, most of the world is still governed by authoritarian regimes, and many of the newer democracies in Latin America and elsewhere are hardly robust, stable political systems. In many so-called democracies, elections are more for foreign consumption than domestic effectiveness, and civilian government is at best a threadbare glove that scarcely conceals the iron fist of the military. The fate of the Weimar Republic provides ample warning of the dangers of unstable democratic systems that are jerry-built on volcanic social and economic soils.

For EXPRO authors the end of the Cold War has opened dramatic new possibilities. The last fifty years have laid the groundwork for new forms of relations and conflict resolution at an international level. The irrationality of defining security in military terms and seeking peace through war has become more apparent. The material basis for a new transnational society has been built. But the institutions, political economy, and habits of mind that constitute the war system remain in place. The end of the Cold War will not produce a new era of peace, unless *all* the elements of the war system are dismantled and supplanted by new arrangements that can sustain and nurture peace.

THE PEACE SYSTEM

What are the elements of a durable peace? Answering this question is difficult, because war is such an integral part of our civilization that it is tough to envision a world without it. Idyllic, pastoral images of sheepherders tending to quiet pursuits come quickly to mind. When imagining how this Garden of Eden might be reached, there is a widespread tendency to envision a terrible cataclysm — a war to end wars, a natural catastrophe. For many EXPRO participants, however, cataclysm would more likely produce the grotesque, violent world depicted in the post-apocalypse Mad-Max movies that were popular in the 1980s. EXPRO therefore sought paths to a durable peace that could be built gradually, a peace that could withstand inevitable conflict and turmoil.

Most EXPRO members assumed that a peace system must be grounded less on nobility than on self-interest, and it must be built on the assumption that humans are not saintly but frail. Progress towards a peace system cannot wait for universal disarmament or a sudden conversion of humanity to nonviolence. Indeed, just as the war system has survived periods of peace, a peace system would have to be able to survive the periods of war. Mechanisms would have to be developed to isolate and channel conflicts. EXPRO authors tried to envision a peace system with all the complexity and internal dynamism of the war system. The U.S. Joint Chiefs of Staff define "strategy" as "the art and science of developing and using political, economic, psychological and military forces as necessary during peace and war to ... increase the probabilities and favorable consequences of victory and to lessen the chances of defeat."[23] Just as war strategists systematically plan the complete mobilization of social forces for modern warfare, EXPRO participants assumed that a peace system would entail dramatic social transformations, revamped security doctrines, new habits of mind, and many interrelated political, economic, and cultural policies to reinforce the possibility of peace.

The "tracks" of the EXPRO investigation — on security, democracy, ecology, economics, and community — ultimately made many recommendations for new policies and institutions, some of which are discussed in the essays that follow. From these can be drawn a set of common-sense strategies for peace, guideposts by which current or proposed policies may be assessed.

Common Security: Mutually Assured Survival

Any system of peace must be grounded on a far broader conception of defense than that of the warrior states. In the Cold War system, national security was defined primarily as a matter of meeting military threats through military means. Yet, today's threats to security come from many sources. Economic dislocation, environmental degradation, cultural and nationalist antagonisms may all be as much a source of violence as hostile military forces.

Just as the nature of threats needs to be redefined, so does the response. The dominant strategic paradigm has been deterrence through military superiority.

War planners assumed hostility and prepared for a "worst case" scenario, building sufficient forces not only to deter attack but also to insure victory in the event of attack. Their assumption was that we will be more secure if our adversaries are more vulnerable. This has led us to create provocative, threatening military postures that have generated equally provocative responses from our adversaries. As Dietrich Fischer writes, "Security sought at the expense of others cannot last. If others feel that we pose a threat to them, they will naturally wish to counter that threat. That in turn reduces our security."[24] Provocative security policies lead an adversary either to match our armaments, which fuels a wasteful arms race, or to launch a preemptive first strike, which means war.

A peace system, EXPRO participants suggest, should be grounded on the concept of common security, in which all nations seek mutually assured survival. Common security is based on two related principles. First, nations should actively try to prevent and resolve conflicts long before violence occurs. And second, nations should try to increase the security of all nations, especially their adversaries. These principles are not utopian. They assume that countries and peoples will act in their own self-interest, and that they will have differing interests, some complementary, some not. Even if conflicts are inevitable, they need not end in war. Through conscientious peacemaking efforts, mutually satisfactory arrangements for resolving disputes can be found.

Active Peace Policy

A first element of a common security strategy would be to embrace what Dietrich Fischer has dubbed an "active peace policy." This entails a fundamental commitment to crisis prevention instead of just crisis management. Nations carrying out an active peace policy would seek to anticipate and defuse potential sources of conflicts, to mediate or otherwise resolve those that do arise, and to isolate those that become violent.

Many mechanisms for conflict resolution already exist, but they are starved for respect, resources, and recourse. The arts of diplomacy, mediation, arbitration, law, and litigation — the civilizing mechanisms for resolving conflicts that were so often disdained during the Cold War — must be given far greater priority by leaders, media, and citizens. An active peace policy would seek to weave a web of institutions and relationships charged with anticipating, defusing, and mediating conflict. The budget of U.N. international agencies would grow as the budgets of national military establishments declined. The United Nations would be given the mandate and resources to monitor the peace and to bring reports on potential conflicts to the world's attention. U.N. mediation, World Court adjudication, and a host of informal and formal forms would be mobilized, along with world attention, to prevent a dispute from turning violent. U.N. peacekeeping forces would receive the political and financial support they needed. The Cold War divide effectively blocked the use of these mechanisms for over four decades, but now, with the Cold War over, there is a new opportunity to revive them.

In the idealist conception, a world government enforcing the rule of law has often been seen as the prerequisite for any system of peace.[25] But world government presumes a global order of universal legitimacy and acceptance that, if ever achieved, will only be the end product of a very long process. An active peace policy, in contrast, does not depend upon a settled legal order. It emphasizes initiatives at a range of levels — citizen diplomacy, municipal foreign policy, state-to-state mediation, regional security arrangements, international institutions — that can prevent and resolve conflicts long before they explode into war. Active peace initiatives would consciously seek to develop what might be called a common law of peace, a body of precedents upon which is built an international legal order through practice, not declaration. Collective military security would be under-taken with international sanction only as a last resort. The goal would be, not to demonstrate that military prowess can enforce a legal order, but to perfect peaceful mechanisms that can successfully resolve conflict at a lower cost.

Perhaps the best example of the potential of an active peace policy has been provided by the "new thinking" of Soviet President Mikhail Gorbachev. Anxious to end Soviet isolation internationally and to gain breathing space for internal reform, Gorbachev launched a series of efforts to defuse tensions with his adversaries. He sought to settle ongoing regional conflicts in Central America, Angola, Afghanistan, and Southeast Asia. He proposed cooperative projects with the West to address the "common concerns of mankind" — hunger, disease, and environmental depredation. He unleashed a blizzard of exchanges, negotiations, and unilateral initiatives, all designed to increase cooperation and calm fears. He supported the U.S.-led collective response to the Iraqi invasion of Kuwait. He allowed democratic revolutions to sweep Eastern Europe, even as they united Germany and brought the Warsaw Pact to an end. As a result, he has gained political space and foreign assistance for reforms inside the Soviet Union and increased the nation's security from external attack at a time of internal discord and upheaval.

With the collapse of the Warsaw Pact and the transformation of the East, Europe is now developing a wide range of security and economic arrangements that could provide something of a model for active peace policies in other regions. The Conference on Security and Cooperation in Europe (CSCE) could provide a forum for anticipating and defusing conflicts caused by traumatic economic changes, nationalist revivals, and ethnic tensions. The European Economic Community could expand its membership to insure growing economic integration of Eastern Europe with the West. The pan-European environmental institution proposed by

Gorbachev could provide minimum standards for ecological protection. The Bank for European Reconstruction and various national aid programs could help channel aid toward sustainable development in the East. The Council of Europe and an expanded European Parliament could monitor compliance of all European nations with regional legislation on human rights. These diverse institutions could provide the basis for isolating and limiting conflicts in Europe, while leaving enough political space for national diversity. As economic integration and political coordination grow, national sovereignty will be weakened, and thus movements for local autonomy or even independence — for Croats or Lithuanians, Welshmen or Scots — will become less threatening or disruptive. It becomes possible to envision a regional civic order that can resolve conflicts without violence, or at least insures that violent upheavals are met with an active, regional response.

An active peace policy requires a change in policy and priorities among the industrialized nations. As Michael Shuman, Hal Harvey, and Daniel Arbess have pointed out, the United States now spends an estimated 21 times as much on military forces as on various diplomatic and peacekeeping functions.[26] The Reagan Administration was particularly contemptuous of the United Nations and its adjunct bodies. The United States and the Soviet Union have generally cooperated with the United Nations only when it was convenient, and currently the United States is the largest scofflaw in unpaid dues to the U.N. system. The United States has refused to commit itself to the jurisdiction of the World Court and has essentially ignored the Court's ruling on its illegal covert war against Nicaragua. The unilateral use of force in Grenada and Panama and the rush to war in the Persian Gulf also contradict any commitment to building a common law of peaceful conflict resolution.

Commitment to international mechanisms would be complemented by the spread of a wide range of private and nongovernmental peace initiatives. Citizen diplomacy, for example, can help break down misconceptions and provide novel solutions to conflicts. Efforts by the National Resources Defense Council to monitor Soviet underground nuclear testing, for example, have helped lay the groundwork for a comprehensive test ban treaty. Similarly, it was "détente from below," the dense network of relations formed between dissident groups in Eastern Europe and peace groups in the West, that helped sustain the democratic movements in the East that eventually took advantage of the political space opened up by Gorbachev's "new thinking."

A Disarming Process

Another component of an active peace policy is the systematic reduction of the role and weight of military force in international affairs. Ever since the Old

Testament's injunction that we turn our swords into ploughshares, peacemakers have considered disarmament as essential to any durable peace. After reviewing the history of arms control, however, many of EXPRO's participants concluded that peace movements had focused too much attention on weapons. Nuclear weapons are so destructive that even dramatic cuts in nuclear arsenals would have little effect on the threat they pose. In the Soviet-American rivalry, moreover, arms control became primarily a tool to manage a continuing arms race.

Complete and general disarmament may be the stated goal of arms control negotiations, but it can only be the product of a long era of peace. Since nuclear weapons cannot be disinvented, disarmament requires either universal trust or perfect verification. In reality, if we are lucky enough to avoid a nuclear cataclysm and build a durable peace system, nuclear powers are likely to retain some nuclear weapons rusting in their silos, like the "shattered visage" in Shelley's *Ozymandias*. The more immediate challenge is how to begin a disarming process that builds down nuclear and conventional arsenals.

Drawing on work done primarily by scholars in Europe, EXPRO authors Mark Sommer, Dietrich Fischer, and Michael Shuman argue that a transition strategy might focus on what B. H. Liddell Hart called "qualitative disarmament," a phased transition to a non-offensive defense posture that would eliminate those weapons and forces sculpted for attack, while leaving or building up those suitable only for defense. At the far end of the process, military forces might even be largely replaced by civilian-based defense, in which an entire population would train in the art of repulsing invaders through small militias or nonviolent resistance.

Any country can transform its military posture to defense unilaterally without waiting for mutual agreements. The impact of Gorbachev's unilateral reductions of Soviet forces in Eastern Europe illustrates the power of the concept. The Soviet Union remains a communist nation with a massive nuclear arsenal, yet its announcement of unilateral withdrawals of 500,000 troops from Eastern Europe in December 1988 radically transformed the West's perception of the Soviet threat.

In a peace system, the elimination of offensive military forces would be combined with a build-up of common security practices. These would include a wealth of confidence-building measures, many of which were invented in the course of the Cold War: risk-reduction centers that link military staffs to explain movements of forces; verification systems that enable international agencies or even civilian organizations to check compliance with disarmament treaties; and international satellite systems that can monitor troop movements, environmental trends, and natural disasters. All of these measures make military forces more transparent to potential adversaries, and thus less threatening.

Non-offensive defense or "defensive defense," was elaborated in the context of the Cold War face-off in Europe, where offensive forward-deployment and "deterrence" strategies fueled a threatening arms race. By the late 1980s, Gorbachev adopted the peace movement's strategy as his own and made "reasonable suffi- ciency" a centerpiece of Soviet military policy, calling for force structures that would rule out "the physical possibility of launching an attack and large-scale offensive operations."[27] This philosophy was at least partially adopted by both sides in the Conventional Forces in Europe (CFE) talks in Vienna.

But by its nature, defensive defense assumed a continued threat by one bloc against another. When the Warsaw Pact collapsed, non-offensive defense became somewhat outmoded. If East joined West, what was the threat that the forces were to defend against? Yet in the agreements forged between the Soviet Union and Germany and those being negotiated in Vienna on conventional forces, non- offensive defense was used as a transitional strategy (even as NATO sought to sculpt a "rapid response" interventionary force for low-level conflicts in Europe). In this regard, non-offensive defense has served effectively as a way station on the road to disarmament. But now, with the end of the Cold War and the transforma- tion of Soviet military policy, dramatic initiatives on disarmament are possible.

The new threat facing the United States and the Soviet Union is the prolifera- tion of weapons of mass destruction. "By the year 2000," estimates Defense Secretary Richard Cheney, "more than two dozen developing nations will have ballistic missiles, 15 of those countries will have the scientific skills to make their own, and half of them either have or are near to getting nuclear capability, as well. Thirty countries will have chemical weapons and ten will be able to deploy biological weapons."[28]

A raft of books and articles have detailed imaginative strategies to enforce and strengthen accords attempting to check the proliferation of nuclear, chemical, and biological weapons. But no attempt to limit proliferation is likely to succeed unless the weapons are made morally and politically unacceptable, as poisonous gas was after World War I. Moral obloquy against nuclear weapons, however, will be difficult so long as the great powers are continually modernizing their own nuclear weaponry. It is necessary, therefore, that the nuclear powers move towards a minimum deterrence posture, in which they would dramatically reduce their own nuclear arsenals, put a halt on the testing and deployment of new weapons, and retain only the minimal number of weapons necessary for deterrence. If both great powers were to move in this direction, the probability of developing a global movement against proliferation would be increased tremendously.[29]

Similarly, conventional arms reduction depends on reducing both the demand for and supply of weapons. NATO and Warsaw Pact nations provide 92 percent of the arms sold internationally. Iraq built the fourth or fifth most powerful military force in the world without manufacturing a screw by purchasing its missiles, tanks, and poison-gas plants from companies and governments, East and West. Military spending in developing countries has risen 7.5 percent a year since 1960, with many of the poorest countries spending twice as much on their military establishments as they do on health and education.[30] Now, with the end of the Cold War, there is an unprecedented possibility of developing multilateral restraints on the arms trade. In developing countries where the wars of the last decades have been fought, military expenditures rose by 35 percent in the 1980s, while per capita social budgets either remained frozen or declined. Japan, now the world's largest donor, has announced that its development assistance will be conditioned on the recipient countries restraining their military spending. Germany has expressed interest in a similar initiative. If other donor countries, along with the World Bank and IMF, were to join in conditioning loans and aid on military austerity rather than social austerity, dramatic reductions in the levels of spending on weaponry worldwide might be achieved.

Together, the Soviet Union and the United States supply close to two-thirds of all the arms in the world sold. This means that simply a Soviet-American agreement on conventional weapons sales could eliminate much of the problem. But they will also have to enlist their allies and new supplier nations like China and Brazil. Developing countries with thriving arms industries will undoubtedly resist efforts to limit them from acquiring the arms (and profits) enjoyed by the industrial nations. To recruit them, at the very least, will require that the industrialized world pledge to restrict its own interventions in the Third World and its own involvement in the arms trade.

None of this can happen, however, unless the supplier nations, particularly the current and former members of NATO and Warsaw Pact, free their own economies from the profits of continued arms sales. Currently, trade in weapons and military services accounts for over five percent of U.S. exports. American producers of military hardware increasingly view foreign sales as essential to their business; purchases from abroad help sustain production lines and reduce unit costs. During the war in the Persian Gulf, U.S. arms producers rejoiced when Saudi Arabia indicated its desire to purchase some $20 billion in modern weapons. One congressional aide described it as the "defense industry relief act of 1990."[31] Other nations are similarly hooked on the arms trade. When Václav Havel took office, he vowed to end Czechoslovakia's arms sales. But by the end of his first year in office, the promise had been withdrawn. With the Czech economy in increasingly dire straits and nationalism on the rise, Havel quietly permitted his industries to pursue arms deals again.

Any disarming process also requires a clear commitment to economic conversion from military to civilian production. In the United States, there are approximately 35,000 prime contracting firms and about 100,000 subcontractors working on military contracts. The Pentagon employs 500,000 people simply to manage the contracting process. In the mid-1980s military production accounted for twenty percent of U.S. manufacturing.[32] Arms production is a lifeline for nearly seven million U.S. workers — roughly 6.4 percent of the labor force — and it constitutes an important income supplement for 1.2 million others. Military imperatives also provide a continued justification for deficit spending in order to give a Keynesian boost to demand in the economy. Without conversion there is little hope for any long-term progress toward reducing military spending or halting the arms race.

Another kind of needed conversion concerns international aid flows. For decades, U.S. military spending has provided a fiscal stimulus to the global economy, which in recent years has been underwritten by foreign investors lending money to cover U.S. deficits. A dramatic reduction in global military spending could cause a global recession if it is not replaced by an increase in other forms of government spending. Military Keynesianism must be supplanted by social and environmental Keynesianism.

If nation-states progressively limit their militaries to defense and significantly reduce the level and capacity of offensive weaponry, who will defend the weak against the strong? Who will police the global order?

For realists, international order is always determined by the strongest powers, but a debate is now raging among realists about the capacity of the United States to police the new world order on its own. Charles Krauthammer, among others, argues that the United States is the "unipolar power," well equipped to enforce global order with its military prowess. Henry Kissinger, reflecting more sober views of the limits of U.S. power, argues that the United States can best play a "balancing role" with others by insuring that no threats get out of control.

For idealists, imperial policing of any variety insures the continuation of the war system. The goal must be to build collective security arrangements, both regionally and internationally. Within the EXPRO community, most concluded that a stable peace ultimately requires an international force to uphold international law. Providing the United Nations with adequate peacekeeping forces would greatly limit the legitimacy and temptation of any country intervening unilaterally into low-level conflicts. Other EXPRO members, however, warned of the dangers of an international coercive force. A U.N. military command could be both too inactive—if held up by the veto—or too intrusive. A peacekeeping force operating under the U.N. Security Council as presently constituted could easily become a tool for the North to police the South. The manner in which the United States used the United Nations to gain international authority for what was essentially a unilateral military operation in the Persian Gulf illustrates the concern.

The aftermath of the war in the Gulf suggests the need to strengthen collective security arrangements through the United Nations. Arguably, if the allied forces in the Gulf had been put under U.N. command, as the Soviet Union requested, the conflict might have been settled without a war and certainly without the ground assault launched in the face of Iraqi efforts to negotiate. Instead of the United States asserting its desire to police the new world order and pressuring Germany and Japan to provide forces and funds for such efforts, a stronger United Nations could have provided a vital counterweight to U.S. inclinations toward intervention.

Sustainable Development

Another component of an active peace system would be to redress the underlying causes of instability. In a world of fundamentalist religious passions, of violent ethnic, racial, and nationalist rivalries, of economic upheaval and growing tensions over trade, the sources of conflict and fragmentation are many and expanding. In broad-reaching explorations, the EXPRO tracks on the economy and the environment ended up focusing on the challenge of sustainable development — how the growing divide between rich and poor can be closed in an era of environmental constraints.

Conservatives, flushed with victory in the Cold War, assume that the integration of more and more of the world into the global marketplace will spread the blessings of prosperity. The growing threat to the environment is dismissed as a question of getting the prices right. The magic of the market, it is assumed, will produce new technologies to clean up pollution and to replace depleted resources with cheaper synthetics.

EXPRO authors Arjun Makhijani and David Orr, however, both paint a harsher picture and argue that the growing immiseration of the South cannot be divorced from the prosperity of the North. Makhijani compares the global system of capitalism to that of South African apartheid, arguing that if we view the global economy as a whole, the disparities in income, health, life expectancy, and literacy between North and South are remarkably similar to the disparities between Whites and Blacks in South Africa. In both cases, twenty percent of the people control most of the resources. And in both cases inequalities are enforced with restraints on labor mobility and the ideologies of racism and sexism.

For much of the Third World, the 1980s was the "lost decade." Mounting debts, IMF-enforced austerity, declining prices for many commodities, and unfavorable integration into a competitive global marketplace have all produced growing desperation, especially for countries in Africa and Latin America. The World Health Organization (WHO) estimates that eleven million children die every year in the "developing world" from easily treatable diseases. WHO director general Hiroshi Nakajima calls this the "silent genocide," a "preventable tragedy because the developed world has the resources and technology to end common diseases worldwide" — but lacks the will to do so.[33]

The North, however, is no longer immune from the misery of the South. For example, migration from poorer to richer countries is now a global phenomena that will produce growing tensions in the industrialized world. Remittances sent back by migrant laborers are now major portions of the national income of developing countries from Sri Lanka to Haiti. As legal and illegal waves of migrants transform their societies, nations in the North will awaken to the desperation of the South. The initial response by many nations in the North has been to tighten their borders. In Europe, the warm welcome given to the first refugees from Eastern Europe has been replaced by fear and hostility. We may be seeing the beginning of a new iron curtain, only this time the barbed wire will be strung by the democracies of the West against a flood of thirty-to-fifty million possible migrants from the East.

The desperation and inequality that generates migration, environmental destruction, terrorism, and violence will not get better without a dramatic transformation of the global economy. Environmental constraints only exacerbate the economic crisis facing the world's poor. David Orr notes that the global economy advertises a pattern of consumption that cannot be shared or sustained. Technological development and the population explosion have produced a deadly assault on the earth's ecosystem — and the window of environmental tolerance is closing. Addressing ecological sustainability is no longer a choice but a necessity.

A fundamental challenge of our time is whether sustainable development — defined by the World Commission on the Environment and Development as "development that meets the needs of the present without compromising the ability of future generations to meet their own needs" — is attainable, and on what terms.

Sustainable development is not a problem for the developing countries alone. To address the twin crises of poverty and ecological degradation will require, in the words of Jessica Tuchman Mathews, "social and institutional inventions comparable in scale and vision to the new arrangements conceived in the decade following World War II."[34] Sustainable development will require a dramatic transformation of the basic production systems in both the North and South. New technologies and new ways of organizing an economy must be developed. Concerted efforts must be made to reduce the use of fossil fuels, to reforest large areas of the earth, and to develop renewable energy sources. And new international treaties, institutions, and enforcement mechanisms will be necessary.

Ultimately, sustainable development may even require a fundamental transformation of "our way of life," particularly in the developed nations of the North, which not only are the largest consumers of resources and the greatest sources of pollution but also are responsible for imposing an unsustainable model of development on the South. David Orr concludes that "economic development is driven as much by comparison as by logic. Until sustainable development is no longer thought of as 'second class development,' it will not be widely accepted."[35] Current economic arrangements benefit elites in both the North and the South, while ignoring the growing desperation of the poor everywhere. Until the hold on power by elites is broken, sustainable development has little prospect of succeeding.

Both Orr and Makhijani argue for international efforts to alleviate the immediate crisis. If the nations of the South are ever to stop ravaging their environments in order to produce commodities for export earnings, Third World debt will have to be relieved. Collective international action from both the South and the North is needed to limit damage to the ozone layer and to reverse our plunge toward global warming. And the United Nations Environmental Program might be strengthened to monitor global threats to the environment and organize international responses. In the longer term, neither Orr nor Makhijani believes that peaceful transitions can rely on either centralized managerial solutions or the marketplace. Makhijani suggests that working people in both developed and developing countries must find new ways to wrest control over the economy from dominant elites. Unless they are challenged, these same elites will insure that the burden of environmental and economic adjustment will fall most heavily on those least able to afford it.

What is needed, according to Makhijani, is a strong international commitment to basic human rights — not only commonly accepted political and civil rights but also a minimum standard of economic well-being, respect for nature, and acceptance of diversity. To achieve this, Makhijani argues for a restructuring and democratizing of international monetary and trading organizations to ensure a fairer global marketplace.

New international controls on global corporations and banks are also necessary. Just as the growth of the national economy and large corporations at the end of the nineteenth century forced the United States to build national institutions to regulate banking, to protect consumers, and to insure basic rights for labor, so the growth of a global economy dominated by multinational banks and corporations must lead to global regulation. Without such standards, corporations will continue to play countries off against one another, "harmonizing" downward global standards for product safety, environmental protection, and labor rights.

Sustainable development also must focus on strengthening democratic movements that seek to expand the level of local planning and self-reliance. Makhijani illustrates the extraordinary difference such efforts can make with the case of Kerala, one of India's poorest states, whose population of 27 million is greater than that of most developing countries. Beginning in 1957, a succession of progressive state governments implemented sweeping reforms in land ownership, agriculture, health care, and literacy. When conservative governments were voted in, citizens organizations were strong enough to ensure enforcement of existing laws. While Kerala has one of the lower per-capita income levels in India, it boasts rates of life expectancy, literacy, infant mortality, and birth that are closer to those of the

United States (where the GNP is one hundred times higher) than to the rest of India.

In the end, sustainable development will depend upon democratic movements in both the North and South making common cause with one another. Makhijani and Orr argue forcefully that thus far capitalism has not provided an acceptable model for sustainable development. But it may well be that there is no "one path" to development when so many dramatic changes must be made in so many different countries, including the wealthiest ones. International regulations—which include setting standards for the environment, regulating trade and capital flows, and protecting basic economic and social rights — must be combined with diverse national and local modes of economic organization and development. Ultimately, sustainable development must be built from the bottom up by an engaged citizenry acting locally, or else it may entail the brutal imposition of drastic controls from the already privileged. New forms of international regulation are inevitable, but if not grounded in democratic movements, they may well become additional sources of conflict.

Democracy and Participation

The spread and renewal of democracy is another element central to the construction of a durable peace system. As EXPRO writer Michael Shuman, an attorney and grassroots organizer, notes, peace requires "leader control." Wars are generated in no small part by warrior elites whose careers and status depend on the perpetuation of the war system. While popular passions can be roused to support war, or at least to acquiesce to them, an informed, democratic populace can help to limit a leader's ability to wage war. During the Cold War leaders sought maximum discretion to dictate foreign and military policy and viewed popular participation as a dangerous impediment to the proper fulfillment of their global responsibilities. A peace system would reverse this relationship. The challenge would be, not to manipulate the public more cleverly, but to build new structures of accountability and promote new modes of popular participation that would undermine the ability of leaders to define crises and wield military force. Leader control also would require a dramatic reduction in secrecy and a broader flow of information.

Conservative commentators share this enthusiasm for democracy — but only for other countries. For some, the aggressive export of democracy should become the central organizing principle for U.S. foreign policy. The U.S. victory in World War II, for example, helped produce successful democracies in Japan and Germany. The timely intervention of the U.S. Air Force in 1989 deterred a coup attempt against President Corazon Aquino in the Philippines. U.S. covert operations and a tight economic boycott eventually forced the Sandinistas to hold an election that they wound up losing. Active intervention on behalf of democracy, conservatives argue, can ultimately oust the kinds of mischievious dictators and trouble-makers that cause war.

Democracies have frequently justified intervention and wars by claiming to defend or spread democracy. For the EXPRO authors, however, the export of democracy at the end of a bayonet is a contradiction in terms. Stable democracies must be grounded upon a legitimate internal order, one that is very difficult to impose by external force. The U.S. intervention in Japan after World War II was successful because it had remarkably little effect on the Japanese governing system.[36] Moreover, neither the United States nor any other country is likely to be consistent or principled in its support for democracies, as illustrated in our recent rescue of Kuwait and Saudi Arabia, the most feudal of all regimes in the Persian Gulf. More likely, any foreign policy built around the export of democracy will become an updated excuse for sustaining the war system at home.

What really makes the U.S. experiment so alluring around the world is its example of material prosperity and political freedom. Indeed, to the extent that sustaining the war system weakens U.S. economic competitiveness, saps resources from cities, and leaves the environment fouled, it undermines the attractiveness of American-style democracy. For many industrial countries, the Japanese system of mercantilist state capitalism, with an elite rule barely tempered by a one-party electoral system, is a more compelling model.

None of this means that democracy is not central to the process of creating a peaceful world. Over the past decade, profound changes have been set in motion by popular, generally nonviolent movements that have challenged entrenched authoritarian governments. Popular movements do not always produce enlightened democracies, as Iran's experience attests, but democratic citizen movements provide the best hope for producing legitimate governments with a minimum of violence.

Shuman suggests that a peace system must be built upon democratic reconstruction of foreign policy, both at home and abroad. Although any peace system must be global in scope, its resilience depends upon the degree to which all decisions, including those concerning foreign policy, can engage citizen participation and democratic control. People-to-people contacts, city-to-city relationships, the bonds of trade, and academic exchange can all help mitigate the easy demonization of foreign enemies that is necessary to engage popular support for war.

The Culture of Peace

Finally, a stable system of peace depends upon building a global civic culture that rejects the barbarism of war. This requires a transformation of popular culture, which too often glorifies aggression, violence, and domination. The global communications network that has helped to make the world smaller and brought pictures of distant corners into our living rooms is brimming with images from American culture. CNN brought the news of the Gulf War to nations (or at least hotel rooms) across the world, but its news focused on military technology and battle maneuvers to the virtual exclusion of political, social, and historical context. Even more destructively, perhaps, the networks competed to market the war as entertainment — a bloodless, high-tech diversion, in which citizens became a passive audience, incapable of participating in a democratic dialogue about policy.

Writing from the vantage point of Detroit, where the war system has virtually gutted a once vibrant metropolis, EXPRO writers Grace Boggs and Sharon Howell decry popular American culture, which routinely romanticizes violence, conflict, and military prowess. They question the value of spreading the habits and rituals of what the Senate Judiciary Committee concluded was "the most violent and self-destructive nation on earth," where over 23,000 people were murdered last year. If global culture becomes homogenized around U.S. values, it could spread the primacy of violence and apathy rather than any shared sense of a global commons.

But new communications technologies are also helping to foster a new, vibrant, transnational civic culture. Citizen movements armed with computer networks, faxes, and video cameras are already having major influence on the consciousness of citizens and the policies of nations. The best example is the extraordinary spread of the global environmental movement and the development of what U.N. Secretary General Peres de Cuellar has called "earth patriotism."

Any peace system must be grounded in a new global civic culture, one built at the grassroots. The human rights movement, led by Amnesty International, has had a remarkable civilizing influence. The peace, labor, and dissident movements in Europe created a process of "détente from below" that snowballed into the popular revolutions that transformed the East. Indeed, one of the characteristics of our time is that it is generally nonviolent, mass movements — in the Philippines, Eastern Europe, Iran, Haiti, and elsewhere — that are overturning encrusted old orders. Even as militaries grow more powerful and dictatorships more efficient, unarmed popular uprisings are becoming the engines of political transformation.

Remaining Puzzles

This sketch of the basic elements of a peace system reveals some of the contradictions with which those seeking peace must struggle. For example, there is a continued tension between community-based, democratic decision-making and the development of international law and institutions. As the global economy grows increasingly integrated, as challenges from the environment to the proliferation of armaments become more global in scope, stronger international regulations and institutions will be necessary. But the farther these institutions get from the community level, the greater the likelihood of domination by elites and the weaker the checks and balances of democratic accountability. Poorer nations have already become accustomed to negotiating with international technocrats about the details of their national economic policies. Now, the hitherto domestic policies of industrial democracies are coming under the influence of international institutions as well. The largest reform among major banks in the industrialized world recently took place without fanfare in an agreement initialed at the obscure Bureau of International Settlements. Trade negotiators haggling over the General Agreement on Tariffs and Trade have begun to set ground rules limiting the ability of countries and their local governments to restrict commerce on environmental or health grounds.

International networks of citizen organizations can insure a modicum of accountability and participation in these institutions. But with rare exceptions, global citizen networks are too often dominated by the affluent offspring of the same elites running the international institutions. Even Greenpeace, the fiestiest global environmental organization, is dominated by young men and women from predominantly white, upper-income families.

EXPRO authors assert that the principle of subsidiarity — that is, that decisions should be made as close to the community as possible — must be the cornerstone of any peace system. But it is less a question of principle than of power and practice. A central challenge to any peace system will be whether democratic accountability can be built into international organizations when the basic building blocs of democracy are thousands of miles apart from one another.

The question of accountability is particularly vital because of a second tension — the tension between sovereignty and intervention. An active peace system must be interventionist to protect human rights and provide for basic human needs, to mobilize international concern for internal upheavals and civil conflicts, and to organize global constraints on arms transfers, military maneuvers, environmental pollution, and economic growth. As the global economy generates more upheaval, an active peace system will increasingly seek ways to undermine the sovereignty of nation-states and to limit the power of leaders to act without accountability to the international community. EXPRO's writers are not isolationists. They envision the construction of a transnational network of institutions, laws, regulations, and transactions that will constrain the choices of individual states and communities.

Yet throughout the EXPRO writings is the conviction that international intervention in the name of peace cannot become a new rationale for the strong to dominate the weak, especially through the use of force. EXPRO authors consistently looked for decentralized, self-reliant, nonviolent means to achieve international change, such as civilian-based defense, energy independence, decentralized development, and citizen diplomacy. For each of these policies, democratic, engaged citizen movements are seen as a vital bridge for transcending national boundaries without causing new interstate conflicts.

THE NEW WORLD ORDER

For President Bush and his aides, victory in a Cold War that was assumed to be permanent was deeply disorienting. At the height of World War II, government agencies and citizen organizations undertook elaborate planning for the peace to come. Yet throughout the four and a half decades of the Cold War, while scenarios were plotted for every conceivable military contingency, virtually no preparations were made for the possibility of peace.

The initial response of the Bush Administration to Soviet "new thinking" was denial. Despite the transformation of Soviet-American relations since 1985, George Bush ran for President in 1988 on a Cold War platform, journeying to Fulton, Missouri, the site of Churchill's famous 1946 "Iron Curtain" address, to announce that the Cold War was still on. The much celebrated fundamental "security policy review" at the beginning of the Administration reaffirmed the standard containment policy, what the President termed "the status quo plus." As late as 1989, Marlin Fitzwater, the President's spokesman, was dismissing Gorbachev as a "drugstore cowboy." Only by 1990, after popular revolutions had transformed Eastern Europe, did the President and his aides begin to acknowledge the possibility of a "post-containment era."[37]

The Bush Administration adjusted hesitantly to the new era taking shape, content to reap the public benefits of the sea change in Soviet-American relations that could not be denied. The imminent collapse of the Soviet Union was a triumph for U.S. foreign policy. With the Soviet Union in chaos, the United States was the sole remaining superpower. It faced far fewer constraints on its foreign policies than ever before.

At the same time, the end of the Cold War shattered the case for U.S. leadership. If military prowess were less important than economic strength in the post-Cold War era, where did that leave the United States? In the decade of the Reagan Administration, the United States had gone from creditor to debtor status; record trade deficits accompanied a hemorrhaging of manufacturing jobs. In industry after industry, the United States seemed unable to compete with the rising economic power of Germany and Japan. The Cold War is over, went the quip, and Japan won. The trading rivals seemed to grow more assertive with each passing month. Chancellor Helmut Kohl sealed the deal on German reunification with Gorbachev without consulting the United States. At the 1990 economic summit of the leading industrial nations in Houston, the Japanese and German leaders rebuffed the pleas of President Bush for coordinated policies on relations with the Soviet Union and China. British Prime Minister Margaret Thatcher decried the growing rivalry between the "yen, mark, and dollar blocs."

As President Bush and his advisors struggled to adjust U.S. policy to fit the rapidly changing world, their initiatives had little to do with the peace policies EXPRO prescribed. As Gorbachev sued for peace and worked to limit Soviet commitments abroad, the Administration was happy to help settle long-standing conflicts in Angola and Nicaragua on U.S. terms. Yet the Administration was hesitant to embrace a new role for the United Nations or active peace initiatives. Aid continued to support covert operations in Afghanistan and Cambodia, the economic boycott of Cuba was tightened, and funds for low-intensity conflict in El Salvador were sustained. The United States remained the leading scofflaw at the United Nation, failing to pay over $800 million of owed dues. And with its invasion of Panama and its refusal to recognize the World Court's judgment against its covert war on Nicaragua, the United States displayed a cavalier disdain for international law that made even hawkish senators like Daniel Moynihan blanch.

In Europe, where change was inescapable, the Bush Administration was happy to rely on its Europeans allies to take initiatives toward the East. Its major concerns were how to sustain U.S. forces in Europe and how to integrate a united Germany into a NATO military alliance that had lost its purpose with the collapse of the Warsaw Pact. The United States sought to use aid to the Soviet Union and Eastern Europe as a stick to encourage rapid transition to market systems and integration with the world economy. The Polish government's "shock treatment" was rewarded with U.S. support for dramatic debt relief, but for the most part, the Administration was unprepared to provide the East with the kind of financial assistance that insured the rapid recovery of Western Europe after World War II.

From its first days in office, the Bush Administration faced pressures for action to halt global warming and ozone depletion. Although progress was made, the United States was a notorious recalcitrant. Administration spokesmen discounted concerns about global warming and resisted efforts to provide aid to developing countries to reduce their dependence on ozone-destroying chemicals. The United States did encourage debt-for-nature swaps and some debt relief, but in general it continued to push export-oriented development, domestic austerity, and debt repayment — the very policies that promote environmentally destructive production and investment.

The President's primary focus was to reassert the war system for the post-Cold War world. "The world," the President warned, "would remain a dangerous place." U.S. interests would continue to be threatened by "terrorism, hostage taking, renegade regimes, and unpredictable rulers." If global communism was no longer a threat, "instability" would surely take its place. And to counter instability in the emerging world, "we need forces able to respond to threats in whatever corner of the globe they may appear." The President began campaigning for a "lean, mean military," including a new generation of nuclear weapons.[38]

Despite the enormous opportunities presented by the unilateral initiatives of the Soviet Union and negotiations on conventional and nuclear force reductions, the Bush Administration showed no interest in moving towards a less provocative defense posture. The Administration ignored the invitation of the Soviet Union to join in a nuclear test ban. It pressed for the development of a new generation of nuclear weapons systems — the MX, advanced cruise missiles, and the B-2 bomber. Rather than seizing upon new Soviet interest in conventional arms limits, perhaps by creating a suppliers' cartel that could limit arms exports, the Administration seemed more interested in ensuring that U.S. weapons manufacturers would capture a greater market share.

The U.S. military services responded to the threat of peace by identifying new security threats that mandated continued vigilance. Long before Iraq marched into Kuwait, the commander of the U.S. Marine Corps, General A. M. Gray, argued that "the underdeveloped world's growing dissatisfaction over the gap between rich and poor nations will create a fertile breeding ground for insurgencies [which] have the potential to jeopardize regional stability and our access to vital economic and military resources." Not surprisingly, the General discovered that the post-Cold War world required a strong Marine Corps. Or in his military language, "if we are to have stability in these regions, maintain access to their resources, protect our citizens abroad, defend our vital installations, and deter conflict, we must maintain . . . a credible power projection capability with the flexibility to respond to conflict across the spectrum of violence throughout the globe."[39] The Army, Navy and Air Force all weighed in with their own white papers, invoking a similar range of threats to justify their continued existence. Throughout these plans ran a constant theme: rather than moving towards a less provocative, more defensive posture in the post-Cold War world, the United States needs forces that are more mobile, lethal, and interventionary.

The Bush Administration added that the willingness to use military force would remain the hallmark of U.S. greatness. What makes America different, Defense Secretary Richard Cheney argued, "is that we're willing to put troops on the ground . . . .Americans are willing to risk their lives to insure the security of our friends and allies."[40]

As if to demonstrate the point, the first months of the post-Cold War world featured a remarkably diverse assortment of U.S. military interventions. The President ordered the invasion of Panama in the world's biggest drug bust. The Pentagon claimed a new role for fighting coca farmers in the Andes and began setting up bases and poisoning crops in Peru, Colombia, and Bolivia. In 1989, the

Navy patrolled the Persian Gulf to guard oil tankers at the end of the Iran-Iraq War and the Air Force helped suppress a coup in the Philippines. The military was installing itself as the only cop on the global beat.

When Saddam Hussein invaded Kuwait in August 1990, the Administration quickly saw an opportunity to assert U.S. leadership and prowess. "In the life of a nation," President Bush declared as the first U.S. troops were arriving in the deserts of Saudi Arabia, "we're called upon to define who we are and what we believe." The crisis in the Gulf was called the "defining moment" (later expanded to "hour") that would set precedents for the new world order. Yet, in every aspect the Administration's policy was to reaffirm the basic elements of the old war system.[41]

The crisis reaffirmed, as the President boasted to a joint session of Congress, "that there is no substitute for American leadership." "We remain," Secretary of State James Baker told the Senate Foreign Relations Committee, "the one nation that has the necessary political, military, and economic instruments at our disposal . . . to mobilize global efforts to curb international lawlessness."[42] The President then assembled an international coalition and gained U.N. authorization for the war in the Gulf, but his deeper purpose was to demonstrate the power of the United States to enforce its will halfway around the world.

The international coalition put together in response to the Iraqi invasion and the action of the U.N. Security Council demanding Iraqi withdrawal and authorizing recourse to force were examples of what could have been the beginning of a new world order against aggression. But the White House acted to insure that the crisis reinforced, not a new system of keeping the peace, but the old system of mobilizing for war. The United States acted unilaterally when it placed forces in the desert, began military enforcement of economic sanctions, and pushed coalition forces toward an offensive mission. Economic sanctions were abandoned just when the CIA concluded they were beginning to have serious effect. Negotiations were avoided as the President insisted that there was nothing to negotiate about. Soviet suggestions that forces be put under U.N. command were flatly dismissed. Despite all the pious talk about collective security, the Administration did little more than "make sure to dress unilateral action in multilateral clothing," as Charles Krauthammer later argued.[43]

At home, the President cloaked his actions with the authority of the United Nations, but he carefully asserted a Presidential perogative to act independently in military matters. The "line was drawn in the sand" and the first 200,000 troops were dispatched on the President's order with Congress out of town, despite the fact that the United States had no treaty commitment to Kuwait and no U.S. forces were at risk in the Persian Gulf. The reinforcements that transformed Desert Shield into Desert Storm came on a presidential order issued before the November elections —

but announced afterwards. Even as Congress finally bowed to the inevitable and "authorized" the use of force, the President openly asserted that he could take the country to war no matter what the legislative branch decided.

The war itself displayed the new sophistication of the Pentagon in feeding and managing public opinion and the media. Television turned warfare into a spectator sport, as Americans thrilled to the high-tech accuracy of smart bombs zooming through doorways and down chimneys, only to learn after the war that eighty percent of the bombs dropped on Iraq did not hit their targets. Reporters, as *New York Times* correspondent Malcombe Browne later testified in frustration, were transformed into "unpaid employees of the Defense Department" and enlisted into the battle to control the hearts and minds of the American public, which was as successful as the war itself. The media turned the conflict into entertainment; the Pentagon even announced that its Gulf War highlights video would be produced by National Football League (NFL) films. The massacre of a hundred thousand Iraqis, the ecological catastrophes caused by oil spills and burning wells, the pronouncement by a U.N. team that the "near-apocalyptic" destruction of the Iraqi infrastructure was causing the spread of plagues and hunger, the regional chaos that has ensued since — all of these results were washed away in an elongated victory celebration that surely will last in one form or another though the 1992 presidential election.

For the President, the victory over Iraq defined U.S. leadership after the Cold War. We alone would continue to police the globe. And our "increased credibility" would mean that we would not have to use force often, for the nations of the world now understand that, in the President's words, "what we say goes."

The Administration painted the war as the solution for many of the problems plaguing the country. The remarkable military victory reaffirmed public faith in national institutions and leadership; the President's popularity soared to record heights. The triumph silenced talk about the German and Japanese challenge. The President even suggested that the war would pay dividends in future economic negotiations, giving the United States "persuasiveness that will lead to more harmonious trading relationships." Financial contributions of allied countries provided some short-term relief for the nagging U.S. trade deficit. U.S. companies were rewarded with a significant portion of the $50-100 billion the Kuwaitis would spend to rebuild their country. And, given the awesome display of U.S. military technology, U.S. weapons were once again in high demand around the world. Before the war even ended, the Administration informed the Congress of its intent to sell $18 billion of high-tech weapons to allies in the region. The Administration then pressed for new authority to use Export-Import Bank credits to finance arms transfers to less developed countries. Alan Greenspan, Chairman of the Federal Reserve, further suggested that the resounding victory in the war would help the nation climb out of a recession. Consumer confidence would rise, oil prices and interest rates would fall, and the economy would bounce back. The stock market soared as the run-up to the war began.

In reality, as the EXPRO essays that follow show, the war did little more than shore up the war system. The United States would sustain a "high-tech, highly mobile [military] force," the President declared, "and it ain't going to come cheap."[45] The Pentagon recovered in public esteem much of what had been lost in Vietnam. The military-industrial-research complex would be reinvigorated by arms sales abroad and continued defense spending at home.

The war punctured hopes for an emphasis on sustainable development. The President's energy program, issued as the war came to a close, embraced continued reliance on imported oil, while giving energy efficiency and renewable sources of energy little attention. The United States moved toward a permanent military presence in the Gulf, allied with feudal sheikdoms having an abundance of oil and a paucity of people. The Emirates quickly demonstrated that they had little desire to implement democratic reforms and little interest in promoting sustainable development in the region. Talk of a regional development bank that could alleviate some of the misery of impoverished Arabs was quickly squelched by the Saudis. U.S. military force would guard "our way of life" for the foreseeable future. The President was updating the old system for the new order, leaving its war institutions, prerogatives, and habits of mind intact.

But if the war system is the answer, then surely war is the future. In the Middle East, the war generated new hatreds and divisions, and sowed the seeds for future conflict. One month after the Iraqis were routed, the Israelis and Syrians were edging towards war in Lebanon, and the hopes for a viable peace process were dissipating far quicker than the smoke and fumes from Kuwait's burning oil wells. The brutal Iraqi suppression of civil uprisings by both the Kurds and the Shiites had stilled any pronouncements of a new era of peace. U.S. arms sales would feed a renewed arms buildup.

Worse, the demonstration of U.S. military prowess generated predictable reactions from shaken military establishments abroad. In Europe, France was calling for a European interventionary force independent of NATO (and the United States). The Germans and Japanese were debating whether to loosen the constitutional limits on the use of their military forces. NATO itself was calling for creation of a new mobile expeditionary force to use against undetermined threats. In Pakistan, the foreign minister called for the purchase of high-tech weaponry to compete with the capacity displayed by the United States. Hardline Soviet generals and party reactionaries, stunned by the effectiveness of U.S. high-tech weapons, began challenging Gorbachev's military cutbacks and diplomatic initiatives, impeding progress on Soviet-American nuclear and conventional arms negotiations, and arguing that the United States had only taken advantage of Gorbachev's "new thinking." In August 1991 these right-wing forces almost overthrew Gorbachev — and almost derailed the new era of superpower cooperation he supports.

War is contagious and self-perpetuating. Each war inflicts wounds and creates new threats that lead to the next war. War feeds on itself, drawing nourishment from blood that is spilled. If the President has his way, the new world order will reassert the war system for another generation.

ANOTHER WORLD ORDER?

It is useful to speculate on how an EXPRO peace system might have treated the Persian Gulf crisis. First, the conditions that produced the conflict would have been far different. Instead of a ten-year process of prepositioning arms and building bases for U.S. interventionary forces in the Gulf, the United States would have sought to limit the arms build-up in the region. Supplier boycotts might have kept the Iraqi arsenal much smaller. Kuwait would not have boasted of a U.S. commitment to its security, but instead would have developed its own defensive forces and strategies. If Kuwaiti defenses had been stronger and more self-reliant, the Iraqi invasion would have been more difficult and less likely, or at least the possibility of stalemate or protracted fighting would have been much greater.

The economic situation also would have been different. Greater energy independence in the industrialized world would have changed the nature of the threat. Iraq's invasion might have been condemned as a direct affront to international law, but it would not have posed a threat to "our way of life." Progress toward sustainable development in the Middle East — and greater regional peace — would have eroded the widespread resentment many Arabs felt about the oil rich emirates. The deep-seated antipathy of Iraqis toward the wealthy Kuwaitis — for relying on the West, for exceeding their OPEC quotas, for claiming disputed territories and oil deposits — could have been mitigated by more rational and cooperative development policies.

Second, an active peace policy would have sought to prevent the crisis from escalating. Instead of the Administration ignoring or discounting signs of growing antagonism between Iraq and Kuwait, instead of assuming that Iraqi moderation was being purchased by trade credits and arms sales and that Kuwait's protection was being insured by an ambiguous U.S. commitment, the United States would have sought to mediate and resolve the dispute through regional and international bodies *before* war ever occurred. Saddam Hussein would not have been told by the U.S. Ambassador to Iraq, April Glaspie, that the United States had no stake in "Arab-Arab conflicts." Instead, his substantive claims would have been given attention through well-developed informal or formal processes of mediation and adjudication.

Had the invasion still taken place, the United Nations' role would have been stronger. The international forces would have been assembled under a U.N. mandate and command. They necessarily would have been defensive, designed to deter further intervention while economic sanctions took effect. The President, in contrast, was haunted by a political hourglass. He could not afford alienating U.S. public opinion by sustaining a major expeditionary force indefinitely in the desert. Once the large force was deployed, it had to be used or reduced. He purposefully set the conditions for a ultimatum under the pressure of time. An international force would have been far more sustainable financially and politically; it could have bought enough time for sanctions and conflict resolution to work. Negotiations would not have been shunned but sought. The public would have expected the United Nations to find a peaceful settlement, rather than passively watch the President's manhood drive the coalition toward war.

Greater democratic accountability would have limited and informed the President's actions. Any deployment beyond our normal commitment to U.N. forces would have received full debate and approval in Congress. The decision to adopt an offensive mission would have been debated prior to the dispatch of additional forces. A more thorough democratic debate surely would have revealed the depth of the doubts held by many military commanders (including the Chairman of the Joint Chiefs of Staff, Colin Powell) about the purpose of the intervention, about the environmental and other risks involved, and about the likelihood of chaos following the invasion.

At the same time, citizen efforts, which for too long have neglected the Middle East, would have been under way for many years. Human rights organizations would have been monitoring and reporting on Iraqi and Kuwaiti atrocities. U.S. sister-city programs with Iraq and other Middle Eastern countries would have informed more people about various national perspectives and concerns. A dense web of human relationships might not have prevented Saddam Hussein's march to war, but it might have raised the potential costs and made the likelihood of Western opposition far clearer.

Saddam Hussein was a character from central casting. Where else could one find a brutal dictator heading a warrior state and building a military large enough to be threatening but backward enough to be vulnerable. His clear acts of aggression, resolute repudiation of world and regional opinion, and bellicose posturing made him an easy scourge to oppose. With no democractic checks and balances within Iraq, he might have still sought to invade Kuwait even under a peace system. But there is little doubt that a peace system would have been more likely to remove the causes of the conflict and to limit and resolve the dispute once it took place. Surely, it could not have done worse in preventing war than the war system did.

A durable peace must be able to withstand the outbreak of war. It cannot depend on any one leader or nation. Instead, it must generate a momentum — like that of the environmental movement — to which recalcitrant leaders must eventually bend.

It is vital that citizen movements act to prevent the war machine from continuing to be fed. In Europe and the Soviet Union, strong efforts are needed to resist a remilitarization of relations and to extend the process of peaceful reconstruction across the borders of the East. In the United States, citizen movements must make clear the terrible costs of the Persian Gulf War, and underscore its failure to produce the promised peace and stability for which it was fought. Perhaps most important, the slow process of building links between citizens of rich and poor countries must be accelerated. In many ways, the war in the Gulf may be viewed as the first conflict between the industrialized North and the restless South. If progress cannot be made on building a democratic movement for sustainable development, it will not be the last.

NOTES

1.   George Bush, State of the Union Address 1991, press copy.

2.   A list of publications by Expro participants is provided in Appendix A and Appendix B.

3.   Robert A. Irwin, *Building A Peace System* (Washington, DC: Expro Press, 1988).

4.   Rousseau, among others, makes the connection between domestic order and war: "[E]ach one of us being in the civil state as regards our fellow citizens, but in the state of nature as regards the rest of the world, we have taken all kinds of precautions against private wars only to kindle national wars a thousand times more terrible." Quoted in Mary Kaldor, *The Imaginary War: Understanding the East-West Conflict* (London: Basil Blackwell, 1990).

5.   *See, e.g.*, Henry Kissinger, "False Dreams of a New World Order," *The Washington Post*, February 26, 1991, p. A21.

6.   Paul Kennedy, "The United States and Grand Strategy," in Paul Kennedy, ed., *Grand Strategies in War and Peace* (New Haven, CT: Yale University Press, 1991), p. 191.

7.   Andrew Bard Schmookler, *The Parable of the Tribes: The Problem of Power in Social Evolution* (Berkeley, CA: University of California at Berkeley Press, 1984).

8.   Quoted in Ronnie Dugger, *On Reagan: The Man and His Presidency* (New York: McGraw-Hill Book Co., 1983), p. 353.

9.   *See*, in general, Richard J. Barnet, *The Rockets Red Glare: When America Goes to War* (New York: Simon and Schuster, 1990).

10.   *See*, in general, Fred Halliday, *The Making of the Second Cold War* (London: Verso Editions,1983).

11.   John Lewis Gaddis, "The Long Peace," *International Security*, Spring 1986, p. 142.

12. Ruth Legar Sivard, *World Military and Social Expenditures, 1989* (Washington, DC: World Priorities Inc., 1989).

13. Mary Kaldor, *The Imaginary War: Understanding the East-West Conflict* (London: Basil Blackwell, 1990).

14. Francis Fukuyama, "The End of History?," *The National Interest*, Summer 1989, no. 16, pp. 3-19.

15. *See*, in general, John Mueller, *Retreat from Doomsday: The Obsolescence of Major War* (NewYork: Basic Books, 1988).

16. Edward Luttwak, "Bush Has the Momentum, But What about His Mess at Home," *The Washington Post*, August 19, 1990, p. D1.

17. Richard J. Barnet, "Reflections: The Uses of Force," *The New Yorker*, April 29, 1991, p. 82.

18. David Orr, *infra*.

19. William M. Arkin, Damian Durrant, and Marianne Cherni, *On Impact: Modern Warfare and the Environment: A Case Study of the Gulf War* (Washington D.C.: Greenpeace, May 1991).

20. William Pfaff, "Redefining World Power," *Foreign Affairs*, 70:1, 1990-1991, p. 47.

21. Henry Kissinger, op cit.

22. William Ophuls, *Ecology and the Politics of Scarcity* (San Francisco: W. H. Freeman, 1977), p. 3.

23. Quoted in Sissela Bok, *A Strategy for Peace* (New York: Vintage Books, 1989), p. 99.

24. Dietrich Fischer, *infra*.

25. *See*, e.g., Harry B. Hollins, Averil L. Powers, and Mark Sommer, *The Conquest of War: Alternative Strategies for Global Security* (Boulder, CO: Westview Press, 1989).

26. Michael S. Shuman, Hal Harvey, and Daniel J. Arbess, *Security without War: A Post-Cold War Foreign Policy* (Boulder, CO: WestviewPress, 1992).

27. Quoted in Mary Kaldor, *op. cit.*, p. 247.

28. Charles Krauthammer, "The Unipolar Movement," *Foreign Affairs*, 70:1, America and the World 1990-91, p. 30.

29. Contrast this with the crackpot realism in the suggestion that the United States gird itself to stop proliferation by destroying the weapons production facilities of Third World countries, as Israel did in Iraq. *See, e.g.,* Alan Tonelson, "What is the National Interest," *Atlantic Monthly,* July 1991, p. 51.

30. Steven Mufson, "Study Faults Third World Priorities," *The Washington Post*, May 23, 1991, p. A39 (citing United Nations Development Program, *Human Development Report, 1991.*)

31. For a more detailed discussion and source of the statistics on arms trade, *see* William D. Hartung, "Breaking the Arms-Sales Addiction: New Directions for U.S. Policy," *World Policy Journal*, 8:1, Winter 1990-91, p. 1-26.

32. William Grieder, "The Economy: What Went Wrong and Who Is to Blame," *Rolling Stone*, January 1, 1991.

33. Quoted in Ruth Legar Sivard, *World Military and Social Expenditures, 1990* (Washington, DC: World Priorities Inc., 1990), p. 23.

34. Jessica Tuchman Mathews, "Redefining Security," *Foreign Affairs*, 68:2, Spring 1989, p. 173.

35. David Orr, *infra.*

36. James Fallows, "Is Japan the Enemy," *New York Review of Books*, May 30, 1991.

37. *See,* in general, Robert Borosage, "Bush and NATO — Comes the Reformation ," in Dan Smith ed., *European Security in the 1990's* (London: Pluto Press, 1989).

38. Robert Borosage and Andrew Leff, "The Gulf Crisis: Implications for the

U.S.," in *Crisis in the Gulf* (Washington DC: Institute for Policy Studies, October 1990), p. 24.

39. Quoted in Michael T. Klare, "The New World War," *The Progressive*, November 1990, p. 14.

40. *Ibid.*

41. Robert Borosage and Andrew Leff, *op. cit.*, p. 23.

42. Secretary of State James Baker, Testimony before Senate Foreign Relations Committee, prepared statement, September 5, 1990.

43. Charles Krauthammer, *op. cit.*, p. 26.

44. Quoted in Dan Balz, "Bush Sees Mild and Brief Recession," *The Washington Post*, February 2, 1991, p. A4.

SECURITY

Dietrich Fischer is an Associate Professor of Computer Science at Pace University and author of several books on defense policy, including *Preventing War in the Nuclear Age*. Fischer has long argued that various features of the security system adopted by Switzerland, his native country — including non-provocative defense, civilian militias, and strict neutrality — could benefit the United States.

Fischer recommends that we develop security policies that are capable of not only deterring war but also building peace. The key components of an "active peace policy" are conflict prevention, conflict resolution, and self-defense. Fischer then applies these approaches to Iraq's invasion of Kuwait in 1990 to demonstrate how the Persian Gulf War was an unnecessary conflict. He concludes by outlining steps the United States can take to reduce the root causes of conflict and global instability.

AN ACTIVE PEACE POLICY

Dietrich Fischer

The Romans used to say, if you want peace, prepare for war. But the Romans and their adversaries had no nuclear, chemical, or other such devastating weapons. Today, relying simply on military force to deal with conflicts has become too risky. We now must develop the structures, institutions, and policies of a peace system that can prevent war with non-military means. A peace system must anticipate potential conflicts and seek to prevent or resolve them long before they escalate to the use of force. And it must rely on military force only as a last resort.

The traditional discourse about war and peace has focused primarily on "national" security, military threats, and military means to achieve security. These foci, however, are much too narrow. To achieve true security it is necessary to look at the entire range of threats to human survival, not just intentional military aggression. It is also necessary to examine a broad range of means to achieve security, not just the option of military defense.

Given how few people advocate violence, poverty, inequality, and war, why do we suffer from so many of these problems? One answer is that the old political institutions of sovereign nation-states are rapidly becoming obsolete. Global warming, stratospheric ozone depletion, nuclear war, terrorism, drug trafficking, and Third World debt are all problems that defy national solutions and can be solved only through global cooperation.

Addressing these problems requires an open mind and the capacity to learn and adapt to new conditions. We must discard rigid ideologies and seize new opportunities presented by an increasingly interdependent world. We need new thinking, a *perestroika* of the international system. Everyone in the North, South, East, and West must participate in this effort to imagine and shape a better future, because no individual or group has the complete answer. As Patricia Mische has observed, "Today there are very few governmental leaders offering a compelling, positive vision of the planetary future . . . .We must generate our own vision of a preferred world."[1] Robert C. Tucker has emphasized that anyone able to diagnose a problem and offer a solution can provide leadership, even without possessing official power.[2]

The first advanced civilizations emerged some six thousand years ago because individual households could no longer solve their own problems. No one farmer could prevent the recurrent droughts and floods in the ancient Nile and Euphrates valleys. Large-scale cooperation was required to build dams to control the flow of these rivers. These initial acts of cooperation led to higher forms of social organization, the emergence of written language, mathematics, and science, the codification of law, and the flourishing of music and poetry. Today, as we face more and more global problems that can no longer be solved by any one nation-state alone, greater global cooperation is essential. As the Brundtland Commission Report stated, the separate histories of the world's nations are now entering into a common future.[3]

Nothing has done more to inspire new thinking about peace than the astounding changes that have taken place in the Soviet Union and Eastern Europe since Mikhail Gorbachev became the Soviet General Secretary in 1985. Emblematic of these changes was the fate of Václav Havel. After more than five years in jail for criticizing his government's human rights record, Havel was released in the spring of 1989 and six months later he was elected President of Czechoslovakia. As democratic, contested elections swept across the Soviet Union and Eastern Europe, even hardliners such as Ronald Reagan pronounced the Cold War over. The bitter confrontation between two blocs with hostile ideologies has given way to a free flow of ideas, people, and goods between East and West.

Forty years earlier, the Soviet Union was ruled by Stalin's iron fist. In 1948, Stalin imposed client regimes on Eastern Europe and blockaded Berlin. George Kennan warned of the dangers of Soviet expansionism and formulated the strategy of containment. As Western Europe became increasingly terrified about the possibility of a Soviet invasion, the United States decided to form a series of military alliances, including NATO and SEATO, encircling the Soviet Union with a ring of foreign military bases.

Today, even though we face a very different Soviet Union, the remnants of the Cold War mentality are still alive in Washington. In 1990 the Bush Administration excluded the Soviet Union from taking loans from the new European Development Bank and denied it access to technology and tariff reductions that were made available to China (despite the Tiananmen Square massacre). At the same time the Administration committed $70 billion to the stealth bomber, a plane designed to hit targets in the Soviet Union after an initial nuclear exchange, and requested $5 billion more for "star wars" research and development. Bush also requested that spending by the Department of Energy for designing, testing, and producing new nuclear weapons be raised by 35 percent to $13.9 billion over the next five years.[4]

Confronting today's Soviet Union as if it were still Stalin's Russia is as absurd as treating today's Germany as if it were Hitler's Third Reich. Evolution teaches us that those who adapt to new environments thrive, while those who cling rigidly to outmoded forms of behavior are doomed. Thus far, the concept of a peace system has been almost completely overshadowed by discussions of military strategy. NATO must now begin to develop security policies in Europe that are capable of not only deterring war but also deliberately building peace.

One such change would be a commitment not to use armed intervention or coercion. We have almost forgotten that the recent political changes in Eastern Europe had to begin in the Soviet Union. When Alexander Dubcek introduced reforms in Czechoslovakia in 1967-68, his government was crushed by Soviet tanks. Even if the governments of the Warsaw Pact wished to do so, they were in no position to initiate reforms and defend themselves against a Soviet military response. Reforms could not succeed until a leader like Dubcek emerged in the Soviet Union itself. This, of course, happened when Mikhail Gorbachev came to power and launched his initiatives for democratization, *glasnost*, and *perestroika*.

For similar reasons, a radical change in policies in the West — toward less reliance on military force in international relations and greater reliance on peaceful relations — must now begin in the United States. To be sure, the United States has not suppressed reforms undertaken by its allies with the dispatch of tanks, but it *has* exercised subtle economic pressures. For example, I asked a Japanese friend why his country did not increase its trade with the Soviet Union for mutual benefit. He replied, "It is not so much that we are afraid of the Russians; we are more afraid of how the Americans might react if we increased trade with Moscow. We are highly dependent on the U.S. market for exports. This is why we don't dare to cooperate more closely with the Soviet Union." Even though the U.S. economy is highly dependent on Japanese credit today, Japan's history of being occupied after World War II and given a new constitution by General MacArthur seems to have influenced a succession of Japanese governments to bow to the leadership of the United States. It is noteworthy that Japan did not dare to open relations with China until after the United States took the lead in 1972 (though recently Japan has begun to pursue a more independent foreign policy with respect to China). Another way the United States exercises control over many smaller countries, such as El Salvador, is through subsidies. This is obviously not as heavy-handed as sending tanks, but it is no less effective. And as the invasion of Panama has shown, the United States will not refrain from using force when economic sanctions fail to have the desired effect. Therefore, the United States may in some ways exercise as much control over the West as the Soviet Union traditionally did over Eastern Europe.

The United States also has the power to change the security policies of the West, just as the Soviet Union has the power to change the security policies of the East. But how exactly can the United States or other powerful countries promote peace? What kinds of new security policies should be put into place?

NEW THINKING ON PEACE AND SECURITY

It has been widely asserted that nuclear weapons have helped keep the peace since 1945, but this is contrary to historical facts. The five nations possessing nuclear weapons have been involved in more wars since 1945 than almost any other country. Table 1 ranks all countries by the number of wars they have been involved in since 1945.[5] Table 2 lists the wars in which each nuclear-weapons nation has been involved during this same period. The tabulation does not include military actions that have resulted in fewer than one thousand battle deaths, such as the U.S. interventions in Guatemala (1954), Lebanon (1958), Grenada (1983), or Panama (1989), or the Soviet-led invasion of Czechoslovakia in 1968. Additionally, the list does not include instances in which nuclear nations have financed wars, such as U.S. support for the Bay of Pigs invasion in 1961 or U.S. military aid for the Contra war against Nicaragua throughout the 1980s.

Table 1   **Countries Involved in Wars from 1945 to 1991 (Interstate Wars, Civil Wars and Interventions Resulting in More than 1,000 Battle Deaths)**

# of wars	Countries
7	Egypt
6	China, France, India, Syria, U.S.A., Vietnam
5	Iraq, Israel, U.K.
4	Jordan, Kampuchea, Philippines
3	Cuba, Ethiopia, Laos, Turkey
2	Algeria, Australia, Belgium, Canada, El Salvador, Indonesia, Iran, South Korea, Lebanon, Netherlands, Saudi Arabia, Pakistan, Thailand, Turkey, Uganda, U.S.S.R.
1	Afghanistan, Angola, Burundi, Colombia, Cyprus, Dominican Republic, Greece, Guatemala, Honduras, Hungary, North Korea, Kuwait, Libya, Madagascar, Mauritania, Morocco, Nicaragua, Nigeria, Rwanda, Somalia, Sri Lanka, Sudan, Tanzania, Yemen, Zaire, Zimbabwe
0	all others

Table 2   **The Five Nuclear Powers' Involvement in Wars from 1945 to 1982**

China (6)	Civil War (1946-50), Korea (1950-53), Tibet (1956-59), India (1962), Cultural Revolution (1967-68), Vietnam (1979)
France (6)	Indochina (1945-54), Madagascar (1947-48), Korea (1950-53), Algeria (1954-62), Sinai (1956), Iraq-Kuwait (1991)
Soviet Union (2)	Hungary (1956), Afghanistan (1979)
United Kingdom (5)	Indonesia (1945-46), Korea (1950-53), Sinai (1956), Falkland Islands/ Malvinas (1982), Iraq-Kuwait (1991)
United States (6)	Korea (1950-53), Laos (1963-73), Vietnam (1965-75), Dominican Republic (1965), Kampuchea (1970-75), Iraq- Kuwait (1991)

The five nuclear powers have been involved in *eight times* as many wars, on average, as all the nonnuclear countries since 1945.[6] Perhaps the possession of nuclear weapons by the United States and the Soviet Union has helped prevent a direct military clash between the two superpowers, but nuclear weapons came at the expense of exorbitant military spending, a number of devastating proxy wars, and an ongoing risk to human survival. Four of the neutral and nonaligned countries of Europe (Austria, Finland, Sweden, and Switzerland), in contrast, possess no nuclear weapons, are under nobody else's "nuclear umbrella," and have not been involved in a single war during the nuclear age. This indicates that factors such as refraining from foreign military interventions and actively seeking to develop good relations with other countries have been more decisive in maintaining peace than nuclear weapons.

Only two countries in the world have been free from war since the time of Napoleon — Sweden and Switzerland.[7] Several other countries have had no wars since their independence, but they have not been part of the international system for as long. Both Sweden and Switzerland have maintained a strong conventional defense relative to their strategic importance, but they have strictly observed their promise never to fight abroad (except for Sweden's participation in U.N. peace-keeping operations). The lesson from these two countries is clear. To prevent war, a country must make a potential aggressor understand: (1) if he attacks, the costs will far outweigh the expected gains, and (2) as long as he does not attack, he has absolutely nothing to fear. The first point is widely heeded, but the second point is often overlooked. A concept known as "non-offensive defense" emphasizes both points equally.

A careful observer visiting Switzerland will notice that every few miles along the highways, from the border inward, there are rows of covered holes in the pavement. If Switzerland ever believed it was in danger of being invaded, these holes, typically located in tunnels or next to steep cliffs, would be filled with thick steel-rods to block advancing tank columns. There is not just one such row but a dozen or more in some areas. If one is broken, there is the next one, and another one, and so on. Switzerland seeks to protect itself against aggression through *redundant* defenses.

The countries involved in the largest number of wars have not simply defended their borders; they also have pursued various global "missions." Johan Galtung[8] has stressed that both superpowers are convinced that they have not only the right but the duty, at times a burdensome and holy duty, to bring the "truth" to others. And if persuasion fails, force must be applied. The Soviet Union's goal in the past has been to spread the gospel of socialism. The United States' policy has been to save the rest of the world from the evils of Marxism and to integrate every country into the international system of free trade. Both countries also have pursued economic interests, such as better access to foreign sources of raw materials and to foreign markets.

The Soviet Union has now renounced its long-standing goal of making other countries copy itself. Gorbachev has declared that the pursuit of universal human values must now take precedence over "class struggle." He has emphasized that ideology and the threat or use of force cannot and must not play a role in international relations.[9] When will other leaders follow suit?

As long as a country seeks either to expand its territory or to bring its political system and culture to other countries, by force if necessary, it pursues a goal that is incompatible with other countries' pursuit of the same goal. Such policy goals have been called "self-incompatible."[10] The pursuit of self-incompatible goals tends to lead to war. If a country, instead, were only to defend its borders against foreign aggression, this would not prevent any other country from pursuing the same goal. If every country only defended itself from its borders inward, war would cease to exist. A non-offensive defense posture seeks to achieve this goal by sharply reducing or eliminating arms that could be used to invade and hold territory, such as tanks, self-propelled artillery, armored personnel carriers, bridge-building equipment, ground-attack aircraft, and helicopters. Purely defensive arms, such as anti-tank and anti-aircraft weapons in fixed positions, would be retained or even strengthened.

There are some who claim that it is impossible to distinguish between offensive and defensive arms. Whether a weapon is offensive or defensive depends entirely on its intended use, they argue. For example, when Gorbachev announced a restructuring of Soviet forces to a more defensive military posture, Henry Kissinger commented, "When they say they are shifting to a defensive posture, nobody really knows what that means precisely. For example, a tank has been called an offensive weapon. But it is also said that the best defense against a tank is a tank. . . ."[11] Of course, there exist some borderline cases of arms that can be used either in defensive or offensive ways. But there also exist arms that can be classified unambiguously. For example, a tank barrier in a fixed position cannot be used to invade another country. A first-strike weapon, such as a bomber on an unprotected air field, which has to be used quickly in an attack or else it will be destroyed, is an offensive weapon. To cite one example in order to claim that a distinction cannot be made is as if someone were to say, "There is no distinction between light and dark colors. Take, for example, the color grey."

Non-offensive defense has a number of advantages over a strategy that envisages defeating an enemy by vanquishing the enemy's forces deep in its home territory. It can better prevent escalation of a war that begins by accident or misunderstanding, and it provides little incentive for an arms race or for preemptive strikes. A military force that does not have the capability for offensive operations poses no threat to other countries. This then reduces the pressure on each side to initiate a preemptive attack.

NATO's Follow-On-Forces Attack (FOFA) strategy was called defensive, but it envisioned deep strikes into the Warsaw Pact's territory to destroy staging areas and command posts at the first sign of hostilities. It effectively gave the Soviet Union every incentive to maintain the initiative in combat if war should ever start, because Soviet hesitation would allow NATO forces to advance into Eastern Europe and the Soviet Union. If two neighboring countries have military strategies designed to push any fighting back onto the territory of the other side, even an accidental border violation could rapidly escalate into a full-scale war. But if one side defends its territory up to the border and not beyond, the adversary has every incentive to withdraw. NATO's current defense planning does not provide this incentive. In a region like Europe strewn with many "usable" nuclear bombs as well as a range of increasingly devastating conventional weapons, it is important to have a strategy to de-escalate war.

The competition between two opposing military alliances to build larger and increasingly powerful offensive forces is essentially driven by mutual fear. Purely defensive measures that pose no threat to an adversary, in contrast, cannot fuel an arms race. It is hard to imagine how fortifications in fixed positions, for example, could be perceived as a threat by anyone. Some have sought to discredit a defensive conventional posture by pointing to the failure of the Maginot line. But a good defense would be widely dispersed and cover territory in depth; it would not be concentrated only along the border. The Maginot line resembled a thin egg shell; once broken or bypassed, it was worthless. A good defense should resemble a solid rock; even if the surface has been penetrated it is just as hard to proceed.

Some advocates of an offensive military posture argue that if fighting occurs it is better if it takes place on the adversary's side of the border. But assuming there *will* be war is the wrong premise. A purely defensive posture is aimed at preventing war in the first place.

While a strategy of non-offensive defense remains an important element of a country's efforts to keep out of war, it is not enough. Any country with strong defenses could still be attacked by nuclear weapons and totally destroyed. A country must do more than build strong defenses — it must also pursue an *active peace policy* [12] that searches for causes of conflict and removes them. Non-offensive defense, while an important component of an active peace policy, must be supplemented by a comprehensive set of economic and diplomatic policies aimed at creating a climate in which war becomes unlikely.[13]

An active peace policy should have three main components: cooperation, conflict resolution, and self-defense. Greater international cooperation, especially between countries with a history of hostility towards each other, can create an atmosphere of better understanding and trust and can increase interest on both sides to maintain mutually beneficial relations.[14] If conflicts erupt nevertheless, as they undoubtedly will from time to time, there are a wide range of conflict-resolution techniques to settle disputes without war. And if these fail — if an adversary refuses to resolve a conflict peacefully and then resorts to the use of violence — non-military defenses and non-offensive military defenses can deflect the aggression without escalating the war. The following ten sections, summarized in Table 3, contain brief observations about each of these components of an active peace policy.

Table 3   **Ten Components of an Active Peace Policy**

A. Conflict Prevention

    (1) International Cooperation

B. Conflict Resolution

    (2) Unilateral Concession

    (3) Negotiation

    (4) Good Offices

    (5) Mediation

    (6) Arbitration

    (7) International Law

C. Self-defense

    (8) Invulnerability

    (9) Dissuasion

    (10) Non-offensive Defense

CONFLICT PREVENTION

In the famous Robbers Cave experiment, social psychologist Muzafer Sherif and his associates found that one of the most effective ways to overcome a climate of mutual hostility and distrust is for two groups to work together to achieve a super-ordinate goal, something that is in both sides' interest but cannot be accomplished by either side alone.[15] At the 1985 summit meeting in Geneva, Ronald Reagan said to Mikhail Gorbachev that if the planet were invaded by aliens, the two superpowers would surely become allies to fight them. But there is no need to wait for an invasion from outer space. There are plenty of problems right here on earth that can be solved only if the two superpowers and all major industrial countries cooperate: ending the arms race, promoting equitable Third World development, halting destruction of the ozone layer, preventing the spread of nuclear weapons to terrorist groups, and many more.

There are a range of other problems where international cooperation is not absolutely necessary but would be of great benefit, particularly in the areas of economics, culture, and science. For example, with the help of international participation and financing, an international research center in Mexico has developed higher-yield varieties of wheat. Unfortunately, this "green revolution" technology is prohibitively expensive for poorer farmers, and thus far the spread of this technology has led to greater income disparities between rich and poor farmers. Clearly it would be helpful if international cooperation made these technologies available to *all* farmers regardless of their economic status. International scientific cooperation is another example of the benefits of sharing technology. Consider how CERN, the European center for experiments in particle physics, has enabled all its participants to undertake advanced research at a lower cost than if each European nation had constructed its own particle accelerator separately.

Jean Monnet foresaw that a mutually beneficial common institution could pave the way in overcoming the century-old hostility between France and Germany. He conceived of the Coal and Steel Union, which benefited all six initial members, including Germany and France. This agreement formed the nucleus out of which the European Community grew, and it ultimately made war between France and Germany unthinkable.

Similar projects are now required to begin a gradual dissolution of the East-West divide in Europe. Advocating a new Marshall Plan for Eastern Europe, Mark Sommer has argued that if someone is dying from suffocation, he needs oxygen now, not five years from now.[16] Sommer sent copies of his proposal to a number of politicians, including California State Representative John Vasconcellos, who then ordered fifty more copies, distributed them to his colleagues in the state assembly, and invited Sommer to speak before a legislative committee. The members were especially enthusiastic about Sommer's proposal to establish a sister-relationship between Czechoslovakia and California, and drafted a corresponding law (Unfortunately, it became a victim of the $15 billion California budget deficit, and was never funded).

A successful example of a cooperative venture between East and West is the construction of a gas pipeline from Siberia to Western Europe. The Reagan Administration asserted that the proposed pipeline would make Western Europe dependent on the Soviet Union and tried to block it. However, the Soviet Union was as much interested in maintaining an incoming flow of hard currency as Western Europe was in the flow of gas. Since its completion, this project has been mutually beneficial and increased both sides' stake in maintaining good relations.

There is, of course, a long list of other cooperative projects that could strengthen East-West relations:

~ Joint development of better scrubbers for coal-burning plants would reduce acid rain and enable damaged forests to regenerate.

~ Extending the tracks of high-speed trains into a pan-European network would encourage greater use of public transportation and less use of polluting private automobiles.

~ Expanding the free flow of people, ideas, and information technologies (including integrated telephone lines and computer networks) across the East-West border would increase cross-cultural understanding and foster greater cooperation.

~ Joint efforts to find cures for cancer, AIDS, and other diseases and to eliminate hunger and illiteracy in the Third World would greatly expedite solutions to these problems at a fraction of the cost.

Cooperation in all these areas could set in motion a benign escalatory process. The more joint undertakings succeed, the greater the mutual desire to go further.

Obviously, some forms of cooperation are more fruitful than others. For example, China learned through bitter experience that buying entire manufacturing plants from another country was riskier than entering joint ventures. In the early 1970s China bought from foreign firms a number of complete plants, including a steel rolling mill. Soon after it had paid for the plant, China discovered that it was built on soft ground and, as a result, the mill's machinery had become unaligned and no longer functioned properly. When Chinese officials asked the foreign construction firm to correct the problem, they were told that the plant now belonged to them and its maintenance was their responsibility. From then on, China relied on joint ventures in which the supplier of a plant is not paid in cash but instead receives a certain share of the profits. This gives the supplier every incentive to insure that the plant remains in good working order and that there exists a strong market for the product, regardless of what is specified in the contract.

It has been argued that Eastern Europeans and the Soviets wish to buy a great deal from the West but have only low quality goods to offer in return. The same could be said about Chinese products when Beijing opened its borders to trade with the West in the early 1970s. Few people in the West were interested in buying grey Mao uniforms. But several Western textile manufacturers went to China and showed the Chinese how to manufacture Western-style clothing. The Chinese were eager to learn. As a result, Western assistance not only has provided cheaper clothing to American and European consumers but also has helped to improve the quality and variety of textiles available in China. Today, many Eastern European and Soviet entrepreneurs want to learn how to produce goods for a Western market, and if we help them in this endeavor, everyone can benefit from higher quality goods and lower prices.

The importance of Western cooperation is demonstrated by the Japanese "miracle." In 1946, Japan's per capita income was less than $100[17] compared to $1,264 for the United States.[18] By 1988, Japan's per capita income reached $21,020, exceeding that of the United States, which was $19,840.[19] Over time, Japanese industries went from producing textiles and bicycles to a broader spectrum of goods, such as cameras and radios, always being careful to keep their prices cheaper than competing products made in the West. When the transistor was invented in the United States, the technology was made available to Japan and other countries. This coupling of American inventiveness with Japanese production techniques gave people throughout the world inexpensive, battery-operated radios. Japan has since applied this strategy to the production of cars, television sets, video-recorders, computers, and many other products. Our act of sharing technologies with Japan dramatically improved the living standard not only of the Japanese but also of millions of people in many other countries. Today, the same lesson can be applied to trade between North and South. If countries with low wages are given access to the North's production methods, their standards of living can be raised and the rest of the world will benefit from the availability of higher quality goods at lower prices.

International cooperation helps to create common interests and a climate of mutual understanding that make war less likely. This is, of course, far from setting up a world government. As the examples have shown, countries can mutually benefit from voluntary agreements, unenforced by any global police force.

The principle of *subsidiarity* is useful for deciding whether an agreement or venture should be pursued at the international level. Every political decision ought to be made at the lowest level of government that includes all those affected by it. If the decision-making level is lower than that, "external effects" are not taken into account, which means people will tend to engage in too many activities that are harmful to others and not enough activities that are beneficial to others. For example, policies concerning acid rain require international agreements. If they are made only at the national level, insufficient funds will be allocated for pollution cleanup because damage inflicted on other countries will most likely be ignored. If decisions are made at a higher level than is needed, unnecessary delays and avoidable conflict will result. People directly affected by a decision tend to have more accurate and up-to-date information about local conditions than someone far removed. Even if they make a wrong decision and suffer the consequences, they have only themselves to blame and will choose more wisely next time. If a bureaucrat in the ministry of agriculture orders a farmer to plant wheat when the farmer knows that by planting tomatoes he could earn three times as much, the farmer will have legitimate reasons to be upset. This explains why excessively centralized and authoritarian systems are filled with tension and often rely on political repression to keep disputes from flaring up openly. Conflict *prevention* requires that decisions be left to only those affected by them.

Another reason why overly centralized decision-making can be harmful is that it suppresses healthy competition. It is now generally accepted that the former socialist economies of Eastern Europe, in which most economic decisions were made by a central ministry, were not sufficiently flexible to adapt to new realities and consequently suffered many serious blunders. But the same type of exclusive monopoly over decision-making in another area, foreign relations, is assigned to a foreign ministry in nearly all nations today, with perhaps even more catastrophic consequences in the form of high military spending, excessive secrecy, covert actions, armed interventions, and wars. Citizen diplomats, who establish friendly contacts and mutually beneficial cooperation with people in other counties, play the same role in improving international relations as small private enterprises in Eastern Europe and the Soviet Union play in improving their economies. If many ideas are allowed to compete, those that work best tend to prevail in the end.[20]

There exist, of course, some problems that can be solved only at a higher than national level. Jan Tinbergen has estimated that about three percent of world's GNP would be required to deal adequately with such problems as preventing war through peacekeeping, saving the global environment, and eliminating world hunger.[21] Many governments are reluctant today to join such global projects for fear of losing some of their national sovereignty. But that fear is misguided. No government today, for example, has sovereign control over the ozone layer. If a single country continues to release major quantities of chlorofluorocarbons into the atmosphere, people around the world will suffer from more skin cancers. By forming a global authority that can allocate emissions quotas and enforce them, we do not give up any control over our destiny that we now possess, but we gain added control that we cannot achieve by ourselves. Joining such a global authority is not a loss but a gain of sovereignty.[22]

While it might be valuable for cooperating nations to form as tight a political union as presently exists in the European Economic Community (EC), even a fairly loose organization, such as the Organization for Economic Cooperation and Development (OECD), which includes Western Europe, the United States, Canada, and Japan, can provide a useful forum for discussing common problems. It is not a coincidence that no OECD country plans or fears war with any other OECD member. If this type of minimal organizational structure could span the entire globe, war might gradually disappear as an instrument of international politics.

CONFLICT RESOLUTION

When I once spoke about the benefits of international cooperation, a military officer said, "You live in a world of illusions. As long as civilization exists, there will always be conflict," and from his grim look it was clear that he meant armed conflict. Certainly, conflicts in the form of differences of opinion and interest will always be with us. But this does not mean that we have to kill each other to resolve them. IBM and AT&T are currently engaged in an intense struggle over the conquest of the computerized telecommunications market, but they would never dream of bombing each other's headquarters or slaughtering each other's employees. There exist more civilized ways to wage conflict, including lowering prices, improving products, and occasionally battling it out in court.

The members of the EC often have conflicts among each other, but they have developed legal and political mechanisms to solve them nonviolently. When the British government felt it had been overcharged in its contributions to the EC, Prime Minister Margaret Thatcher negotiated an agreement with Francois Mitterrand, who was then President of the EC, to reimburse Great Britain with less than Thatcher had originally sought but still a reasonable amount. Neither side ever thought of resorting to heavy artillery. There is no reason why disputes between other countries or regions cannot be settled in a similarly sane manner.

There are at least six approaches to conflict resolution when dealing with conflicts of increasing intractability: (1) unilateral concession, (2) negotiation, (3) good offices, (4) mediation, (5) arbitration; and (6) a court of law. Unilateral concession, by definition, involves only one of the parties to the conflict. Negotiation aims to involve all the parties to the conflict (usually two). The other methods involve all the parties plus an impartial outsider. Someone providing good offices supplies a neutral meeting ground or carries messages back and forth between two conflicting parties without making any suggestions. A mediator tries to come up with a sensible compromise but leaves the decision whether to adopt it to the conflicting parties. An arbitrator makes a final decision, but only after both parties have pledged in advance that they will accept the verdict. And a court of law is like an arbitrator, only it also has the power to bring sanctions against a party that refuses to accept its decision.

A brief example for each of these six methods illustrates how they work. The goal of conflict resolution is to begin with the first, and gradually go down the list if the previous method has failed.

Unilateral concession: When a fire at a Swiss chemical warehouse near Basel poisoned the Rhine river, killing fish and polluting drinking water for many French, German, and Dutch communities along the river, Switzerland did not wait to be taken to court. Nor did the Swiss government attempt to negotiate with neighbors over compensation. Instead, in an effort to defuse public anger, it simply announced that it would pay for the cleanup.

Removing the cause of a grievance is an important way to prevent a conflict that can lead to war. In the Third World perhaps the most common grievance is unjust land tenure. Up until the late 1970s, for example, the ruling Somoza family owned about half the land in Nicaragua, while most of the country lived in extreme poverty. This imbalance provoked a popular struggle that ultimately brought about the dynasty's downfall. Other Central American countries, such as El Salvador, Guatemala, and Honduras, still have very unequal distribution of land, and consequently are facing uprisings by those who have little or nothing to lose. Real land reform undertaken unilaterally could go a long way toward solving these conflicts. It is not sufficient to carry out a one-time land reform, however, if large landholders can repurchase their tracts. For example, even though Bangladesh instituted land reform when it became independent in 1971, land holdings have since become concentrated again. After a major flood a few years later, many poor peasants who desperately needed money to feed their families sold their land titles to rich landlords for a pittance. South Korea instituted an interesting system to discourage landlords from re-accumulating land—a progressive land tax. A person owning twice as much land pays more than twice as much in taxes. This makes it unprofitable for anybody to keep huge land holdings over a prolonged period. Other developing countries would be wise to adopt this kind of system as a means to prevent violent revolution or civil war.

To preserve the peace, a government must treat all groups within the country fairly. Remarkably, it was Moshe Dayan, commander of the Israeli army in the Six-Day War of 1967, who became a prominent critic of the Israeli government's subsequent policy of replacing elected mayors in occupied Palestinian towns with Israeli officers. He warned that even though this might seem expedient in the short run, it was bound to create enormous problems in the long run. The recent uprising of Palestinians on the West Bank, widely known as the *intifada*, has shown that Dayan was right. Power sharing, a method that gives all groups within a country a voice commensurate with their size, can help prevent or end such conflicts. The recent elections in Namibia that brought the black majority to power, for example, ended the long guerilla struggle waged by SWAPO against the white minority government that had been installed by South Africa.

Negotiations: If we wish to conclude negotiations successfully, we must make proposals that offer something attractive to both sides (win-win solutions). If our proposals are too one-sided, there is little incentive for our negotiating partner to accept them. And failure to reach agreement hurts our own interests.[23]

The recent measures taken by the South African President F. W. de Klerk to free Nelson Mandela and begin talks with the African National Congress are important steps toward defusing a potentially explosive situation. Ultimately, the unjust system of apartheid must be dismantled to achieve peace or a full-scale civil war may occur. Mandela's promise of a role for whites in a more democratic South Africa has helped reduce white fears and begin the transition to racial equality. The success of negotiations in facilitating the relatively peaceful shift to majority rule in Zimbabwe, a former apartheid state where a black majority and white minority now coexist peacefully, provides a helpful precedent.

Good Offices: When Finland hosted the 1975 Conference on Security and Cooperation in Europe, this was a wise investment. It probably contributed far more to Finland's security than adding a new tank division. Moreover, it did not threaten Finland's neighbors; indeed, it improved the security of all the countries of Europe.

Mediation: An emissary of the Pope was able to mediate the dispute between Argentina and Chile in 1984 over the Beagle Canal. In 1988, U.N. General Secretary Perez de Cuellar mediated a cease-fire in the Iran-Iraq War. Mediation is useful because accepting a proposal made by one's adversary is sometimes seen as a sign of weakness or defeat and can cause the negotiating government to lose face before domestic public opinion. It is often easier for parties involved in a dispute to accept a proposal made by a neutral player.

Arbitration: When the United States and Canada were unable to negotiate an agreement over fishing rights off their coasts they submitted the dispute to a panel of judges from the International Court of Arbitration in the Hague.[24] Both parties announced in advance that they would accept the judges' verdict, and ultimately they did.

Court of Law: When France announced that it planned to end the special status of a duty-free zone surrounding Geneva, where the residents of Geneva could buy agricultural products tax-free, Switzerland took its case before the World Court. In the end France accepted the court's decision that it ought to maintain the zone. When the United States mined the harbors of Corinto, El Bluff, and Puerto Sandino, Nicaragua filed a complaint before the World Court and won. Unfortunately, the Reagan Administration's refusal to accept the decision impaired U.S. credibility on other issues of international law and undermined the ability of future Administrations to submit international disputes to the World Court.

The World Court could ultimately become an important arbiter of global conflicts, provided that several reforms are undertaken.[25] Judgments of the World Court should be enforced by tougher sanctions, both material and moral.[26] When our government ignored the World Court's decision in the case brought by Nicaragua, Japan and the countries of Western Europe, to whom we are heavily indebted, should have openly condemned our contempt of court and withheld further credits until we complied with the court's decision. The ease with which the Reagan Administration walked away from the World Court's verdict may encourage other nations to do the same.

It is a welcome sign that the Soviet Union has recently announced that it will accept the World Court's jurisdiction over disputes involving the conventions on genocide, slavery, racism, torture, and women's rights.[27] The United States has ratified only one of these conventions, the Genocide Treaty, and it has declared that it would not submit to any ruling of the World Court in matters it deems governed by "national sovereignty." Of course, the actual implementation of human rights is more important than their formal adoption, but our government's refusal to accept the jurisdiction of the World Court sets a bad example for other countries. The more countries that rely on the World Court, and the more areas in which they accept its jurisdiction, the less likely it is that any dispute will lead to war. It is best not to wait until a serious conflict becomes violent before turning to the World Court, but instead to practice using the option now with relatively non-controversial cases, so that it becomes a matter of routine — just as military defense is regularly practiced in maneuvers.

With an active peace policy, we would not simply wait until a conflict became acute and then resort to legal proceedings to solve it. Instead, we would seek negotiations over any disagreements at an early stage, when it is generally much easier to find an amicable solution. In fact, in choosing topics for negotiation, it is best to begin with areas where there are clearly visible and immediate benefits to both sides (win-win solutions), such as trade, technology sharing, and cultural exchanges. Success in these areas can create a climate of trust in which it becomes possible to resolve more difficult disputes. Ross Perot, a Texas oil billionaire, once criticized the Reagan Administration's confrontational approach toward the Soviet Union by saying, "If I sit down at the negotiating table and wish to strike a business deal, I don't begin by breaking the teeth of the person sitting across from me. That will not bring me any agreement. I search for common interests." Political leaders should learn from successful businesspeople.

So far, there has been a strange asymmetry in law, both at the domestic and international level. Law focuses on the prevention of wrongdoing exclusively through the threat of punishment or sanctions, but fails to encourage desirable behavior through the promise of rewards. Legal systems seek to deter actions that are harmful to others by punishing those who cause harm. They fail, however, to encourage people to do something extraordinary for the benefit of society or the international community. Laws do not reward those who improve the lot of others. There is, in fact, a rudimentary approach to solving this problem. Someone who has discovered a new cure for a disease or who has made a significant contribution to world peace may receive a Nobel Prize. But this is as if once a year we were to choose "the criminal of the year" from around the world for exemplary punishment, while every other culprit went scot-free. We would hardly consider this an adequate legal system. There is a need to develop what might be called "remunerative law" as a complement to our current system of punitive law. It would reward not just the victims of wrongdoing but also those who make sacrifices for the benefit of others and society as a whole. Psychological studies have found consistently that people respond better to praise and rewards than they do to criticism and punishments.[28] Such a transition may be comparable to the shift from slavery, where the motivation for work was the fear of punishment, to wage labor, where the motivation became a monetary reward. This is a great task waiting for us in the future.

SELF-DEFENSE

No matter how many precautions are taken to avert war, prudence dictates that a nation must prepare to defend itself against blatant aggression, should it occur. In the long run, this responsibility should be assigned to the United Nations. Today's situation, where every country maintains its own military defense, is as wasteful as every house in a community maintaining its own fire engine. The U.N. Secretary General should have a standing peacekeeping force at his or her disposal. Such a force should consist of individually recruited troops whose primary loyalty is to the United Nations, instead of national contingents whose primary loyalty is to their own government.[29] Such a peacekeeping force should be ready to be dispatched at a moment's notice to any place in the world where fighting has broken out, or is about to break out, without having to wait for approval after a lengthy debate in the U.N. Security Council. (Imagine if each time a crime victim cried out for help the town council would have to meet first to deliberate over whether to recruit a police force to deal with the emergency!)

Until a sufficiently effective global peacekeeping force has been established, countries will need to rely on self-defense or collective self-defense. Even defense, however, involves many non-military measures. Self-defense includes not only the military policies of non-offensive defense but also the non-military policies of invulnerability and dissuasion.

Invulnerability

One means of discouraging aggression is through invulnerability. Bomb shelters and underground hospitals, for example, are not weapons, but they can reduce losses in the event of an attack. A country also can make itself less vulnerable by having a decentralized decision-making apparatus that cannot easily be "decapitated." Similarly, a dense, redundant transportation network with numerous alternative routes is much harder to disrupt than a highly centralized network with only a few principal arteries.

Reserves of food and other vital materials, along with stand-by plans to produce imported goods domestically, can help protect a country against an interruption of imports. It may be more expensive to produce such goods domestically than to purchase them on the world market, but it will be far less expensive than going to war. Plans to ration in case of a crisis can help ensure that the most essential needs are covered.

Self-reliance is perfectly compatible with a high volume of mutually beneficial trade during peacetime. For example, Switzerland imports about fifty percent of the food it consumes, yet it also has a standby plan to become self-sufficient should food imports ever be cut off. Not only does Switzerland maintain food reserves that are constantly renewed to bridge any temporary shortfall, but it also has plans to convert grassland into farms producing potatoes and other high-yield crops.[30] What's more, the Swiss maintain storage depots of oil and other raw materials, and a standby rationing plan to reduce consumption of fuel and everything else. There is a difference between complete autarky and the option of self-reliance if needed. Someone who is self-reliant keeps candles in the house in case the electricity is cut off, whereas someone who practices autarky only uses candles for fear that the electricity might be cut off some day.

Dissuasion

This strategy seeks to avert war by convincing a potential aggressor, without evoking fear, that peaceful cooperation better serves its interests than going to war. A country can make peace more attractive by increasing the benefits of mutual cooperation or by voluntarily removing injustices that are offending the adversary. Similarly, war can be made less attractive by increasing the losses an aggressor would suffer and by reducing any benefits it might hope to gain.[31] Military defense only focuses on inflicting greater losses on an aggressor and neglects the other three strategies.

Even if the objective is only to inflict losses on an aggressor, non-military methods can be effective. It has been said that the construction of a United Nations office complex in Vienna saved Austria two army divisions. Any country that invaded Austria would quickly earn the enmity of the 168 nations whose diplomats might be harmed.

To reduce the gains from aggression, one also can deny an attacking force control over the population and economic resources. Sweden deterred a German invasion during World War II by threatening to blow up the hydroelectric dams powering its iron ore and coal mines. Switzerland informed the Nazis that it would respond to any aggression by blowing up its bridges and Alpine tunnels. Nonviolent resistance also has proven effective in deterring attacks in several instances of history, even though this method has rarely been planned or funded in advance of a war. When the Philippine dictator Ferdinand Marcos, who had just lost an election, sent tanks to crush an army unit that had joined the popularly elected opposition in 1986, half a million unarmed civilians successfully defended against the attack. The tank drivers refused to roll over nuns kneeling on the ground in prayer. Had they been opposed by armed soldiers they might have moved on with little hesitation. No invader can govern a country unless its citizens cooperate voluntarily to some degree. If a soldier needs to stand next to every worker, a country becomes effectively ungovernable.[32]

Wilhelm Nolte[33] has proposed the concept of "autonomous protection," a combination of civilian-based defense in cities and non-offensive defense in rural areas. This proposal is based on a simple observation: During World War II those cities with important military installations were generally bombed, while demilitarized cities were largely spared and provided a safe haven for refugees from the fighting in the countryside. Since trying to defend population centers with military means appears to invite their destruction, Nolte recommends keeping most weapons outside cities.

Another way to dissuade an adversary from attacking is to increase the benefits of sustained peaceful cooperation. A country can deliberately seek to make itself indispensable to its adversaries. Some have argued that what helped Switzerland stay out of World War II was not so much its military defenses but the fortunate circumstance that both sides in the war needed a neutral place to deposit funds and to exchange information. Swiss defense documents reveal, however, that this was a deliberate component of its security policy, aimed at persuading surrounding countries that an invasion of Switzerland would only hurt their interests. Who would wish to bombard his or her own bank deposits?

Despite its very vulnerable position, Hong Kong also has used dissuasion to bolster its security. Clearly, Hong Kong could not possibly stand up to China's Red Army. In fact, if China turned off Hong Kong's water supply, it could force the city to surrender within a few days. But by becoming one of China's main sources of foreign-exchange earnings, Hong Kong has seen to it that it is not in China's interest to threaten the city.

These methods of dissuasion can work even at the interpersonal level. When Steven Spielberg, producer and director of a number of top U.S. films, was in school, a big bully constantly harassed him by pushing him, punching him, or shoving his head under the water fountain. Spielberg was too small to resist and had no friends to defend him, but one day he had the idea of making a movie in which he needed someone to play the role of a bully. He asked the bully if he would play the role and his antagonist gladly agreed and played the part very well. After that, he became Spielberg's friend and defended him against other boys.[34]

With some imagination, individuals and countries can develop new ways in which they can play a useful role to others, so that others will wish to maintain good relations with them. During peacetime, a country should seek out potential grievances and remove them before they explode into open conflict. From this perspective, the former Rumanian dictator Nicolae Ceausescu's plan to raze small hamlets containing Rumania's Hungarian minority and move the inhabitants into larger towns was highly provocative. The new Romanian government has wisely abandoned the plan.

Non-offensive Defense

If dissuasion fails to change the mind of a would-be aggressor, the last resort is to deflect and stop the attack. But this must be done in a way that is not perceived as a threat by the aggressor; otherwise, the aggressor may feel compelled to attack preemptively and eliminate the threat if war seems imminent. In the 1960s, President Nasser developed an air force he believed would make Egypt militarily stronger and more secure, but in fact it did just the opposite. Both Egypt and Israel possessed bomber fleets that were parked on unprotected airfields in the desert. Each side knew that in case of war whoever struck first could destroy the other side's air force on the ground. Thus, when tensions increased in 1967, Israel felt it had no choice but to destroy Nasser's air force in a surprise attack before his planes could attack Israel. Sweden and Switzerland deliberately did not acquire any long-range bombers before World War II because they feared that these weapons might invite a preemptive air attack; instead, they concentrated on short-range interceptors and anti-aircraft defenses.[35]

Weapons in space, as envisaged under the Strategic Defense Initiative (SDI), would be even more destabilizing than bombers on the ground. The very space stations that are designed to intercept incoming warheads with laser beams or kinetic-energy projectiles could just as well destroy an opponent's space stations.

Since each station would be able to destroy many targets, the side that struck first would gain a military advantage. Deployment of a system like SDI therefore increases the chances of war during a crisis.

SDI would also increase the risks of an accidental war. Decisions to fire space weapons would have to be made within seconds after an opponent's missiles were launched, leaving no time for consultation with political leaders. Entrusting the fate of the world to computers is exceptionally risky. Between January 1979 and June 1980 the computerized NORAD system generated 3,804 warnings of a Soviet nuclear attack on the United States — all false.[36] No such figures have been published since then so as not to "frighten the public." The crew of the USS Vincennes also relied on an automated warning system, the Aegis, and wound up accidentally shooting down Iran Air Flight 655. This is a warning about what could happen with SDI.

Whereas disarmament must be bilateral to improve a country's security, a shift from an offensive to a defensive military posture, which some have called *transarmament*, improves a country's own security even if it is undertaken unilaterally. Recognizing this, Mikhail Gorbachev announced in 1988 a unilateral reduction of 500,000 troops and 10,000 tanks, along with plans to restructure the Soviet Union's armed forces into a more defensive configuration.[37] Other countries have found it politically easier to undertake transarmament through bilateral negotiations.

A willingness to negotiate in good faith is probably a necessary precondition to induce two or more adversaries to scrap offensive weapons. Unfortunately, many Americans believe that inflexibility in negotiating is the only way to achieve favorable arms-control deals. For example, many Americans concluded that the INF Treaty of 1987 was reached because Reagan made a one-sided proposal and did not yield. I find it hard to believe that if the Soviet leadership had called Ronald Reagan a "liar and a cheat" and the United States an "evil empire," the President would have decided that the Soviets were tough and serious and that he had better give in to reach an agreement with them. That is not human nature! If Washington had been less inflexible, we might have had many more East-West agreements by now besides just the INF Treaty. The list could have included a comprehensive nuclear test ban, a fifty-percent reduction in strategic nuclear weapons, naval force limitations, and a prohibition of weapons in space, all with stringent verification measures. These were all treaties that the Soviets offered and we rejected.

Another component of non-offensive defense is the creation of zones on both sides of a border that are free of tanks and heavy artillery.[38] A difficult issue is how violations should be treated. One possibility is to regard any tanks reintroduced into a forbidden zone as a "casus belli," which would give the other side the right to destroy the tanks, perhaps through aerial bombardment. However, this action would increase the likelihood of war, even if the violation happened by accident. A tank-free zone may not be as clearly marked with barbed wire fences and border checkpoints as the borderline itself. It is conceivable that a tank unit could take a wrong turn in fog, in the rain, or at night and enter the zone by mistake. If this is detected by radar from an observation satellite and immediately treated like a deliberate attack, World War III could be set off. Obviously, it would be preferable to assign a neutral fact-finding commission the task of establishing what exactly happened. If one side makes accusations of a violation and immediately retaliates, there is a risk of an accidental war being set off by a false alarm. Imagine a legal system in which the person who makes an accusation also judges the merits of her or his own case, decides on a punishment, and carries out the sentence. That would be a travesty of justice. The principle of separating defendant, judiciary, and police has long been recognized as essential for a legal system to be fair. It is even more important at the international level where the consequences of a mistake could be far graver. Violations must be treated seriously, but with a proportionate response. For example, a violation could be reported immediately to a neutral investigating body, and a warning could then be issued to the party responsible for the violation. Or some tanks could be reintroduced into the zone facing the violator, just as a precaution. This would provide essential time to clear up any misunderstanding and defuse the crisis.

One of the most important steps to dismantle offensive forces in Europe is for the United States, Great Britain, and France to join the Soviet Union and China in adopting a policy of no first use of nuclear weapons. NATO's traditional philosophy was that the threat to escalate a conventional war to a nuclear conflagration would help deter an attack by the Warsaw Pact. This assumed that war can only begin through deliberate aggression. But unlike Hitler's march into Poland in 1939, many wars are unintentional. World War I was triggered by a lone assassin's shot at Austrian Archduke Franz Ferdinand in Sarajevo. In addition, it is often unclear which side really started a war. In the Vietnam War, the United States and North Vietnam both called each other the aggressor. Egypt maintains that Israel started the 1967 Mideast war by bombing Egyptian air fields; Israel maintains that Egypt started the war by blocking Israeli ships at the Bay of Aqaba. It is always possible to find something the other side did first. If any war, regardless of which side is the aggressor, escalates to the use of nuclear weapons, it may well lead to the total destruction of both sides. Despite all the political changes in Eastern Europe, NATO continues to threaten the first use of nuclear weapons to deter a conventional attack, only now it calls the threat a "last resort." This is analogous to trying to prevent traffic accidents by packing a car full of dynamite, putting a trip wire around it, and telling everybody, "Don't hit me, or my car will explode and kill you (and me too, of course)." This should indeed deter anyone from hitting the car intentionally. But if we have the slightest collision for any other reason, it would be our demise.

To prevent war, it is important to oppose aggression firmly but not to overreact. Before World War I the prevailing wisdom was that the best way to avoid war was to prepare to win it. The key to victory was thought to be quick and decisive action at the outset of hostilities. The objective was to surprise and defeat the adversary's forces before they could be fully mobilized. The result of this philosophy was the bloodbath of World War I. Many then concluded that avoiding war required a more conciliatory attitude. Neville Chamberlain probably thought he had learnt the lessons of World War I when he yielded to Hitler's demands in Munich in 1938. As we now know, the consequences proved to be even more disastrous, and after World War II the pendulum of opinion swung back full cycle. Emphasizing the risks of appeasement, both NATO and the Warsaw Treaty Organization vowed that they would react strongly to the first sign of aggression. The Soviet Union, which had been attacked from the West three times this century, espoused a doctrine of "strategic defense, tactical offense." In anticipation of war on the central front, NATO planned a "follow-on forces attack," the destruction of command posts and staging areas deep inside Eastern Europe. By threatening quick retaliation and deliberate escalation, these strategies sought to deter intentional aggression. But they actually increased the probability of a war caused by accident or miscalculation. Clinging to the lessons of Munich, both sides seemed to forget the lessons of Sarajevo.

If a country or an alliance fully implements non-offensive defense, even unilaterally, it can avoid both types of war. By providing a strong defense, this strategy makes it possible to resist the type of aggression that initiated World War II. And by avoiding offensive weapons and war plans, it would help prevent the automatic escalation of fighting that led to World War I. Whenever two potential adversaries adopt a posture of *mutual defensive superiority*, where each side is able to defend itself but is unable to attack the other side, the risk of war, even during periods of severe tension and conflict, is greatly diminished.

THE GULF WAR

While it is always easy to look back after a war has been fought and observe with 20/20 hindsight how it might have been averted, it is still an important exercise to help prevent the recurrence of similar wars in the future. Now that the smoke has cleared from the Persian Gulf War, we should ask what might have dissuaded Saddam Hussein from ordering his troops to occupy Kuwait on August 2, 1990. How could each of the principles discussed above have been applied by Kuwait, the international community, and the United States to prevent Iraq's aggression?

Looking at the three approaches to security — conflict prevention, conflict resolution, and self-defense — we can see that the Persian Gulf War was truly an unnecessary war.

Conflict Prevention

Totally unprincipled and ruthless leaders such as Iraq's dictator Saddam Hussein present a grave threat to international security. People who do not shy from blatant aggression if they believe it serves their purposes must be prevented from becoming leaders — or they must be removed from power if they seize it.

There were several striking parallels between Saddam Hussein and Adolf Hitler. Both displayed incredible brutality against their own people. Hussein, like Hitler and Stalin, murdered numerous suspected enemies and innocent scapegoats to increase his hold on power. Besides employing well-known measures of repression such as torture and execution, Hussein's most blatant and well-documented abuse was the use of poison gas against Iraq's Kurdish population in 1988, which claimed the lives of five thousand civilians. Like Hitler, Hussein also had a history of committing aggression. On September 20, 1980, he invaded Iran and began a bloody eight-year war in which one million people were killed. In a speech on July 18, 1990, Hussein accused Kuwait of undermining Iraq's economy by depressing the price of oil, and he solemnly stated, "It is better to cut off necks than to cut off people's source of livelihood . . . . Allah, be witness that they have been warned."

For a long time, Amnesty International and Iraqis in exile sought in vain to draw the world's attention to Saddam Hussein's gross violations of human rights. During the Iraq-Iran war, Iran offered a cease-fire if Hussein resigned. At a meeting of his cabinet ministers, Hussein asked for frank opinions about what they thought of the offer. Everyone urged him to stay on. He then repeated his question, this time more insistently. Finally, the health minister suggested, "Why don't you resign and then take office again a few months later?" Hussein thanked his colleagues, ended the meeting, and promptly arrested the health minister. The health minister's wife asked the wife of Hussein, a close friend of hers, to plead with her husband to release the minister. She then received a phone call from Hussein, who asked her if she would like to have her husband back, and she enthusiastically replied "yes." He asked her if she would like to see him tomorrow, and she thanked him profusely. The next day, soldiers brought her a black plastic bag, and when she opened it, she found the body of her husband, cut into small pieces.[39] This is only one among many atrocities Hussein has committed. He also has forced fathers to shoot their sons if they refused to go to war, and executed the fathers if they refused to kill their sons. Only after the invasion of Kuwait, when oil prices were at stake and not just innocent people's lives, were these brutalities widely reported and raised as a matter of international concern.

To prevent such flagrant violations of human rights in the future, international law must be strengthened. According to the Nuremburg principles, individuals must be held accountable for the crimes they commit in the name of their governments. These principles should be reinforced by supplementing the World Court, in which governments can file suit against other governments, with an international criminal court. There individuals who cannot find justice in their own country still would have the opportunity to expose their tormentors, even if the human rights violations were committed by their own government. This may sound utopian now, but one can easily see how the present notion of absolute national sovereignty is absurd. Under Roman law, the head of the household, the *pater familias*, had "absolute sovereignty" over the members of his family. He could beat his children, sell them into slavery, or even kill them, and nobody had the right to interfere. He was prohibited from hurting someone else's children, but not his own. Today we find it hard to comprehend that such juridical concepts ever prevailed. In the years ahead we may wonder how people ever allowed human rights abuses in the name of protecting national sovereignty.

Of course, one must avoid a situation where a government which has a human rights complaint can set itself up as judge and mete out punishment, as noted earlier. Determination of wrongdoing must be established by a non-partisan international tribunal. If a government refuses to cooperate with a legitimate international investigation, it should be a cause for suspicion — and further international pressure should be applied to uncover any illicit activities. Government officials found guilty of crimes, or guilty of obstructing an on-site investigation of crimes, must be held individually accountable. Those who support or protect torturers and murderers should face penalties as well.[40]

The ease with which Saddam Hussein could disregard domestic and international law was only part of the reason for the crisis in the Gulf. What else might have been done to avoid the conflict? Consider the widespread discontent in the Arab world over the extremely unequal distribution of the region's oil wealth. By skillfully exploiting this dissatisfaction, Hussein garnered the support of many Arab citizens, though not their governments. Hitler similarly used the misery of unemployed workers in Germany during the Great Depression and the national feelings of humiliation after losing World War I to rouse his own masses by promising jobs and renewed national glory. Hussein's rhetoric, however, was based partly on reality. The royal families of Kuwait, Saudi Arabia, and several of the Arab Emirates are fabulously wealthy, while most Arabs, including most Iraqis, live in abject poverty.

In Kuwait, prior to the invasion, only one in four residents were regarded as citizens and shared in the annual revenue from oil. These citizens paid no taxes, received an annual stipend, and enjoyed free medical care, free education, and other public services. Through this limited effort to share the wealth, the royal al-Sabah family was supported by Kuwaiti citizens, though not by the majority of people living in the country. Excluded from these riches were the 1.6 million foreigners working in Kuwait, many in menial jobs that Kuwaitis were unwilling to perform. Even though these workers earned a higher income in Kuwait than they could have in their home countries (such as Egypt, Jordan, India, Pakistan, Bangladesh, and the Philippines), they had few political rights and felt like second-class citizens. Some of them reportedly spied for Iraq.

Saudi Arabia is governed even more autocratically by its royal family, which controls about $800 billion in oil wealth, and there is no sharp dividing line between the assets of the state and those of the royal family. Saudi Arabia has no free press, no political parties, and no parliament. Despite a high average national income (the 1987 per capita GNP of $6,200 ranked 24th among the 131 countries with over 1 million population), its mortality rate for children under five years old was 98 per 1000 in 1988 (ranking 76 among the same countries), and its female adult literacy rate in 1985 was only 31 percent (ranking 105).[41] These data indicate that the Saudi's wealth has been unequally distributed and has not been used effectively to meet basic human needs.

Nations like Kuwait and Saudi Arabia with severe injustice create envy and political instability, both within their borders and in the region as a whole. If the oil wealth had been used more systematically to improve the living conditions of Arabs in the region, and if the oil-rich Gulf states had democratic institutions giving ordinary people a voice in how to use that wealth, it would have been more difficult for Saddam Hussein to incite a large number of Arabs against the ruling families of Kuwait and Saudi Arabia. He also would have had more difficulty projecting himself as a champion of the poor, which in fact he was not, since he squandered Iraq's oil wealth on fighting a costly war against Iran.

Another way to have averted the war would have been to address the long-standing border dispute between Iraq and Kuwait. This border was imposed on the region by the British. After World War I and the fall of the Ottoman Empire, Britain controlled Kuwait as a protectorate and had mandatory power over Iraq that was sanctioned by the League of Nations. In 1922, Sir Percy Cox, Britain's steward in the Gulf region, redrew the boundaries of Kuwait, Saudi Arabia, and Iraq, leaving Iraq with no secure access to the Gulf.

There certainly were ways this border dispute could have been settled. Iraq wanted control over the islands of Bubiyan and Warbah in order to have secure access to the waters of the Gulf. For Kuwait, which has a major seaport in Kuwait City, these islands are not of strategic importance. But it is understandable that Kuwait was not prepared to give up territory without compensation. If Iraq had offered to exchange the two islands for a larger piece of territory further inland, both sides would have gained. Kuwait would have enlarged its territory, and Iraq would have achieved its long-sought access to the sea.

Conflict Resolution

The immediate issue that Saddam Hussein used as a pretext for his invasion was that Kuwait had exceeded its OPEC quota of 1.5 million barrels of oil a day by fifty percent, which helped depress oil prices on the world market. This was imprudent of Kuwait, since its financial security did not require additional oil revenues and it knew that exceeding the agreed production limits would only anger other OPEC members, especially Iraq. Similarly, Kuwait would have been wise to have cancelled at least some of the staggering debt it was owed by Iraq, which Hussein accumulated during his eight-year war with Iran. Before invading Kuwait, Iraq intimated that it would not repay the debt because of the depressed price of oil. Kuwait could have made concessions, and at a minimum it could have entered negotiations. By saying this, I do not mean to blame the victim of aggression; the responsibility for the attack rests entirely with Iraq. But potential victims of aggression are usually more motivated to prevent war than the aggressor. Therefore, it is always useful to explore what the victims could have done.

President Hosni Mubarak of Egypt and King Hussein of Jordan tried to mediate between Iraq and Kuwait, but both were misled by Saddam Hussein's false promises that he would not invade Kuwait. President Carter was more successful in his effort to mediate between Israel and Egypt at Camp David in 1978, but he enjoyed an advantage that the Egyptian and Jordanian leaders did not have — he could promise both sides billions of dollars in assistance if they reached an agreement. (To this day, Israel and Egypt are by far the largest recipients of U.S. military aid.) Furthermore, unlike Saddam Hussein, Presidents Begin and Sadat were honest and reliable negotiators, even if their interests differed.

In yet another dispute over oil from the Rumaila oil field, which straddles the border between Iraq and Kuwait, direct negotiations or mediation had been attempted for many years and failed. Arbitration could have been tried but would have required Iraq's acceptance of an arbitrator with the power to make a binding decision — an unlikely possibility. A better option would have been for Kuwait to bring the dispute before the World Court. There is, of course, no guarantee that Iraq would have accepted a decision by the World Court or even participated in the proceedings, but it would have put Kuwait in a better position to show that it had the support of the international community.

Conflicts over resources or territory are among the most difficult to resolve, because they are zero-sum games. What one side gains, the other loses. But there were also elements of a positive-sum game in the conflict between Iraq and Kuwait. Some compromise might have been possible, for example, if both sides had emphasized their common interest in increasing oil revenues through higher prices. A model for how Iraq and Kuwait might have settled their conflict over the Rumailia oil field is provided by the way England and Norway share oil reserves in the North Sea. They jointly pump out the oil, export it through England, and share the revenue according to a fixed percentage. This leaves no room for disputes over who extracted how much.

Self-Defense

One way Kuwait could have better defended itself, as already noted, would have been to adhere scrupulously to OPEC rules. The oil-consuming countries of the world, especially the United States, also could have made themselves less vulnerable to a sudden reduction in the world oil supply by investing more in energy conservation. The United States could save about $200 billion per year if it used energy as efficiently as the Western Europeans do.[42]

Another means of self-defense is dissuasion. But many countries over the past decade have done exactly the opposite — they have actually aided and encouraged Iraq's aggressive tendencies. When Iraq invaded Iran on September 20, 1980, the whole world failed to condemn this clear act of aggression. Throughout the 1980s, many industrial nations, especially France and the Soviet Union, responded by selling large quantities of arms to Iraq. The United States did not supply Iraq with weapons, but it did provide militarily usable technology and billions of dollars in food credits, which freed up Iraqi resources to purchase weapons from other countries. When Iraq used poison gas against Iranian troops, and then against its own Kurdish citizens in Iraq, the world again failed to take any action. President Reagan blocked an attempt by Congress to impose economic sanctions. And in January 1989, at an international conference on chemical weapons in Paris, the United States strongly opposed naming Iraq as a violator. President Bush continued to oppose sanctions against Iraq up until the very day it invaded Kuwait.

The world also ignored the clear signs that Iraq was preparing to invade Kuwait, from Hussein's initial threat to Kuwait on July 18, to his massive buildup of troops along the Kuwaiti border in the days that followed. Hussein sent over 100,000 soldiers, along with numerous tanks and heavy artillery pieces, all under the open eyes of the superpowers' satellites and ground-based U.N. observers who were policing the cease-fire with Iran. U.N. officials warned that this buildup was not just a simple show of force to put negotiating pressure on Kuwait, as Western intelligence organizations asserted. Despite these foreboding signals, the American ambassador to Baghdad, April Glaspie, spoke in shockingly subservient language to Hussein during a meeting on July 25, one week before the invasion, when she was summoned by Saddam Hussein to convey a message to President Bush. Hussein had complained about an editorial on Voice of America naming Iraq in a list of undemocratic countries, and the U.S. State Department decided to apologize. According to a transcript of the meeting released by Iraq, Glaspie said to Hussein, "I am pleased that you add your voice to the diplomats who stand up to the media. Because your appearance in the media, even for five minutes, would help us to make the American people understand Iraq. This would increase mutual understanding. If the American President had control of the media, his job would be much easier."[43] Such language is unworthy of the envoy of a democratic nation.

Concerning Saddam Hussein's demand for higher oil prices, Glaspie reportedly said, "We have many Americans who would like to see the price of oil go above $25, because they come from oil-producing states .... I admire your extraordinary efforts to rebuild your country. I know you need funds."

And with regard to the forces massing on the Kuwaiti border, Glaspie was quoted as saying that the United States was neutral in the conflict between Iraq and Kuwait: "We have no opinion on Arab-Arab conflicts, like your border disagreement with Kuwait. I was in the American Embassy in Kuwait during the late 1960s. The instruction we had during this period was that we should express no opinion on this issue and that the issue is not associated with America." This statement was comparable to Secretary of State Dean Acheson's disastrous omission of South Korea in 1950 when he listed the countries the United States would defend against communist aggression. Acheson's blunder is widely considered responsible for misleading North Korea into believing it could invade South Korea without triggering a U.S. intervention, and it was a mistake that ultimately cost three million lives. This time, the mistake by the U.S. government was even more direct and less excusable. Not only were Iraq's assembling forces a clear and present danger but Glaspie also assured Hussein explicitly that the United States would *not* take sides. Glaspie later explained that she never expected Iraq to take "all" of Kuwait. In other words, if Iraq had taken some of Kuwait's territory, as it had done twice before, it would have been acceptable.

Kuwait also made a grave error by paying billions of dollars to Iraq on two previous occasions in return for Iraq's withdrawal from Kuwaiti territory. In this way, Kuwait succeeded in doing the opposite of what it intended — rewarding and thus encouraging aggression — just as paying ransom for hostages encourages more kidnapping.

Kuwait made a further mistake by allowing Hussein to believe that he could seize Kuwait's oil installations intact. Kuwait could have mined its oil fields, refineries, and pipelines to make it clear that these assets would not fall into an aggressor's hands in working order, similar to the way in which Switzerland and

Sweden prepared to sabotage their own infrastructure before World War II to dissuade Hitler from invading. Unfortunately, it was Iraq that did this after seizing the installations to deter an allied effort to recapture them.

Another serious mistake on the part of the United States was its invasion of Panama in December 1989, which enabled Hussein to argue that it is acceptable international behavior to invade other countries. (Similarly, the CIA's mining of Nicaraguan harbors in 1984 inspired Libya to mine the Red Sea three weeks later.) The United States would have been in a morally and legally stronger position to oppose Iraq's aggression had it not previously invaded Panama, Grenada, and many other countries. To be sure, the United States did not permanently annex these countries. But even if Iraq had followed the U.S. model in Panama and gradually withdrawn its forces from Kuwait after installing a pro-Iraqi government, the United States would have found these actions intolerable.

Alone, Kuwait's small army was clearly not capable of resisting the million-man, battle-hardened forces of Saddam Hussein. But Kuwait had enough time to invite United Nations peacekeeping forces, including American contingents, while Iraq was building up its forces along the border. Whether other countries were prepared to assist Kuwait in its defense before the Iraqi invasion is not certain, but clearly it is much easier to deter an attack before it occurs than to reverse the result afterwards. As mentioned earlier, the U.N. Secretary General ought to have a standing peacekeeping force at his disposal for rapid deployment in the event of such emergencies.

Post-Invasion Options

What could have been done after the invasion had occurred? Given Saddam Hussein's ambition to build nuclear weapons and long-range missiles, and given the dangers of allowing him to control half of the world's oil reserves had he been able to march into Saudi Arabia, the initial U.S. response of sending troops into the Saudi desert with the consent of King Fahd was reasonable. A standing U.N. peacekeeping force would have been more desirable, but discussions at the U.N. Security Council on whether to assemble this force could have taken some time. Commendably, the United States did not intervene unilaterally; it sought and received assistance from many other countries, including several key Arab states. After the initial troops were stationed along the Saudi border, however, there was no reason for U.S. forces to dominate the peacekeeping mission. U.S. forces should have been replaced as rapidly as possible by a truly international force. This force could have included U.S. troops, but they would have been under U.N. command.

In addition to preventing further aggression by Iraq, the international community needed to make it clear to Saddam Hussein, and to other future aggressors, that aggression does not pay. The U.N. Security Council's unanimous vote to impose trade sanctions was an appropriate response, though deliveries of food and medicine for humanitarian purposes should have been more clearly exempted. The Security Council rightly insisted that humanitarian shipments be distributed by trusted neutral international relief agencies, such as the Red Crescent, and not by the Iraqi government; otherwise there was no way to ensure that the food and supplies would have reached those in need and would not have been diverted to Iraq's armed forces. Missing from the design of the embargo, however, was compensation for countries bordering Iraq, such as Jordan and Turkey, whose weak economies were seriously damaged by the interruption of trade with Iraq.

Given enough time, these sanctions probably would have evicted Iraq from Kuwait, and all the other costs of the war would have been averted. One hundred thousand Iraqi troops and a similar number of Iraqi civilians would have been spared.[44] A civil war that killed thousands more and uprooted over a million Kurds would have never occurred. And the ecologically disastrous oil spills in the Gulf and the burning of Kuwaiti oil wells would have been prevented.

When Stalin imposed satellite regimes in Eastern Europe, the United States did not "roll back the iron curtain," as some had advocated. This could have led to nuclear war. Instead, the United States resorted to the strategy of containment, which it later supplemented with the Helsinki process of increasing contacts and promoting human rights. Both policies prepared the way for the Eastern European "velvet revolutions" of 1989. A similar process of patient containment and persistent pressure, accompanied by steady negotiations, might have brought about new, more democratic and more flexible governments in Iraq and elsewhere in the region.

Even if the economic sanctions had not been sufficient to persuade Saddam Hussein to withdraw his forces from Kuwait, they at least could have ensured that Iraq would gain nothing from its aggression. In fact, Iraq *was* worse off than before, because it suddenly lost 99 percent of its outside earnings—about half its GNP. In that limited sense the embargo succeeded. Though it drove up oil prices, the U.N. decision to embargo Iraqi and Kuwaiti oil was beneficial to the long-term interests of the international political community to discourage future aggression.

The Persian Gulf crisis would have been far more dangerous if Iraq had built nuclear weapons, which some experts predicted might have been possible within a few years. If Israel had not destroyed the Osirak nuclear reactor near Baghdad in 1981, it is even conceivable that Iraq could have had atomic bombs usable for global blackmail by August 1990. Imagine the implications of Iraq issuing a warning that if American forces were sent to Saudi Arabia, New York or Washington would be blown up.

Six months before the crisis Iraq was caught trying to import nuclear-weapon triggers from London. To prevent Iraq and other dangerous countries from acquiring nuclear weapons, on-site inspection of all of their nuclear facilities must be demanded. The 1968 Non-Proliferation Treaty (NPT), in which most non-nuclear nations agreed not to build or acquire nuclear weapons in exchange for a promise by nuclear nations to disarm their arsenals, must be strengthened, and every nation must be pressured to adhere to it. But for this to happen, the United States must fulfill its own obligations under the treaty by banning all nuclear weapons tests and taking other steps toward nuclear disarmament. The United States' refusal even to begin negotiating a test ban may well jeopardize renewal of the treaty when it expires in 1995. The U.S. government has fallen prey to the "fallacy of the last move" by only considering the immediate advantage of further developing its own nuclear arsenal, while ignoring the natural reaction of other countries to build their own nuclear weapons.

If the purpose of U.N. sanctions and containment was to create a "new world order" without aggression, that message would have been far more credible if the United Nations (and the United States in particular) had opposed aggression with equal determination wherever it occurred. Aggression cannot be stopped if it is only challenged when precious resources are at stake. Nor can it be checked if countries are unwilling to criticize aggression by their allies. Double standards have seriously weakened any global norm for nonaggression. But it is never too late to begin correcting past mistakes.

In the cease-fire negotiations after Iraq was routed out of Kuwait, the U.N. Security Council rightly demanded that Iraq pay reparations to compensate victims and restore property that was destroyed or stolen. While this suggestion may appear to contradict my earlier praise of the Marshall Plan for how well it dissipated animosities in Europe, a fundamental difference exists between the peace settlement at the end of World War II and the situation after the Persian Gulf War. The Marshall Plan was not offered to Hitler but to a successor government that disavowed Hitler's policies. If a new government comes to power in Iraq that rejects Saddam Hussein's tyranny and aggressiveness, *then* it will be time to seek better relations and help rebuild Iraq.

In a certain sense, the essential elements of a good security policy resemble those of a good education: adhere to moral principles; do yourself what you preach to others; and do not vacillate but remain consistent. I once observed a three-year-old boy on a playground who threw sand into a baby's eyes. The boy's mother, who witnessed this, did not scold her son, but simply tried to comfort the baby. Two minutes later, the boy did the same thing again.

Since the world essentially did nothing to oppose Saddam Hussein when he invaded Iran in 1980 and again when he used poison gas against the Kurds, we should not be too surprised that he resorted to brutal tactics in Kuwait. A little more foresight and consistency could have prevented this war and the heavy human casualties and environmental damage that accompanied it. Hopefully, the world's leaders will draw appropriate lessons.

Some, however, have learned the wrong lesson. They point to Iraq's aggression as a reason for building stronger military forces to deal with other aggressors. This is analogous to observing the misbehavior of a poorly educated child and arguing: "This proves that you need a stick for education, otherwise these rascals do whatever they want." Clearly, if education is undertaken properly, a stick may never be needed. Likewise, if we skillfully pursue a comprehensive peace policy, military force may not be needed either.

APPLICATION TO OTHER RECENT CONFLICTS

Could other recent wars have been prevented through the application of these same active peace policies and principles? The Iran-Iraq war was fought ostensibly over control of the waterway in the Shatt-El-Arab. If Iraq and Iran had simply taken their dispute before the World Court and abided by its decision, this costly war could have been prevented. Iraq began the war when it invaded Iran in 1980, but Iran previously made a number of unwise moves that violated all the principles of prudent dissuasion. It had dissolved its army and appeared militarily weak. It had prohibited the use of Arabic in schools in the Arabic-speaking province of Khuzistan, causing bloody street riots. By seizing American hostages it had isolated itself internationally and made it difficult for other countries to provide economic or military assistance. In daily broadcasts Iran had appealed to the Iraqi people to overthrow their government. Imagine if in 1939 Switzerland had dissolved its army, prohibited the use of German in schools in German-speaking cantons, seized foreign diplomats as hostages, and on a daily basis urged the German people to overthrow Hitler. The probability of a German invasion of Switzerland would have been much greater. Even after the Iran-Iraq war had commenced, if either side limited itself to defending its own territory instead of undertaking assaults, the war might have ended much sooner, with much less bloodshed.

It is usually easier to *prevent* wars before they occur than to find a mutually acceptable end once the fighting, the misery, and the recriminations begin. But what can be done when a conflict has become deeply entrenched, such as the conflict between Israel and the Palestinians? Some Israelis claim that it is now impossible to negotiate with the Palestinians because the latter do not want to share a homeland and only want to drive the Israelis into the sea. There may be a few fanatics who harbor that wish, but Israel's continued harsh treatment of the Palestinians in the occupied territories has driven many moderate Arabs closer to the extremists. If Israel wants to isolate those Arabs who advocate violence and terrorism, it must win the sympathy of the majority of the Palestinian people. Israel should give the Palestinians a voice in managing their own affairs, end the much resented practice of replacing elected Palestinian mayors with Israeli officers, provide them with adequate public services, and allow open elections without deciding beforehand who is fit to run for office. Israel also must acknowledge the Palestinians' right to choose for themselves a representative for negotiations. To insist that King Hussein of Jordan, who is widely distrusted, serve as the Palestinians' spokesman can only further infuriate them. Imagine how colonial Americans would have reacted if King George had insisted that only the Governor of Canada could negotiate on their behalf.

Two preconditions are necessary to prevent wars: the underlying causes of a conflict must be addressed, and mechanisms for peaceful change must be established. This applies not only to interstate wars but also to civil wars. If the landless peasants of Central America could get a plot of land from which to feed their families, if they could have a real voice in choosing their own government, if they were no longer massacred by death squads whenever they spoke out against injustice, they would be far less likely to take up arms against their governments.

In Northern Ireland, the British government's efforts to suppress fighting between separatist Catholics and loyalist Protestants with armed force, without addressing the underlying conflict, has had little success. A similar conflict between Catholics and Protestants occurred in Switzerland in the 1950s, when a French-speaking Catholic minority in the Jura region of the Canton Bern felt constantly outvoted in Parliament. A separatist movement developed, and had it simply been met with force there is little doubt that a full-scale civil war could have occurred. But after some initial hesitation the government of Bern held a referendum in the region and granted those districts that preferred to form a separate canton the right to do so. Since then, the conflict has subsided. In general, people do not resort to violence if peaceful mechanisms are available to bring about the desired change. Violence tends to occur when all peaceful avenues for change are blocked.

WHAT THE UNITED STATES CAN DO

There are a number of steps the United States could take to help defuse tense situations that might lead to conflicts and wars. One obvious step would be to stop supporting military dictators, because repressive rule inevitably leads to disillusionment, anger, and political strife. To its credit, the Reagan Administration helped persuade Ferdinand Marcos in the Philippines and Jean-Claude Duvalier in Haiti to step down from power. In Chile, the continued political rule of General Pinochet was ended in a referendum strongly supported by the United States, though his control of the military continues.

Another example of how the United States can promote conflict resolution was the attempt by the Bush Administration in early 1990 to persuade the Israeli government to enter peace talks with representatives of the Palestinians. Now, in the aftermath of the Persian Gulf War, the United States should continue to encourage Israeli-Palestinian negotiations in the hope of finding a peaceful and equitable settlement. U.S. support for the U.N.-sponsored elections in Namibia, which brought independence to the territory after its long, illegal occupation by South Africa, is another positive contribution to conflict resolution. But U.S. interest in strengthening the United Nations has been intermittent at best. The United States should embrace the United Nations more fully by paying its arrears and strengthening the organization's peacekeeping forces. The United Nations in recent years has played a very useful role in ending the Iran-Iraq war, negotiating Vietnam's withdrawal from Cambodia, and patrolling the cease-fire in Cyprus, and with our support a great deal more could be accomplished.

The United States also could help reduce one of the basic causes of conflict and global instability — poverty. This does not mean handing out money to corrupt governments who will only use our largesse to purchase weapons and police their people more effectively. It means creating new opportunities for poor people to lift themselves out of poverty. One of the primary causes of poverty is indebtedness. A Bengali woman needs only a one-time initial investment of $6 to buy twigs for weaving baskets and sell them to increase her daily earnings from two cents to $1.25.[45] By funding small banks that provide micro-enterprise loans to those who cannot borrow money because they do not own any collateral, the United States could help millions of people advance economically.

Lifting trade barriers to imports from poor countries also could be of great help. How can developing countries repay their loans and reduce their high rates of unemployment if they are prevented from exporting textiles and other light industrial goods into our markets? Easing import restrictions also would give U.S. consumers better access to Third World goods at lower prices.

The United States should cancel the debt of the least developed countries, such as those in sub-Saharan Africa. As long as poor countries use most of their export earnings to service national debts, they will remain trapped in a vicious cycle of poverty. The Brady Plan currently in place, which invites U.S. banks to reduce Third World debts on a *voluntary* basis, is not enough. It is also illogical — those banks that cancel their loans get nothing, while those that do not leave open the possibility of some repayment. This is like asking people to pay their taxes voluntarily.

Another way to help Third World countries is to provide them with more efficient production technologies. Unlike physical resources, which must be taken away from someone to be given to someone else, knowledge is not lost when it is shared with others. The United States could help finance a "Network of Applied Technical Universities and Research Establishments" (NATURE) through which researchers from around the world could develop new appropriate technologies and explore better ways to meet human needs.[46] Instead of being poured into weapons research laboratories like those at Livermore and Los Alamos, the billions of dollars we spend each year on Research & Development could be used to develop pollution-free manufacturing methods, new energy sources, cures for diseases, higher yielding and more disease resistant crops, and so on. Some remarkably modest advances, if widely disseminated, could make an amazing difference. For example, a simple clay oven recently has been designed that could reduce the consumption of fuel wood by seventy percent and help save the dwindling forests in the Third World. Oral rehydration with a simple solution of water, sugar, and salt could save the lives of millions of children who die each year from diarrhea. UNICEF[47] has estimated that it would cost less than $1.50 to inoculate one child against all the major childhood diseases, which needlessly kill about three million children annually. To inoculate all the 140 million children born in the entire world annually would cost roughly $210 million, about a quarter of the price tag of a single stealth bomber.[48]

The United States would be wise to devote greater resources to student exchanges with other countries. Friendships forged during youth last a lifetime and can help create a network of kids committed to better worldwide communication and understanding. Alexander Yakovlev, one of Gorbachev's early advisors and an architect of *perestroika*, was one of the first Soviet students to visit the United States in the late 1950s. The United States also might support Gorbachev's proposal[49] for the creation of an international council of leading personalities in science, politics, literature, the arts, and religion to study global problems and possible solutions, a venture that would cost a minute fraction of our military budgets.

Our government should assist with the economic conversion of military industries to civilian ones and break the dependence of numerous firms and communities on military spending. New roles can be found for the military in such areas as disaster relief, toxic waste cleanup, reforestation, major Third World engineering projects, space exploration, vaccination campaigns, or U.N. peace-keeping.

Most importantly, the United States should give up its habit of intervening in other countries' affairs with military force, directly or indirectly. The CIA's participation in the overthrow of the moderately progressive Arbenz government in Guatemala in 1954 brought a series of brutal military dictatorships to power and plunged the nation into an ongoing civil war that has claimed more than 100,000 lives so far. The CIA's 1953 overthrow of the Mossadegh government in Iran (after it nationalized the oil industry) created sharp frustration and resentment among

Iranian intellectuals, who felt they had no voice in shaping their country's future. The dominance of foreign advisers (mostly Americans) in the Shah's government made it easy for Khomeini to seize power by promising to rid the country of foreign influence. If President Franklin D. Roosevelt had overthrown the Mexican government when it nationalized the oil industry in 1938, we would probably have rather tense relations with Mexico today — perhaps we would have even seen a Mexican hostage crisis. The long-term consequences of the recent U.S. interventions in Grenada and Panama remains to be seen. They certainly opened old wounds about U.S. "gunboat diplomacy" and set back our efforts to create relationships of mutual respect with the countries of Latin America.

If the United States insists on intervening each time a foreign government pursues policies not to our liking, whether it is an ally or an adversary, we in fact hand over to people like Khadafi or Noriega the decision of whether our country is at war or at peace. If, as individuals, we constantly broke into in our neighbors' homes whenever they had family disputes and told them how to solve their problems, we would soon get bruised and lose our friends.

When an American serviceman and a Turkish woman died in the bombing of a disco in Berlin in 1986, President Reagan ordered air attacks on Tripoli and Benghazi in retaliation. Later, the bomb was actually traced to Syria rather than Libya. Imagine if the government of Holland had reacted to the French government's sinking of the Greenpeace flagship Rainbow Warrior in New Zealand, which killed a Dutch photographer, by bombing Paris and Marseilles. Or if Managua had reacted to the Reagan Administration's support for the Contras, who killed not just one Nicaraguan soldier but thousands of politicians, teachers, nurses, doctors, and school children, by bombing New York and Washington. We must learn to see ourselves the way others in the world perceive us — as practitioners of double standards — and work toward practicing what we preach.

Use of force by the United States in international relations, from gunboat diplomacy to CIA overthrows, severely limits our ability to criticize the use of force by others. How could the Bush Administration talk seriously about economic sanctions against the Soviet Union for repressing the Lithuanian independence movement when the United States had just invaded Panama and bombarded shanty-towns resulting in hundreds of civilian deaths? It is no wonder that few of our allies were willing to support the invasion of Panama. Actions like these are not conducive to creating relationships of mutual trust and respect among countries.

There are also a wide variety of arms control measures the United States should pursue as part of an active peace policy. The United States should join the Soviet Union and China in adopting a policy of no first use of nuclear weapons — not just "no early use." If nobody uses nuclear weapons first, they will never be used. Eight out of ten American people favor such a policy; indeed, almost as many mistakenly believe that no first use *is* our official policy.[50] As Kenneth Boulding has pointed out, as long as nuclear war remains possible, no matter how unlikely, it is bound to occur sooner or later.[51]

We should accept the Soviet Union's long-standing offer for a comprehensive nuclear test ban. When Gorbachev began a unilateral moratorium on nuclear testing on the occasion of the 40th anniversary of the bombing of Hiroshima on August 6, 1985, the Reagan Administration at first replied that a test ban could not be verified without on-site inspection. Gorbachev then accepted the concept of on-site inspection, and the United States argued that nuclear tests were needed to ensure the reliability of our weapons stockpile. However, that argument is false since high reliability of nuclear weapons is required only to execute a disarming first strike. The failure of a small number of warheads to explode in an attack would still enable an opponent to retaliate. But pure deterrence does not require one hundred percent reliability. No country could ever assume that *all* its adversary's weapons would fail simply because they had not been tested. A test ban would *increase* mutual security by undermining either side's confidence that it could execute a successful first strike.

Many of the weapons systems our government has acquired in the name of deterrence actually undermine U.S. security. Missiles with multiple warheads, such as the MX, are extremely vulnerable and thus a tempting target for attack. Getting rid of such first-strike weapons would not only save money but also enhance our security.

Czechoslovakian President Václav Havel, in his address to a joint session of Congress, said, "I often hear the question: How can the United States of America help us today? My reply is as paradoxical as the whole of my life has been: You can help us most of all if you help the Soviet Union on its irreversible, but immensely complicated road to democracy. . . . And the sooner you yourself will be able to reduce the burden of the military budget born by the American people. To put it metaphorically: The millions you give to the East today will soon return to you in the form of billions in savings."[52] Many U.S. officials oppose helping the Soviet Union on the grounds that an economic crisis forces Gorbachev to cut military spending and turn his attention inward. But Gorbachev and his allies have already made that choice — and now we must help them. In 1919, French Prime Minister Clemenceau naively took advantage of Germany's weakness after World War I by imposing harsh economic sanctions at Versailles. This led to deep German resentment, which Hitler then successfully exploited by promising to abrogate the Versailles Treaty and restore the luster of Germany's military strength. After World War II, the United States learned the lessons of Versailles and decided to implement the Marshall Plan. By helping its former enemies to rebuild their war-torn economies, Germany and Japan were converted into allies. Has George Bush forgotten the lessons of Versailles? Has he forgotten how close a coup came to toppling Gorbachev? It remains in our strong interest to help *glasnost* and *perestroika* succeed.

CONCLUDING OBSERVATIONS

Modern science and technology have given humanity unprecedented capabilities for accomplishing both good and evil. Automation and robotization have greatly increased our productivity and, properly distributed, new technologies could help eliminate hunger and poverty. Solar energy could free us from dependence on exhaustible fuel supplies like oil. A network of glass fiber cables crisscrossing the globe could permit instant communication between people anywhere. Computerized "expert systems" could give doctors or teachers access to the knowledge of the world's leading specialists. We possess the know-how to eradicate many deadly diseases entirely. Smallpox was eliminated at a cost of $80 million, half the cost of a single MX missile. A campaign to rid the world of malaria, from which millions now suffer, would only cost $300 million, roughly two percent of the cost of one aircraft-carrier task force. For the first time, we have a chance to overcome the scourges that have plagued humanity since the dawn of history. But so far, we have failed to make good use of our knowledge and technological advances.

As a Buddhist monk once put it, "Humankind possesses a key that can open the gates to heaven. But the same key can also open the gates to hell." Our advancements have given us the capacity to turn the earth into a radioactive wasteland. We can alter the climate so that lush forests become deserts and densely populated coastal regions are immersed by the rising seas. We are now causing the extinction of plant and animal species at a rate much faster than during the Mesozoic Age, when dinosaurs and many other forms of life died out. We are rapidly using up exhaustible resources that have taken millions of years to accumulate. And we are depleting the ozone layer that protects us from cancer-causing ultraviolet radiation.

In the past, our capacity to destroy the environment was so limited that we had the luxury to wait until damage became visible before we needed to take corrective measures. People could learn through trial and error. Today, however, we can no longer afford to burn fossil fuels until the greenhouse effect melts the polar icecaps, for then it will be too late. Nor can we afford a single nuclear war, deliberate or accidental. The damage would be irreversible.

The way our political system now operates, reacting to problems *after* they manifest themselves, is comparable to driving a car with our eyes closed. Does it make sense to wait until we have driven off the road before we adjust the steering wheel to get back onto the pavement? As long as we travel at a slow speed and with no other vehicles on the road, it may be possible — though not very smart — to operate that way. But at a high speed, this kind of strategy is deadly. We must now foresee dangers awaiting us before we collide, and we must take corrective action to avoid them in time. We must make every effort to prevent wars before they occur, rather than focusing our attention on how to fight wars once they begin. Let us drive with our eyes open.

NOTES

1.   Patricia Mische, "Choosing the Future of the Earth," *Breakthrough*, Fall1987/Spring 1988, pp. 38-42.

2.   Robert C. Tucker, *Politics as Leadership* (Columbia: University of Missouri Press, 1981).

3.   World Commision on Environment and Development (Chaired by Gro Harlem Brundtland), *Our Common Future* (New York: Oxford University Press, 1987).

4. Eugene J. Carroll, "Peace Dividend? The Arms Race is Continuing," *International Herald Tribune*, May 22, 1990, p. 4.

5.   Based on Melvin Small and J. David Singer, *Resort to Arms: International and Civil Wars, 1816-1980* (Newbury Park, CA: Sage, 1982) and data from 1980-1991.

6.   *Ibid.* The probability that this was due to chance is much less than one in a million.

7.   *Ibid.*

8.   Johan Galtung, *There Are Alternatives! Four Roads to Peace and Security* (Nottingham: Spokesman, 1984).

9.   Mikhail Gorbachev, Address to the United Nations, December 8, 1988.

10. Dietrich Fischer, *Preventing War in the Nuclear Age* (Totowa, NJ: Rowman & Allanheld, 1984).

11. "Nightline," ABC Television, December 8, 1988.

12. Dietrich Fischer, Wilhelm Nolte, and Jan Oberg, *Winning Peace: Strategies and Ethics for a Nuclear Free World* (New York and London: Taylor & Francis, 1989).

13. Harry B. Hollins, Averill L. Powers, and Mark Sommer, *The Conquest of War: Alternative Strategies for Global Security* (Boulder, CO: Westview, 1989).

14. Lloyd J. Dumas, "Economics and Alternative Security: Toward a Peacekeeping International Economy," in Burns H. Weston, ed., *Alternative Security: Living Without Nuclear Deterence* (Boulder, CO: Westview Press, 1990).

15. Muzafer Sherif and Carolyn Sherif, *Social Psychology* (New York: Harper & Row, 1969).

16. Mark Sommer, *Reuniting Europe: Economic Integration as a Path to Peace* (Berkeley: Pacific Institute for Studies in Security, Development , and Environment, 1989).

17. *Encyclopedia Britannica* (Chicago: Helen Hemingway Benton Pub., 1974), vol. 10, p. 54.

18. United States Department of Commerce, Bureau of the Census, *Historical Statistics of the United States: Colonial Times to 1970* (Washington, DC: U.S. Government Printing Office, 1975, p. 225). Figures in current dollars.

19. The World Bank, *World Development Report, 1990* (Oxford: Oxford University Press, 1990), p. 179.

20. Gale Warner and Michael H. Shuman, *Citizen Diplomats: Pathfinders in Soviet-American Politics and How You Can Join Them* (New York: Continuum, 1987).

21. Jan Tinbergen and Dietrich Fischer, *Warfare and Welfare: Integrating Security Policy into Socio-Economic Policy* (New York: St. Martin's Press, 1987).

22. Gerald Mische, "To Set Our Leaders Free: Dismantling the National Security Straitjacket," *Breakthrough*, 9:1-3, pp. 33-37.

23. Roger Fisher and William Ury, *Getting to Yes: Negotiating Agreement without Giving In* (Boston: Houghton & Mifflin, 1981).

24. The International Court of Arbitration is different from the World Court, even though both are located in the Hague, Netherlands.

25. Benjamin B. Ferencz, *Planethood* (Coos Bay: Vision Books, 1988).

26. Howard S. Brembeck, *The Civilized Defense Plan: Security of Nations*

Through the Power of Trade (Fairfax: Hero Books, 1989).

27. Paul Lewis, "Soviets to Accept World Court Role in Human Rights," *New York Times*, March 9, 1989, p. A1, A15.

28. Daniel Goleman, "Why Job Criticism Fails: Psychology's New Findings," *New York Times*, July 26, 1988, p. C1.

29. Robert C. Johansen, "Toward Post-Nuclear Security: An Overview," in Burns H. Weston, ed., *Alternative Security: Living Without Nuclear Deterence* (Boulder, CO: Westview Press, 1990).

30. Dietrich Fischer, "Invulnerability Without Threat: The Swiss Concept of General Defense," *Journal of Peace Research*, 19:3, 1982, pp. 205-225.

31. Johan Galtung, "On the Strategy of Nonmilitary Defense: Some Proposals and Problems," in Wim Bartels, ed., *Peace and Justice: Unity or Dilemma* (Nijmegen: Institute of Peace Research, Catholic University of Nijmegen, 1968).

32. Gene Sharp, *Making Europe Unconquerable: The Potential of Civilian-Based Deterence and Defense* (Cambridge, MA: Ballinger, 1985).

33. Dietrich Fischer, Wilhelm Nolte, and Jan Oberg, *op. cit.*

34. This story was told to me by film producer Arthur Kanegis.

35. Adam Roberts, *Nations in Arms: The Theory and Practice of Territorial Defense,* second edition (New York: St. Martin's Press, 1986).

36. Richard Halloran, "Senator's Report False Warnings of Soviet Strikes," *New York Times*, October 29, 1980, p. A16.

37. Mikhail Gorbachev, Address to the United Nations, December 8, 1988.

38. Independent Commision on Disarmament and Security Issues (Chaired by Olof Palme), *Common Security: A Blueprint for Survival* (New York: Simon & Schuster, 1982).

39. Columbia Broadcasting System, "60 Minutes," October 7, 1990.

40. Life-time imprisonment, rather than the death penalty, is a more appropriate punishment to end the cycle of violence. Those who promote justice must clearly distinguish themselves from those who purge their opponents through execution.

41. United Nations Children's Fund (UNICEF), *The State of the World's Children 1990* (New York: Oxford University Press, 1990).

42. Michael H. Shuman, Hal Harvey, and Daniel Arbess, *Security Without War: A Post-Cold War Foreign Policy* (Boulder, CO: Westview Press, 1992).

43. Elaine Sciolino with Michael R. Gordon, "U.S. Gave Iraq Little Reason Not to Mount Kuwait Assault," *New York Times*, September 23, 1990, p. 1, 18.

44. Patricia E. Tyler, "Iraq's War Toll Estimated by U.S.," *New York Times*, June 5, 1991, p. A5.

45. Muhammad Yunus, "Grammeen Bank: Organization and Operations." Paper presented at the World Conference on Support for Micro-Enterprises, Washington, D.C., The World Bank, June 6-9, 1988)

46. Dietrich Fischer, "Non-military Aspects on Security," Report to the United Nations Institute for Disarmament Research (UNIDIR), 1991.

47. United Nations Children's Fund (UNICEF), *op. cit.*, p. 19.

48. The costs of one Stealth Bomber is now estimated to be $860 million. *See* Richard W. Stephenson, "Pentagon Unveils a Stealth Missile," *New York Times*, June 8, 1991, p. 8.

49. Mikhail Gorbachev, "The Reality and Guarantee of a Secure World," *Pravda*, September 17, 1987. Official translation released by the Soviet Mission to the United Nations, New York.

50. *Voter Options on Nuclear Arms Policy — Technical Appendix* (New York: Public Agenda Foundation, 1984), p. 24.

51. Kenneth E. Boulding, *Stable Peace* (Austin, TX: University of Texas Press, 1978), p. 65.

52. Václav Havel, Address to a Joint Session of the U.S. Congress, *Congressional Record - House*, February 21, 1990, pp. H392-H395.

DEMOCRACY

For nearly a decade Michael Shuman, an attorney, directed the California-based Center for Innovative Diplomacy (CID), a coalition of 8,000 people (including 3,000 mayors and city council members) dedicated to increasing direct citizen participation in international affairs. Under his direction CID pioneered the concepts of "citizen diplomacy" and "municipal foreign policy." He is currently a Fellow at the Institute for Policy Studies in Washington, D.C.

In the following essay Shuman argues that participation in peace-making can go far beyond the traditional tools of voting, letter-writing, or marching. The central new objective for the peace movement, he argues, should not be arms control but "leader control." By subjecting leaders at home and abroad to strong civilian checks and balances, wars will become more difficult to wage.

He finally recommends that citizens work through their own communities to promote peace through various non-military strategies — spreading democracy, conserving resources, promoting sustainable development, and practicing citizen diplomacy.

A Separate Peace Movement: The Role of Participation

Michael H. Shuman

THE END OF ACTIVISM?

In June 1989 the staff of *Nuclear Times* sold off their remaining word processors, desks, chairs, and books. For eight years the magazine had served as the principal voice of the U.S. peace movement, a massive grassroots force that had brought a million people to New York City in 1982 to rally for disarmament and had spurred 900 cities, counties, and states to pass resolutions calling for a "freeze" of the nuclear arms race. At the same time, drastic budget cuts were being made at the largest national grassroots peace organization, SANE/Freeze, and the principal funders of the peace movement were moving into other liberal issues, such as environmental protection and reproductive rights. What was most remarkable about all of this was that hardly anyone was even noticing.

When the Berlin Wall came tumbling down in November 1989, the peace movement did indeed seem irrelevant. Many peace organizations blossomed when the United States was pumping up the Pentagon's budget, building first-strike nuclear weapons like the MX and Trident D-5, resuscitating old civil defense plans, casually discussing how to fight limited nuclear wars in Europe, and proclaiming the Soviet Union an "evil empire." By the end of the 1980s, however, even conservatives were heralding the end of the Cold War and rushing to help the Soviet Union and the countries of Eastern Europe transform into liberal democracies. In a celebrated article published in a neoconservative journal called *The National Interest*, State Department analyst Francis Fukuyama trumpeted that the victory of capitalist democracies over socialist dictatorships was now so assured that we had reached the "end of history."[1]

Yet more sober analysts could hardly conclude that we had achieved "peace for our time." Whatever illusions existed about peace "breaking out" were shattered in August 1990, when Saddam Hussein of Iraq invaded the small kingdom of Kuwait and the United States responded by dispatching several hundred thousand troops to the desert of Saudi Arabia. Five months later this crisis erupted into an all out war resulting in tens of thousands of casualties. And Iraqi adventurism, as the other authors in this volume stress, is just one of dozens of major threats that continue to imperil U.S. national security. Global warming, ozone depletion, Third World debt, the proliferation of nuclear and chemical weapons, terrorism, drugs, recession — the list expands every day. A security policy that ignores any of these threats is unworthy of the name. Yet, by and large, the U.S. national security establishment has ignored all of them. So has much of the peace movement.

Like the very men in the Defense and State Departments they criticize, the key thinkers and strategists within the peace movement have been fixated with bombs. Hawks like Caspar Weinberger have wanted more weapons and peace movement intellectuals like Randall Forsberg have wanted fewer, but they have been strangely unified in their conviction that weapons are at the heart of the issues of war and peace. But as international relations scholars have long realized, weapons are merely the symptoms of deeper conflicts. If weapons were all that mattered, we would have armed up long ago against the "British threat" and the "French threat," since both nations possess the nuclear capacities to destroy the United States many times over. Yet any member of Congress advocating a new anti-Tory or anti-French weapons system would be all but laughed out of the chambers. Even arms appropriations aimed at the Chinese Communists — despite the the Tiananmen Square massacre in 1989 — remain politically unthinkable. With each of these countries the United States built *relations* that rendered nuclear war so improbable that military preparations would be ludicrous.

The emphasis of the U.S. peace movement on arms control measures like the "freeze" ironically allowed national security planners to monopolize U.S. foreign policy. By focusing on arms issues, over which they and the public have the least power, members of the peace movement ensured themselves a very limited role in the making of foreign policy — and very limited success. If, instead, the peace movement had defined peace as flowing from appropriate political, economic, and environmental policies, issues over which citizens have a great deal of influence, all Americans could have become active players in U.S. foreign policy.

Many in the peace movement also seemed to accept the common wisdom that national security policy should be the province of the elite inhabiting Washington, D.C. Many leading activists such as William Arkin of Greenpeace and John Pike of the Federation of American Scientists sought to beat national security experts at their own game. While there's nothing wrong with preparing reports and offering testimony to guide national security policy-makers, too often this kind of work has completely crowded out the possibility of the peace movement helping individuals and communities to craft their own foreign policies. The result has been a steady erosion of democratic decision-making over vital security interests. By leaving security policy to the experts, or simply emulating the experts, the peace movement effectively allowed policies to develop that were out of touch with the American

people—policies that emphasized weapons, threats of force, and military intervention. If those Americans most dedicated to preventing war have been content to
allow experts to dominate U.S. foreign policy-making, can we be surprised when
the general population does the same?

The misguided strategy and tactics of the U.S. peace movement reveal a deeper
problem with American political culture—a reluctance of the American people to
participate in national security policy-making. Unappreciative of the links between
nonmilitary actions at home and wars abroad, many Americans believe they are
powerless to affect international affairs. Even those who believe they can have an
impact still look primarily to the formal institutions of national politics to conduct
foreign policy. These beliefs, however, are among the the most pernicious features
of the war system. They are self-fulfilling prophecies of popular impotence that
allow the other gears of the war system to grind on unchallenged.

This chapter suggests that a rededication by Americans to the basics of political
participation could help end the war system. It begins with an exploration of how
nonparticipation perpetuates the war system. It then presents proposals for new
ways people can participate in foreign policy, at home and abroad, and breathe new
life into the peace movement.

PARTICIPATION AND WAR

The war system is characterized by leaders who are able to use military force
easily because they face little or no domestic opposition. The courts, the legislature,
and the people in the war system are all powerless to stand in the way of a decision
to wage war. To be sure, leaders must persuade people that the fight is just, lest they
face defections from the armed forces or civil discontent. But once popular support
has been mustered, the people are effectively barred from debating, challenging,
protesting, or hamstringing battle plans.

These characteristics of the war system are obviously most prevalent in a
dictatorship and least prevalent in a decentralized democracy. According to several
empirical studies of conflicts between nations over the past two centuries, while
democracies and nondemocracies are equally likely to get involved in wars with
nondemocracies, wars *between* liberal democracies are exceedingly rare.[2] One
strains to find two politically well-developed democracies that have come close to
war with one another in modern times.

Intuitively many Americans understand that democratic participation fosters
peace. Americans' collective relief over the emergence of more democratic governments in Eastern Europe, Argentina, Brazil, the Philippines, and South Korea
reflects our recognition that leaders accountable to a vigilant citizenry, and leaders
who respect the rights of the people within their country, are more likely to act

responsibly in international affairs. Conservatives and liberals alike have enthusiastically supported *glasnost* in the Soviet Union, protests by Chinese students, and dozens of other democratic movements abroad.[3]

But what are the underlying reasons popular participation constrains conflict? To begin with, a nation going to war needs to imbue its people with images of a brutal enemy. Since war necessarily involves heinous acts of maiming and killing (especially against civilians in modern warfare), soldiers are less willing to commit such acts and the public is less willing to tolerate them if the enemy seems undeserving of brutality. Where participatory forces operate, including a diverse and free press, exaggerated or dehumanized images of an enemy become more difficult to create and maintain. If the citizens of a democratic country can freely speak and meet with citizens of an adversary, they often discover that the enemy is not nearly as nefarious as government and private-interest propaganda have maintained. This by itself goes far toward explaining why democracies have not fought one another. "Perhaps," writes Yale political scientist Bruce Russett, "our elites cannot persuade us to fight other peoples who we imagine, like us, are self-determining, autonomous people — people who in some substantial way control their own political fate."[4]

Citizens in a democracy also can more easily form valuable relationships with the supposed enemy, and thereby create pressures on both sides for leaders to maintain the peace. Businesspeople want to protect their trade contracts, scientists and academicians want to complete their joint research projects, and artists want to continue their cultural collaborations. After President Carter imposed an embargo on grain sales to the Soviet Union in January 1980, many midwestern farmers who had benefited from earlier grain sales to the Soviets became vocal advocates of restoring economic relations. By 1983, according to William Bundy, then editor of *Foreign Affairs*, President Reagan "responded to heavy domestic political pressures from the U.S. farm belt" when he scrapped the embargo and signed a new five-year contract that prohibited interruptions for political reasons.[5]

The web of relationships made possible by U.S. pluralism also helped reduce American hostility toward China. Widely regarded in the late 1960s as a "yellow menace" against which the United States considered building a "light" ABM system, China became America's ally because of what Arthur W. Hummel, Jr., the U.S. Ambassador there in the early 1980s, has called "an amazing web" of relationships. These people-to-people ties, said Hummel, "perhaps the majority of them having nothing to do with the U.S. government [are] a genuine stabilizing force and a force which through the decades will produce much better understanding."[6] Even after Chinese troops killed thousands of pro-democracy demonstrators in and around Tiananmen Square in June 1989, these relationships gave Americans the opportunity to express anger and disappointment to Chinese officials through dialogue, protest, and divestment, rather than through a renewed nuclear arms race.[7]

A third way democracy promotes peace is by permitting citizens to take peacemaking initiatives with leaders in the adversary nation that constructively supplement and improve official relations. In formal negotiating, leaders make worst-case assumptions about an adversary's intentions. But informal negotiating, according to Joseph V. Montville, a Foreign Service officer in the State Department, and William D. Davidson, a psychiatrist specializing in foreign affairs, is "always open-minded, often altruistic, and . . . strategically optimistic, based on the best-case analysis. Its underlying assumption is that actual or potential conflict can be resolved or eased by appealing to common human capabilities to respond to goodwill and reasonableness."[8] Thus, during the late 1950s the democratic nature of the United States enabled *Saturday Review* editor Norman Cousins to launch the annual Dartmouth Conferences — high-level, off-the-record Soviet-American discussions which played an important role in helping the superpowers reach formal agreements to expand trade, ban above-ground nuclear tests, install the original "hot line," and allow direct commercial air service between the United States and the Soviet Union.[9]

Finally, war is far more fatal and costly to ordinary people than it is to the leaders promoting and planning it. The public in a democracy usually has a limited tolerance for military adventurism. As the Vietnam War demonstrated, popular support in a modern democracy for far-off wars crumbles as young friends and neighbors return maimed or in coffins, as news reports graphically depict atrocities on the front lines, and as international opinion leaders condemn the supposedly just cause. In a democratic culture negative news easily spreads to the people, who then can more readily pressure their leaders to avoid or halt the war. Thus political pressures against the Vietnam War were able to build more rapidly and decisively than did analogous domestic pressures in the Soviet Union against its misadventure in Afghanistan. Once Mikhail Gorbachev's policies of *glasnost* began, however, Soviet public outrage over the 10,000 young Soviet men killed and 20,000 others wounded surfaced and spread rapidly through anti-war rallies, essays, poetry, and films.[10] Democratic political structures allow the public to end hated wars.

Together, these explanations suggest how public participation can reduce the probability of a nation entangling itself in war. Democracy can render leaders accountable to a more informed set of views about the enemy, and make them more aware of the benefits of peacetime relationships and the human costs of warfare. And public participation acts as a check against abuse, zealotry, and rash exercises of power.

But democracy today has played only a limited role in preventing war because of its scarcity. By one conservative count, fewer than 50 of the world's 160-plus nations can be described as democratic.[11] In fact, even those 50 countries have room for substantial improvement. Political participation in America, for example, faces profound obstacles that have inhibited the development of a real peace movement. Consider three sets of problems now besetting U.S. democracy:

~ The U.S. two-party system, institutionalized in every state through a vast web of laws and traditions, has prevented the articulation of sharp and innovative positions on most issues, including those relating to peace. While the Social Democrats, the Greens, and dozens of other parties have become important advocates for significant changes in the foreign policies of Europe's parliamentary democracies, the two-party system has produced relatively indistinct foreign-policy positions and effectively gagged advocates of change.

~ The United States is one of the few western democracies that makes voting difficult for the average citizen. While most countries hold elections on weekends to ensure that workers can vote on a day off, the United States clings to the tradition of holding elections on Tuesdays. And while most countries allow some form of quick or instant registration, most Americans must register months before an election or lose the right to vote.[12]

~ In contrast to many democracies in Western Europe that publicly finance elections or closely regulate campaign expenditures, the U.S. Supreme Court has declared that an individual's right to spend as much as he or she wishes on political campaigns is a constitutionally protected right of free speech.[13] In 1988 it cost $393,000 on average to obtain a seat in the House of Representatives and $3 million to win a seat in the Senate.[14] Money, of course, not only dominates U.S. elections but also feeds the special interest lobbyists, political action committees, media consultants, direct mail houses, and advertising firms that chart the direction of U.S. legislation.[15]

These three general problems with U.S. democracy help explain why emerging democracies are actually choosing parliamentary forms of government over the U.S. model. They also explain why more and more Americans are disaffected with the whole political process. In contrast to European and Latin American democracies where 80 to 90 percent participation rates are not uncommon, the percentage of eligible U.S. voters showing up at the polls has steadily declined from 62.8 percent in 1960 to below 50 percent today.[16]

Falling participation directly influences the propensity of the nation to use military force. Americans refusing to vote are disproportionately female, young, poor, less educated, and nonwhite — precisely those groups most disadvantaged.[17]

These groups are also much more skeptical than the general population about the value of using military force in U.S. foreign policy. For example, the one constituency that was consistently critical of U.S. military involvement in the Persian Gulf was that of African Americans.[18] If Americans continue to disengage from the political system, the president and Congress will feel greater latitude in deploying and using force irrespective of the views of the populace.

Because of the increasing importance of money in reelection campaigns, the positions of many U.S. politicians are also increasingly driven, not by political principle, but by major donors. On the issues of war and peace the financial coffers of arms manufacturers and other Department of Defense contractors have been able to overwhelm the political influence of the peace movement. The entire peace movement, broadly defined, probably has no more than twenty registered lobbyists on Capitol Hill; the firm of General Electric, in contrast, has a lobbying office in Washington, D.C., with a staff of 150.

These problems are compounded by the specific obstacles facing those wishing to participate in U.S. military and foreign policy. When it comes to "external affairs," the United States — like nearly all nations — is run as if it were a monarchy. Americans have readily accepted that their military and foreign policy should be set by the president and a small group of appointed officials in the National Security Council. This, however, was never the original intent of the Founding Fathers of the nation; the Constitution is full of provisions allowing various kinds of public participation in foreign policy.[19] A representative legislature, not the president, was given the right to declare war, regulate foreign commerce, set up national defenses, and define and punish violations of international law. The federal judiciary was empowered to review a wide range of cases with international implications, including those involving treaties, ambassadors, the high seas, international law, and foreign nations or citizens. According to the Tenth Amendment, "The powers not delegated to the United States by the Constitution, nor prohibited by it to the States, are reserved to the States respectively, or to the people." These include the unfettered rights of citizens, as well as cities and states, to speak, organize, research, educate, lobby, give grants, boycott, divest, and meet with leaders abroad on foreign policy matters.

But the tragic reality is that all kinds of Americans — legislators, judges, local officials, journalists, and citizens — have voluntarily surrendered their foreign policy powers to national government, primarily to the executive branch. Congress has relegated itself to denying or approving budget authorizations for certain weapons systems or military operations. The judicial branch has dismissed military-policy and foreign-policy lawsuits as raising "political questions" that it is incompetent to answer, no matter how glaring the violations of actual law.[20] Most cities still regard local involvement in foreign policy as "improper" or "meddling."

The press has sometimes been an important source of independent scrutiny, but too often has uncritically reported official "disinformation" and been reluctant to challenge official policies for fear of alienating official contacts.[21] Meanwhile, the public, as noted, is disengaging from the political system altogether.

The result has been a runaway foreign policy establishment, geared toward continuous military mobilization and giving only minimal attention to public opinion that might point security policy in a new direction. Polls indicate that most Americans are generally satisfied with presidential conduct in foreign affairs but profoundly disenchanted on a growing number of specific security issues. For instance, although between seventy and eighty percent of the American public in the early 1980s favored a bilateral nuclear weapons freeze,[22] the Reagan Administration consistently refused to put a freeze proposal on the negotiating table. Polls also suggest that the American public has been less enthusiastic about nuclear arms buildups and most military interventions than their leaders have been.[23]

The danger of politically uncontrolled leaders entering wars, therefore, is not merely a feature of totalitarian and authoritarian states. It is also a feature of western democracies that have authoritarian foreign policy structures, where it arguably poses even greater dangers. In countries clearly lacking democratic institutions, citizens have learned to treat their government's pronouncements on foreign policy skeptically. Until quite recently, for example, citizens in such countries as Czechoslovakia, Poland, and the Soviet Union knew that the newspapers and history books were filled with lies, and that far more reliable sources were dissidents like Václav Havel, Lech Walesa, and Andrei Sakharov. But in the West, where people are seemingly free to speak, organize, and vote, official catechisms are questioned less frequently and dissenters are readily vilified. Efforts to end the war system through democratization, therefore, must begin vigorously in our own backyard.

PROMOTING PARTICIPATION AT HOME

Addressing the defects of U.S. democracy, one by one, could improve the prospects for peace. Building third parties could give advocates of a peace system a clearer voice and more clout in the electoral process. Mandating day-of-voting registration would help open the political process to the economically disadvantaged members of our society—those most likely to question military adventurism. Restricting the power of money to buy elections or votes on particular pieces of legislation would undermine the political power of Pentagon contractors to perpetuate arms races and military conflicts.

Yet even within the political system that exists today there is much that can be done to strengthen checks and balances over decisions to go to war. At least three different strategies might accomplish this: giving Americans greater access to foreign-policy information; strengthening the political restraints on the government's war-making powers; and harnessing communities to carry out more peaceful foreign policies.

Increasing Foreign Policy Information

With better information, Americans can assess the magnitude of threats to national security and the value of competing policies. Unfortunately, under the rubric of "national security," U.S. leaders have been able to keep an enormous amount of important information away from the American people, causing many to feel left out, disaffected, and powerless. Attempts to restrict public access to information reached a new height in late 1986 when the Reagan Administration unsuccessfully tried to create a new "sensitive" category of classification, giving every federal department the power to withhold from public scrutiny "those unclassified matters that are related to the national defense or foreign relations of the U.S. government."[24]

Officials continually warn that we should avoid releasing information that will embarrass allies, endanger agents and their sources, or provide opportunities for adversaries or terrorists to weaken state security. Yet the national need for secrecy must be continually weighed against its costs, not only to our civil liberties but also to the quality of our foreign policies. In many instances U.S. leaders have used secrecy, not to outwit adversaries abroad, but to silence critics at home. A telling example is the U.S. Navy's policy of refusing "to confirm or deny" the presence of nuclear weapons on its ships. Because Soviet intelligence no doubt knows a great deal about the status of the ships it tracks, this policy results in the American people's knowing less about American security policy than the Soviet military does.[25] The U.S. government has clung to secrecy even when the lives of American citizens have been at stake. After the September 1980 explosion of a Titan II silo near Damascus, Arkansas, despite local fears about releases of radiation, the Pentagon refused to acknowledge whether the accident had occurred and whether there was any danger to public health.[26]

This closure of the U.S. foreign policy-making apparatus has not served security interests very well. In a climate of more open dissemination and evaluation of information, some of the most serious foreign-policy blunders in modern U.S. history might have been avoided. If the public had known the strength of the Viet Cong, which the Pentagon deliberately underestimated to present a more sanguine picture of the American military effort in Southeast Asia, the Vietnam War might have been cut short by several years.[27] President Carter's secret agreement to bring the Shah of Iran into the United States for medical treatment triggered the takeover of the American Embassy in Tehran and brought down Carter's presidency.

President Reagan's Iran-Contra scandal involved secret deals to trade arms for hostages and funnel profits through Swiss banks to help the Nicaraguan rebels wage war against the Sandinista government. In all of these instances the public was excluded or deceived, not out of a principled concern for Americans' interest, but because successive administrations concluded that their policies could not have withstood informed public scrutiny. To view these events simply as misjudgments within each administration is to miss the larger point. Scandals and bad judgment are inevitable without vigorous public scrutiny, and the more they are covered up, the worse they become.

Besides often being counterproductive, secrecy also may be increasingly irrelevant. We are living in an era of expanding mass communications. Smart, agile reporters are roaming the globe. Broad networks of people are communicating with one another through telephones, radios, and computers.[28] A growing number of "eyes in the sky" satellites are making high resolution photos available for private purchase.[29] Very little information can now remain under national lock and key, even information within relatively closed societies. Prior to *glasnost*, for example, American technical visitors to the Soviet Union were able to tell Soviet experts facts they did not know about their own country's military capabilities, facts which were widely published in the United States.

The accountability of American leaders could be improved with greater public openness about our strategic doctrines, weapons deployments, and intelligence activities abroad. This might be accomplished by narrowing the national security exceptions to the Freedom of Information Act. Another helpful reform would be to force the Pentagon to identify more of its "black" budget—line items for highly classified facilities and operations that are virtually immune from congressional scrutiny. Currently these hidden line items total more than $35 billion annually.[30]

U.S. national security advisors would be well advised to listen to—and not just lecture—the general public. A good model is the National Environmental Policy Act (NEPA), which requires environmental impact statements and public review before any major federal action can proceed. Just as NEPA often has led to decisions that are less expensive and environmentally more sound, an analogous process requiring national-security impact statements with public review for any major shifts in foreign or military policy could help prevent costly mistakes.

Restraining Military Adventures Abroad

A second strategy for making U.S. leaders more accountable to the people would be to put more checks and balances on the president's ability to commit military forces abroad. The president has accumulated the power to involve the United States in warfare far in excess of what the Framers of the Constitution envisioned. The Founding Fathers placed war-making powers in the hands of the Congress to prevent precisely the kinds of military adventures and entanglements that presidents have launched throughout the twentieth century. Alexander Hamilton, one of the most stalwart advocates of a strong executive, once said, "The history of human conduct does not warrant . . . [committing] interests of so delicate and momentous a kind, as those which concern [a nation's] intercourse with the rest of the world, to the sole disposal of . . . a president of the United States."[31] Yet, displaying unwarranted confidence in presidential wisdom in foreign policy, Congress has allowed its war powers to be bypassed and undermined. According to Eugene V. Rostow, former director of the Arms Control and Disarmament Agency, presidents ordered U.S. armed forces into combat more than two hundred times between 1789 and 1973, while Congress made only five declarations of war.[32]

Congress tried to retrieve its checks on presidential adventures in 1973 with the War Powers Resolution. Enacted over the veto of President Nixon, the act requires the executive to notify Congress within 48 hours whenever he sends U.S. troops "into hostilities or into situations where imminent involvement in hostility is clearly indicated." Congressional consent also is required for the troops to remain in action for more than sixty days, or ninety days if the president certifies an "unavoidable necessity." Unfortunately, however, the War Powers Resolution has done little to give Congress control over military operations and instead has given the president a blank check for short-term wars.

Despite repeated presidential uses of force since 1973, Congress has never once used its sixty- or ninety-day clocks to approve or terminate a military action.[33] One problem is that the War Powers Resolution is vague about when hostilities are "imminent." When President Bush announced to Congress in August 1990 that he was dispatching 100,000 troops to Saudi Arabia, he carefully stated, "I do not believe inolvement in hostilities is imminent." This deliberate effort to evade the law went unchallenged by the legislative branch. If congressional controls over the president are to be made effective, the War Powers Resolution will need radical revision.

At a minimum, writes J. Brian Atwood, one of the authors of the statute, Congress "must make sure that consultations become politically and legally unavoidable *before* United States forces are introduced into hostilities."[34] Presidents have frequently committed U.S. forces with no consultation whatsoever. On March 16, 1988, for example, President Reagan sent 3,200 troops to Honduras to help repel Nicaraguan forces that had chased rebels across the Honduran border — the day after his secretary of state, national security advisor, and chief of staff each had assured Congress that no such policy was being contemplated.[35] Congressional consultation after forces are deployed is usually too late.[36] Atwood has suggested creating a special "leadership committee" made up of both houses' political leadership and the ranking members of the foreign affairs, armed services, and intelligence committees. Another alternative suggested by Donald Robinson of Smith College would be to give some members of Congress seats on the National Security Council.[37] In May 1988 a bipartisan group of Senators proposed setting up a "permanent consultative group" to confer with administration officials before, during, and after a military operation.[38]

Possibly the best reform of the War Powers Resolution would be to follow the original version passed in the Senate — an outright prohibition on the president's use of force without Congressional approval unless a true national emergency exists. "Under this bill," according to Senator Cranston, "the decision to initiate involvement in a war situation — the modern-day equivalent of a declared war — was restored to Congress, as the Framers of the Constitution clearly provided."[39]

However the War Powers Resolution is reformulated, attention needs to be paid to its enforcement mechanisms. An effort in 1987 by 107 House and Senate Democrats to mandate the president to comply with the resolution after deploying forces in the Persian Gulf was rebuffed by a federal court as a "political question" and put back into the hands of Congress.[40] The House and the Senate should seize the judiciary's invitation and write narrow criteria that encourage the courts to review executive responsiveness and allow citizen groups to bring lawsuits in federal court to trigger these reviews.

The most serious yet least discussed presidential usurpation of war powers relates to the command structure controlling nuclear bombs. As Princeton political scientist Richard Falk has written, "War plans and decision procedures involving nuclear weapons are completely cut off from democratic notions of agreed-upon guidelines or modes of accountability, much less citizen or even Congressional participation."[41] That the president can, in his sole discretion, unilaterally launch a nuclear first strike, committing the United States to a war that would kill more people than all previous wars combined, underscores the need to develop greater constraints on the use of nuclear weapons. The trend toward "launch on warning" and other forms of automated launch threatens to remove human decision-makers from the critical question of when the fateful decision to authorize nuclear attack should be made. Jeremy Stone, executive director of the Federation of American Scientists, has suggested that a nuclear planning committee of Congress be established to work closely with the president's national security advisors and to exercise decision-making power over the first use of nuclear weapons.[42]

Short of a major commitment of U.S. troops or nuclear weapons, presidents also have involved the United States in smaller international adventures through covert actions. After World War II, covert actions undertaken by the Central Intelligence Agency became a convenient way for the executive branch to attempt to assassinate foreign leaders, destabilize elected governments, spread disinformation, and implement other policies that could not otherwise win popular support if openly known. When these actions were publicized in 1975 by the Senate Special Select Committee on Intelligence Activities, committee chair Frank Church lamented that they had done little to help the national interest: "I suggest we have lost — or grievously impaired — the good name and reputation of the United States from which we once drew a unique capacity to exercise moral leadership . . . In the eyes of millions of once-friendly foreign people, the United States is today regarded with grave suspicion and distrust."[43]

The Church committee concluded that covert actions are inherently unreliable means for accomplishing foreign-policy objectives. Clandestine operations must be undertaken quickly enough and on a scale small enough to remain secret, which puts severe limits on their usefulness. To preserve secrecy they must be undertaken by a small number of decision-makers, yet this increases the probability of serious errors, such as the misguided belief by the Kennedy Administration that the Cuban people would support the U.S.-backed Cuban exiles over Fidel Castro during the Bay of Pigs invasion. Moreover, as Harvard political scientist Stanley Hoffmann has argued, "When the operations entail the manipulation of foreign elements with their own agenda (the Cuban exiles mobilized for the Bay of Pigs landing, or the Nicaraguan Contras, or the anti-Allende factions in the Chilean military), American ability to control them is often limited."[44] The fact is that most U.S. covert actions substantially hurt the nation's interests. Covert coups undertaken in Iran, Guatemala, the Congo, and Chile, for example, all produced extraordinarily repressive dictatorships and infused opposition groups with a deep hatred of Americans.

While the Church committee seriously considered banning all covert actions, it settled for establishing a permanent structure of intelligence committees to review all covert actions confidentially. The president was obligated to provide "timely notice" of new operations to Congress, which could then raise objections. But the ultimate power of deciding whether to embark upon an action was vested entirely to the president (except, of course, if Congress passed special legislation prohibiting an operation or stripping away funding). Senator Church's argument for allowing some covert actions won the day:

> I can conceive of a dire emergency when timely clandestine action on our part might avert a nuclear holocaust and save an entire civilization. I can also conceive of circumstances . . . where our discreet help to democratic political parties might avert a forcible take-over by a communist minority, heavily subsidized by the Soviets.[45]

Today this logic seems weak. The kinds of national emergencies Senator Church was describing are actually part of the president's constitutionally defined power as commander in chief. Moreover, if Congress wanted to do so, it could exempt emergencies more clearly and still impose a general ban on covert actions (though even in emergencies the president should be required to consult Congress). If the concern is politics abroad, it is hard to see how the overt participation of the U.S. government would be more damaging than the political fallout that occurs when covert operations are unmasked. Leaving aside the inescapability of leaks to the press, few covert operations can long remain secret even under ideal circumstances. Morton Halperin, Director of the American Civil Liberties Union's Center for National Security Studies, has argued, "U.S. arms sales to Iran ... were discussed so often with so many people over so many insecure channels of communication that interested governments and arms merchants all over the world knew about them."[46] That Congress now routinely debates in the open whether to fund covert programs has caused former United Nations Ambassador Jeane Kirkpatrick to conclude "that, within any sensible meaning of the term, covert action isn't a viable policy option in the post-Watergate era."[47]

Perhaps the most important evidence of the futility of allowing covert actions with congressional oversight was the ease with which prescribed procedures were tossed aside by the Reagan Administration as it supported the Nicaraguan Contras. After the Iran-Contra scandal revealed a pattern of officials lying to the intelligence committees, the Administration tried to assure Congress that it would be more cooperative in the future.[48] But many observers have concluded, with Morton Halperin, that prevarication is endemic to covert actions:

> Covert operations breed a disrespect for the truth. Officials start out lying to the enemy, then to the public, then to Congress, then to other agencies and finally to the person in the next office. They lie about the essentials, and once they discover how easy that is, they start lying about other aspects of the operation. ... If it is effective to lie about aid to the contras, why not about an imminent invasion of Grenada or about arms for hostages?[49]

Neither the Congress nor the president is helped by rules that allow some covert actions, some of the time. The current procedures make it difficult for those members of Congress overseeing covert actions to stop a program they dislike. Since opposition to a program means acknowledging its existence, the procedures wind up silencing precisely those legislators otherwise best situated to stop misguided operations. At the executive level the current procedures encourage subordinates not to inform the president about covert operations. Admiral John Poindexter explained during the Iran-Contra hearing that his goal was to allow the president to "plausibly deny" any knowledge of the operations. As the Church committee's final report declared, "Any theory which, as a matter of doctrine, places elected officials on the periphery of the decision-making process is an invitation to error, an abdication of responsibility and a perversion of democratic government."[50]

U.S. democracy would be well served by the complete abolition of covert actions, excepting perhaps a limited, narrowly defined range of national security emergencies. An alternative formulation, articulated by Cyrus Vance shortly before he became secretary of state, would be to allow only those actions that were "absolutely essential to the national security," and then only if no other alternatives were available.[51] Another helpful reform would be to take all remaining military operations out of the CIA's hands and put them under the control of the Department of Defense, where better established procedures for congressional oversight exist.[52] The CIA could then be returned to its original responsibilities for gathering and analyzing information.

These new restrictions on covert action would not compromise covert intelligence gathering, on which roughly 95 percent of the CIA's budget is spent.[53] Nor would the detailed implementation of specific policies have to be made public. But the American public and its elected representatives should be better able to assess carefully the costs and benefits to the nation of involving itself in a conflict abroad before such involvement begins. As former Attorney General Nicholas Katzenbach argued in 1983, an effective U.S. foreign policy "must be based on policy and factual premises which are accepted by the overwhelming majority of the American people."[54]

Decentralizing Foreign Policy

Another way Americans can better exert democratic oversight of their leaders is by moving foreign policy-making closer to the people. In recent years the principles for decentralizing power have enjoyed a bipartisan revival. Conservatives have supported decentralization in the form of "new federalism" and "states' rights," while progressives have supported it in the form of "Green politics," "bioregionalism," and "local self-reliance." To those with democratic sensibilities on either the right or the left, granting exclusive power to remote and largely unaccountable government officials, even the wisest ones, is transparently dangerous.

To counter these problems, many Americans have begun to develop alternative, decentralized mechanisms of foreign policy-making in their own hometowns. Today, more than one thousand local governments in the United States are officially involving themselves in foreign affairs.[55] These "municipal foreign policies," once dismissed as trivial, aberrant, or unconstitutional, are exerting an increasingly important influence on U.S. foreign policy. More than nine hundred local governments passed a nuclear freeze resolution and helped pressure President Reagan to launch the Strategic Arms Reduction Talks (START) in Geneva and the intermediate-range nuclear forces (INF) negotiations in Vienna. By refusing to cooperate with the Federal Emergency Management Agency's "crisis relocation planning" in the early 1980s, roughly 120 cities helped derail the government's civil defense program. By divesting their portfolios of more than $20 billion worth of securities from firms doing business in South Africa, 70 cities, 13 counties, and 19 states helped persuade the Congress to replace "constructive engagement" with limited economic sanctions in 1986.

In the years ahead cities will play an increasingly important role in international affairs through a wide variety of means. Here is a sampling of what is now occurring:[56]

~ *Education*

San Francisco and Boulder County, Colorado, have produced and disseminated pamphlets arguing for a nuclear freeze. New York City and Milwaukee high schools now teach courses in peace studies. The California Department of Education has appropriated money for every local school district to assess and develop curricula for teaching grade-school and high-school courses about "nuclear-age problems." In the United Kingdom, cities' peace-related educational programs have included special newspapers, leaflets, videos, booklets, speaking tours, conferences, workplace seminars, road signs, plaques, advertisements, postcards, banners, badges, peace parks, town shows, exhibitions, adult education courses, special libraries, and "peace shops."

~ *Research*

Undaunted by the absence of nationally funded peace research programs, states such as California, Iowa, and New Jersey have established their own peace programs, and cities such as Los Angeles, Pittsburgh, and Baltimore have passed ordinances requiring their staffs to prepare and publish annual reports on the local economic impact of military spending.

~ *Lobbying*

To convince federal lawmakers of the urgency of eliminating nuclear bomb testing, more than eight hundred U.S. local elected officials have signed petitions for a comprehensive test ban (CTB), nearly two hundred cities have passed CTB resolutions, and the U.S. Conference of Mayors approved a special CTB resolution. Baltimore now has a lobbyist in Washington, D.C., who is trying to reverse the current flow of monies from Main Street to the Pentagon.

~ *Grants*
Cities can become miniature foundations and support nonprofit
organizations carrying out desired international activities. During the
early 1980s the Greater London Council provided tens of millions of
pounds worth of grants to more than two thousand groups, many of
which were involved in peace policy.

~ *Policing*
Nearly thirty cities have passed "sanctuary resolutions" ordering their
police not to cooperate with the U.S. Immigration and Naturalization
Service in its efforts to deport Salvadoran and Guatemalan refugees
back to the war zones from which they fled. After the Soviet Union
shot down KAL flight 007, thirteen states pulled Stolichnaya vodka
from liquor store shelves. Dozens of cities and states are now restricting
the use and sale of products using chlorofluorocarbons and other
ozone-depleting chemicals.

~ *Zoning*
Nearly 170 U.S. cities are "nuclear-free zones," and half of these
actually prohibit the manufacturing of nuclear bombs within their
jurisdiction. A number of jurisdictions, like Chicago and Cambridge,
Massachusetts, have launched projects to assist military contractors in
alternative-use planning.

~ *Contracting and Investing*
Spending $500 billion annually and overseeing $300 billion in investments, many states, counties, and cities are recognizing their power in
selective contracting and investment. Jersey City, New Jersey, and
Takoma Park, Maryland, are among nearly a dozen jurisdictions that
have prohibited any municipal contracts with or investments in firms
producing nuclear bombs.

~ *Sister Cities*
In 1989 Sister Cities International reported that 823 American cities had
active relationships with more than 1,420 sister cities, including forty
with China and thirty with the Soviet Union (another fifty are in some
stage of negotiation). Besides enriching the daily cultural life of participating cities, these relationships help citizens on both sides replace the
ignorance, fear, and hatred that drive arms races and war with understanding, empathy, and trust.

~ *Trade Agreements*
Some two hundred U.S. cities are actively establishing economic city-
to-city ties abroad, promoting their products and attracting foreign
investment. In 1984, for example, Mayor Dianne Feinstein of San

Francisco signed a trade pact with the Chinese city of Shanghai that within a few years resulted in tens of millions of dollars of additional business for the Bay Area.

~ *Political Agreements*

To challenge U.S. military involvement in Central America, 87 cities set up links with communities in Nicaragua. Along with citizen groups, these sister cities provided more humanitarian assistance than the total amount of U.S. aid that went to the Contras. Burlington, Vermont, for example, arranged for a ship to carry 560 tons of supplies to its sister city in Puerto Cabezas, including thirty tons of medical supplies collected from local hospitals.

~ *International Organizations*

To promote their policies on behalf of peace with greater unity and effectiveness, a half-dozen American mayors joined a hundred other mayors from 23 countries in Hiroshima for the First World Conference of Mayors for Peace through Inter-City Solidarity in 1985. Other global organizations that are helping cities coordinate their policies regarding cultural exchange, peace, Third World development, and environmental protection include the United Towns Organisation (Paris), the International Nuclear Free Zone Registry (Manchester), the International Union of Local Authorities (The Hague), and the International Council for Local Environmental Initiatives (Toronto and Freiburg).

~ *Municipal State Departments*

In an effort to consolidate their international affairs activities under one roof, some cities have created special offices with staff, overhead, and funding. The cities of Cambridge, Massachusetts, Washington, D.C., and New Haven have created official peace commissions. The city of Seattle has allocated $225,000 per year for an Office of International Affairs to coordinate both its foreign trade and its relationships with thirteen sister cities (one is Managua and another is Tashkent in the Soviet Union).

These initiatives, if continued and expanded, hold the promise of reorienting U.S. foreign policy in four helpful ways. First, they allow the voices of more Americans to be heard on foreign policy. It is one thing when Americans "speak in one voice" as they did when war was declared against Japan and Nazi Germany. But it is quite another when only one voice is heard because the majority of Americans have been silenced, as happened when President Reagan continued to support the Nicaraguan Contras despite opposition by two-thirds of the public. Municipal foreign policies provide opportunities for all Americans to speak out in international affairs. Those who were once excluded from foreign policy can now work with their neighbors and local officials to devise appropriate education, research, and sister-city programs.

Second, municipal foreign policies are improving the efficiency of U.S. foreign policy. A staggering number of transactions now take place between the United States and other nations in such areas as communication, tourism, trade, investment, and cultural exchange. For example, the Clearing House Interbank Payments System (CHIPS), which is operated by 140 U.S. banks specializing in international finance, conducts several billion transactions daily. Attempts by the national government to control these transactions too tightly inevitably will scare off international trade and finance and stifle domestic economic growth. Municipal foreign policies, in contrast, allow tens of thousands of people, each expert in his or her own area, to take primary responsibility for these policies. National officials already have begun to recognize that the best they can do is to set broad guidelines for the ways in which ideas, people, capital, and goods cross borders and leave the details to individuals, corporations, and local governments. To promote international trade, for example, the Department of State has actually briefed activist governors, assisted state and local representatives through its embassies and consulates, and loaned Foreign Service officers to states.

Third, municipal foreign policies encourage nonmilitary, nonprovocative approaches to international relations — precisely the approaches needed for a peace system. Because local and state governments cannot meet threats abroad by dispatching troops, shipping weapons, and running covert operations, they are forced to develop more nuanced and nonviolent policies.

Finally — and most important — municipal foreign policies enhance accountability in U.S. foreign policy. They provide people at the grassroots with diverse sources of information with which to evaluate, criticize, and improve national foreign policies, and with opportunities to participate directly in international affairs. Municipal foreign policies allow more foreign-policy decisions to be made at a level of government where public scrutiny is high. Unlike national officials, local leaders cannot classify their deliberations or create secret teams in the basement of City Hall. Indeed, most local governments are dogged by scandal-hungry local newspapers and governed by "sunshine" statutes that demand public meetings for important local decisions.

As municipal foreign policies expand, the federal government may be tempted to reassert its primacy in international affairs. Already some commentators are suggesting that the federal government should set up a special desk within the State Department to track, discourage, and police local "meddling" in foreign policy.[57] But given the potential benefits of greater municipal involvement, the federal government would do well to follow several more modest guidelines.

First, the U.S. government should support all local efforts to educate, research, and lobby on foreign policy. In the spirit of the First Amendment of the U.S. Constitution, which protects free speech on foreign policy, and the Fifth Amendment, which grants a broad privilege to Americans to travel abroad, our leaders should be willing to tolerate the freest possible exchange of ideas, people, books, and audio-visual materials. The government has far more to lose if its limits on our basic freedoms and causes outraged Americans to take to the streets. Congress might begin by narrowing presidential discretion in banning of travel abroad and by scrapping the 1799 Logan Act, which has unsuccessfully (and probably unconstitutionally) attempted to discourage Americans from meeting with leaders abroad to discuss controversial issues.[58] Specific travel restrictions, such as those attempting to dissuade Americans from traveling to Cuba or Vietnam, should be lifted. The government might also help fund local consciousness-raising activities by enlarging the coffers of the National Institute for Peace and channeling these monies, with few or no strings, to municipal peace programs.

Second, the federal government should tolerate municipal initiatives unless they pose more than a hypothetical danger to American foreign policy. Cities are passing these initiatives not to meddle in other people's affairs but to meet legitimate local concerns. Municipalities that create nuclear-free zones, for example, are attempting to address the economic impacts of military spending and the health hazards of nuclear-weapons manufacturing. Federal attempts to quash these initiatives will simply anger the people affected and prompt new, equally irksome municipal initiatives accomplishing the same goals. Where municipal initiatives arise that pose more than a symbolic danger to national foreign policy, the federal government should try to work in cooperation with the offending municipality. In the same way that federal officials have worked closely with municipal and state officials to harmonize their trade policies, federal officials should try to involve mayors and other local representatives in the formulation of U.S. policies concerning arms control, resource management, Third World development, and international institutions — all key components of a peace system. Tapping local wisdom not only could transform local protest into constructive assistance but also could help prevent foreign-policy disasters that have occurred because of poor information or inadequate debate.

Finally, the federal government should tighten laws governing those very few kinds of nongovernmental adventurism that have caused serious international mischief. The most obvious activities that come to mind — thus far undertaken by individuals and paramilitary groups, but not by cities — are exports of weapons, ammunition, and other combat equipment to rebels in countries with which the United States is at peace. One possible remedy would be to strengthen the

Neutrality Act by enforcing it through an independent prosecutor rather than relying on the political whims of the Justice Department. States themselves might pass their own versions of the Neutrality Act and make shipments of arms or training of belligerents not approved by the federal government a *state* crime.[59]

Taken together, these proposals could effect fundamental improvements in U.S. democracy. To be sure, members of Congress, local officials, and citizens are no less prone to error or irrationality than the president. But these new tools for citizen participation offer a broader base of political accountability, unprecedented opportunities for the promotion of peace, and badly needed checks on ill-conceived foreign-policy adventures. Whether 250 million Americans can better mold policy than a dozen members of the National Security Council is a matter of political judgment, but it is precisely that judgment which underlies our longstanding faith in democracy. As Thomas Jefferson once wrote, "The good sense of the people will always be found to be the best army."[60]

PROMOTING PARTICIPATION ABROAD

Nearly all the reforms that could strengthen democracy in the United States also could strengthen democracy in other countries and reduce the probability of their going to war. For example, members of the People's Congress of Deputies in the Soviet Union have been debating whether to set up their equivalent of the U.S. War Powers Resolution. A number of U.S. politicians, lawyers, and political scientists have provided assistance in this effort, helping the Soviets establish a powerful legislative safety valve against future Afghanistan wars.[61]

But promoting democracy abroad is a more sensitive undertaking than promoting it at home. Done poorly, it can discredit legitimate democratic movements as foreign puppets and lead to their repression. It can also be used by some Americans as a cover for opportunism, jingoism, and militarism. It is therefore important to formulate some ground rules.

One requirement is that efforts to promote democracy abroad should be nonprovocative. No military interventions or weapons shipments should occur in the name of freedom and democracy.[62] Americans must seek instead to support individuals abroad in their efforts to reform their own systems according to their own values and visions. And we should stand ready to accept the results of democratic processes even when they seem disappointing by American standards. In the past such tolerance would have led U.S. leaders to approve of the Chilean presidential election of 1970, even though it brought to power Salvador Allende, a parliamentary Marxist, rather than to take the view of National Security Advisor Henry Kissinger, who said, "I don't see why we need to stand by and watch a country go communist because of the irresponsibility of its own people."[63]

It is useful to note that most American efforts to democratize the Soviet Union throughout the Cold War were provocative and counterproductive. Hardliners sought a vigorous arms race to jolt the Soviet Union into political change by placing intolerable economic burdens on the Soviet system and forcing the Politburo to turn inward. The arms race did indeed place greater economic burdens upon the Soviet people, but the result, comparable to the consequences of the U.S bombing of North Vietnam or the Nazi blitz on London, was exactly the opposite of what was intended — greater resentment toward the United States, renewed dedication to matching our armaments, and less economic power for all Soviet citizens, including those committed to democratization.

Congress also tried to reform Soviet society when it passed the Jackson-Vanik Amendment to the Trade Act of 1974 (signed into law in 1975), withholding most-favored-nation status for the Soviet Union until it loosened emigration policies. Again the provocation backfired. After the bill was passed, the Soviet Union reduced emigration to a trickle, precisely to show that it would not be pushed around.[64]

A third U.S. approach to pluralizing the Soviet Union — beaming Radio Liberty and Voice of America into the Soviet Union both to spread pro-American information and to foment dissent — has been problematic as well. Many of these transmissions were so clearly antagonistic to the Soviet government that they did little to spawn revolt (imagine Americans' reaction to continuous broadcasts of Radio Moscow).[65] Surveys suggest that fewer than one-in-ten Soviet adults tuned into Radio Liberty once or more a month and that most of these listeners were tuning in to the entertainment programs. Voice of America, which was much less ideological than Radio Liberty, had twice as many Soviet listeners.[66]

Promotion of participation abroad must be grounded in two tactics that are wholly nonprovocative — persuasion and cooperation. The old saw was that Americans using these kinds of "soft" tools were naive and could do little to stimulate reform in the Soviet Union and other "totalitarian" states. In 1985 neoconservative Irving Kristol wrote, "'Liberalization' remains a fantasy. . . . The party still rules supreme, its Leninist orthodoxy intact; the Soviet people remain sullen, intimidated and coerced into passivity."[67] But recent initiatives by American citizens, civic groups, corporations, churches, and local governments have demonstrated that it was the old pundits who were naive.

Americans have found and helped reformers at all levels of Soviet society. Lost in the debate over "linking" various Soviet-American transactions to reformed Soviet human-rights behavior was the fact that many of these transactions *themselves* exert a democratizing influence. Every one of the more than 100,000 Americans to visit the Soviet Union annually has been a walking, talking banned book, expressing facts and attitudes at odds with the prevailing party line. In the early 1980s the good will of American visitors often stood in sharp contrast to the Nazi-like depictions of Americans in *Pravda* and reduced the ability of Soviet leaders to characterize Americans as barbaric monsters worth going to war against. As more Soviets were swept into relationships with Americans — whether economic, scientific, cultural, or personal — they put pressure on Communist Party leaders, in their own small ways, for improved ties with the United States. According to the *Christian Science Monitor*, some exchange experts believe "that 30 years of travel to the U.S. by the Soviet political, cultural, and scientific elite have fueled demand for Gorbachev's reforms."[68] When Americans met high-level Soviets, new possibilities for political cooperation were uncovered. Such encounters in the mid-1980s seemed to play a prominent role in encouraging the Soviets to halt nuclear testing unilaterally for eighteen months, to release prominent dissidents, and to allow on-site inspection of their nuclear test site by the Natural Resources Defense Council, a U.S. environmental group.[69] American "citizen diplomats" also may have nudged the Soviet government toward rejecting nuclear warfighting strategies. Dr. Bernard Lown, co-founder of the International Physicians for the Prevention of Nuclear War, managed to convince Soviet officials in 1982 to broadcast during prime time a frank, uncut discussion among Soviet and American doctors about the medical consequences of nuclear war and the uselessness of the Soviet government's civil defense program.[70] Citizen diplomats even reached the highest levels of the Politburo. According to *New York Times* correspondent Philip Taubman, "Mr. Gorbachev's education about the United States has been rounded by his frequent meetings with delegations of visiting Americans."[71]

Greater Soviet-American trade was another area in which Americans may have helped stimulate Soviet reform. As Soviets encountered more Americans, and more American ideas and products, they began to see the virtues of market-oriented economic systems and became more comfortable with internal economic reform and greater trade with the West. Franz Schurmann, a professor of sociology and history at the University of California at Berkeley, has suggested that the Soviets located the first McDonald's near Red Square to expose their people to the efficiency of American fast food.[72] After PepsiCo recently purchased from the Soviets seventeen submarines, a cruiser, a frigate, and a destroyer for scrap metal, Donald Kendall, the company's president, chided National Security Advisor Brent Scowcroft, "We're disarming the Soviet Union faster than you are."[73]

Another promising leverage point for Americans to empower Soviet citizens has been computerization. As the *Economist* recently argued, information technologies "have shown themselves time and again to be destructive of centralized control, in private companies or dictators' states. A Russia stuffed with Xerox machines, personal computers, and electronic telephone switches humming with too many conversations to be monitored is more the West's kind of Russia."[74] In the early 1980s a number of Americans helped interest top Soviet officials in personal computers and international computer networks, and by late 1988 the Soviet Union agreed to allow Americans to mail computers, diskettes, and video-tape recorders to Soviet friends.[75] IDG Communications began a joint venture in April 1988 to print and distribute a Russian edition of *PC World* magazine to 50,000 paid Soviet subscribers.[76] The result of the dispersion of personal computers, laser printers, and desktop publishing has been the rapid proliferation of *samizdat* (unofficial press) on controversial issues of foreign policy, economic reform, and human rights.[77] Grassroots publications also have been assisted by the emergence of public photocopy shops established by Western companies.[78] In the years ahead, as machines multiply and get smaller, as diskettes move in and out of the country the way audiotapes and videotapes do now, and as computer networks begin connecting to satellites instead of telephones, a whole generation of young Soviet "hackers" will gain access to information at home and abroad that their parents never dreamed possible. A strong case can be made for the United States to subsidize, wherever possible, exports of shortwave radios, video recorders, tele-phones, and telephone directories — every conceivable technology that erodes the government's monopoly on information and empowers individuals to hold Soviet leaders accountable to their own rhetoric for peace.[79]

Outside the Soviet Union, the United States also has begun some useful initiatives for democracy. Between 1985 and 1988, for example, the U.S. Congress and the National Endowment for Democracy (NED) provided more than $5 million in cash assistance to Solidarity and other underground groups to bring into Poland printing presses, ink, publications, radio equipment, microfiches and microfiche readers, and videocassettes and videocassette players.[80] In Chile, NED gave $1 million to help fund parties opposing General Pinochet and to assist voters in getting free photographs for their registration cards prior to the October 1988 election.[81] In Peru and Argentina, the United States successfully discouraged coups by letting would-be military junta leaders clearly know that U.S. economic and political support would be cut off if their democratically elected leaders were toppled.[82] And in countries as diverse as Chile, Haiti, Pakistan, Panama, and the Philippines, private groups like the National Democratic Institute for International Affairs (an affiliate of the Democratic Party) and the Center for Democracy have helped monitor elections for fraud or irregularities.[83]

There are enormous opportunities like these in the years ahead. In Eastern Europe, Americans have unprecedented opportunities for stabilizing new democ-racies by making loans, providing IMF debt relief, and entering joint ventures. In South Africa, Americans might form stronger personal relationships with Afrikaaners to sway them toward abolishing apartheid, while equipping the black majority with technical, financial, and educational assistance that could reduce their vulnerability to apartheid's leaders in Pretoria.[84] Throughout the East and the South, Americans could help developing political cultures draft and adopt constitutions that protect free speech, promote the separation of church and state, check and balance power, and ensure fair judicial review.[85] Now that the Ayatollah Khomeini is gone, relationships with true Iranian moderates might be developed, not for illegal arms transfers, but for joint projects in agriculture, medicine, science, and law. These options are not easy, but they are certainly more promising routes to change than the limited military options presented by the war system.

What must be emphasized, however, is that these initiatives cannot succeed unless they are truly nonprovocative. A good test is the Golden Rule: Would we want others to participate in our affairs in the same ways we are participating in theirs? By this standard, for example, many of the activities of NED would be deemed intolerable. While the United States underwrote the Contra war against the Nicaraguan government that ultimately killed 26,000 people, for example, NED helped finance the opposition paper *La Prensa* and poured millions of dollars into Violetta Chomorro's campaign to beat the Sandinistas at the polls. Americans must ask themselves whether they would have tolerated a concerted effort by the Nazis or Japanese during the Second World War to finance opposition papers or antiwar candidates in the United States. Effective pro-democracy initiatives must be completely free of coercion. And perhaps the best way to ensure this is to take pro-democracy initiatives out of the hands of national decision-makers and put them, instead, directly into the hands of the American people.[86]

HOW PEOPLE CAN ESTABLISH A PEACE SYSTEM

Political participation cannot exist in a vacuum. The one billion people on earth who are illiterate, homeless, and malnourished cannot meaningfully participate in civic life without economic development. Nor can universal participation be possible if ozone depletion, global warming, acid rain, and a host of other environmental catastrophes throw hundreds of millions of people into the prison of poverty. Without economic justice and environmental integrity significant blocs of humanity will be unable to help build a peace system, and without the active participation of the world's poor many nations will continue to be prone to revolution and war.

Participation by Americans can help to bring about the kinds of economic development and environmental protection necessary to boost participation universally. Debating, educating, campaigning, voting, and legislating on these issues are the most obvious opportunities available. But Americans can take direct action as well — as individuals, through their churches and nongovernmental organizations (NGOs), through their businesses, or through municipal foreign policies.

For the sustainable development policies recommended by Arjun Makhijani, we need no longer rely on the IMF, World Bank, U.S. Agency for International Development, or any other national programs. In Western Europe more than one thousand cities are providing schools, medicine, tools, technology, and training directly to towns and villages in Asia, Africa, and South America. Two hundred cities in Belgium have a city councilor responsible for Third World development policies. The eighty largest cities in Holland are spending fifty cents per capita on development cooperation. Following the principles of the 1985 "Cologne Appeal," these city-to-city relationships stress raising the consciousness of people in the North as well as assisting people in the South. The Cologne Appeal also mandates that North-South relationships be based on "equality, reciprocity, [and the] absence of paternalism." There is no reason why the United States' 469 sister-city relationships with the Third World, which are now primarily oriented toward cultural exchange and mayor's junkets, cannot begin hundreds of small-scale, environmentally sound development assisted programs that can replace the misguided megaprojects of the IMF and the World Bank.

Americans can similarly participate in implementing the other components of a peace system. Consider the simple act of saving energy. Across the country communities and individuals have acted in the face of federal neglect. States such as California and Oregon established special energy commissions and revamped their public utility commissions. Many communities have prepared detailed blueprints for a nonnuclear energy future, including: Geneva County, Alabama; Humboldt County, California; Carbondale, Illinois; Franklin County, Massachusetts; Fulton, Missouri; Salem, Oregon; Philadelphia, Pennsylvania; and Madison, Wisconsin. Because of grassroots efforts between 1979 and 1986, the United States obtained more than seven times as much new energy from improved efficiency as from *all* net expansions of energy supply. All this happened with little help and not a little hindrance from federal policy-makers. Despite the fact that energy efficiency has proven itself a far more cost-effective option, federal research and development funds for nuclear fission and fusion are nearly eight times higher than funds for efficiency, and subsidies, as of 1984, were approximately two hundred times as high per unit of energy delivered.[87]

The long-term promise of grassroots efforts promoting energy efficiency is enormous. The full use of the best electricity saving technologies now on the market could save about five times as much electricity as all the U.S. nuclear plants now generate, for less money than the cost of just *operating* those plants.[88] The installation of these technologies would result in net economic savings approaching $100 billion a year, in due time allowing the United States to dispense altogether with all nuclear power plants and probably all coal plants. As an incidental benefit, these technologies (among them superefficient appliances, lights, motors, and building elements) would make Americans more comfortable, let them see better, and improve the reliability and quality of industrial production. U.S. lighting improvements alone, displacing 120 huge power plants, would save their cost (over $200 billion) plus $30 billion a year in operating cost.[89] Cost-effective efficiency would help eliminate four different sources of national insecurity.

To begin with, greater energy efficiency could enable the United States to reduce its dependence on foreign oil supplies and the associated risks of fighting more wars in the Persian Gulf.[90] Before the United States sent its troops to Saudi Arabia in August 1990, the Rocky Mountain Institute calculated that investing *a single year's* budget for the Rapid Deployment Force in efficiency improvements could eliminate the United States' need for Mideast oil, as well as the risks posed by the force itself.[91] Looked at another way, had the United States invested as much as a quarter of the direct cost of the war against Iraq on energy savings, the country could have permanently unplugged itself from the Persian Gulf. Just increasing the efficiency of American cars by three miles per gallon could have replaced all U.S. oil imports from Iraq and Kuwait.[92]

Investing in the least-cost efficiency options would also enable the United States to reduce its contribution to conflicts caused by the environmental impacts of nuclear power and fossil-fuel burning. In contrast to the potential conflicts from more Chernobyls or global warming, the environmental problems associated with conservation are generally small and localized, and most of them can be managed with small-scale technical fixes.[93] Conservation could virtually eliminate the "side effects" of coal and nuclear plants, including nuclear accidents, weapons proliferation, climatic changes, and acid rain — any one of which could cause a major social upheaval in the decades ahead.

Third, reduced reliance on nuclear and fossil sources would reduce the vulnerability of the U.S. energy infrastructure to sabotage and attack (as well as technical failure or natural disaster). Improved efficiency and greater reliance on decentralized renewable sources would eliminate many vulnerable and expensive energy supply sources and distribution nodes. Shut-down nuclear plants would be much less tempting targets for terrorists. Small-scale, dispersed energy sources — sources such as superefficient light bulbs, passive solar houses, industrial cogeneration, and windmills — are inherently more resilient than their expensive, centralized counterparts, and would greatly diminish the destructiveness of attacks on U.S. energy systems by either terrorists or hostile nations.[94]

Finally, increased energy productivity would reduce U.S. insecurity by directly improving our economic well-being. Direct national payments for energy now are about $430 billion per year — two-fifths more than the payments for all military activities. Efficiency gains since 1973 have already reduced the energy payments by about $200 billion per year. Were the United States as efficient as Western European competitors, it could save another $200 billion or more annually.[95] Systematic investments in least-cost efficiency measures could save several trillion of today's dollars by the year 2000 — enough, in principle, to pay off the entire present national debt.[96] The resulting boost to the national economy would shore up the nation's sagging trade position, enhance its economic and political influence abroad, and free resources for other domestic and foreign-policy initiatives.

There is no reason why citizens acting alone or through their cities cannot continue caulking windows, installing more efficient lightbulbs and refrigerators, and scrapping gas-guzzlers — all of which would bolster national security. As David Orr's analysis suggests, similar security benefits would result from grassroots efforts to conserve water and to simplify lifestyles.

Citizens also can help to establish the norms and institutions for conflict resolution discussed by Dietrich Fischer. Because the legitimacy of norms comes ultimately from the people, NGOs have already played an important role in developing them. Amnesty International has helped develop norms against political imprisonment, torture, and capital punishment. INFACT, with its worldwide boycott of Nestle infant formula, has helped create new norms of ethical behavior for multinational corporations. Greenpeace, in its campaigns to save whales and baby seals, has helped establish norms to protect marine life and endangered species.

While many stronger international institutions depend on enlightened action by governments, some may rely on networks of nongovernmental players. For 125 years the International Red Cross has coordinated the work of 146 national organizations and millions of volunteers to provide food, clothing, shelter, medical treatment, and moral support to the victims of war and natural disasters.[97] Cooperative projects to find a cure for AIDS and to promote Third World development have brought together vast international networks of churches, universities, businesses, and foundations. Transnational networks of environmentalists — the International Union for Conservation of Nature and Natural Resources, for example — are developing norms and action projects concerning species protection, sustainable development, rainforest protection, and pollution control,[98] and they are intensively lobbying the leaders of every country to influence national policy, even in the Soviet Union and Eastern Europe. The International Organization of Consumers Unions has member groups in seventy countries pushing for safer products and tighter restrictions on marketing of pesticides, medicines, and baby formula.[99] Analogous networks of human rights activists are taking root to pressure their governments to end various abuses. Many of the 438 prominent dissidents in Eastern Europe and the Soviet Union who linked up in a formal network in 1988 are now in power.[100] The opportunities for citizens to modify the behavior of nations are expanding daily.

Even some of the more ambitious policies for a peace system mentioned by Fischer — establishing stronger international verification and peacekeeping organizations — might also be carried out, at least in part, by citizens. The Natural Resources Defense Council has set up verification systems for monitoring a comprehensive test ban and a cruise-missile ban. As more reconnaissance photos are sold publicly and more private communication networks are formed, military information-gathering functions could also come into the hands of the public. Sweden or India, for example, might launch a satellite verification system financially supported by U.S. cities. With regard to peacekeeping, the church-based organization Witness for Peace played a major observer role in Central America by sending several thousand trained Americans to detail hostilities and human rights abuses throughout Nicaragua. It is conceivable that hundreds of cities globally could assemble contingents of peacekeepers, trained in nonviolent resistance, and dispatch them to trouble spots. So long as such efforts were unarmed and nonviolent, they would be consistent with current U.S. laws of neutrality, as well as with the precepts of a peace system.

Finally, all the strategies for promoting democracy at home and abroad can be carried out by citizens. Any American capable of traveling and talking can meet with people abroad, establish personal relationships, set up exchanges or business ties, and spread computers, laser printers, and telephones. Indeed, most of the examples cited earlier for promoting democracy abroad were of individual Americans acting unofficially with Soviets.

Increasingly, the question facing citizens implementing a peace system will be not what they can do — the number of options are overwhelming — but how they should do it. In recent years, Americans entering the rough-and-tumble of international affairs have discovered that their powers as individuals or as members of NGOs are quite limited. Unlike nation-states, which have vast treasuries derived from taxes, most individuals and NGOs operate on financial shoestrings. Individuals and NGOs also lack the "color of authority" of national diplomats and therefore are much less likely than national officials to get meetings with, let alone influence, powerful officials abroad.

Faced with these realities, millions of Americans seeking world peace have recruited their local elected officials, who, unlike inaccessible national officials, are rarely farther than a telephone call or public meeting away. And they have discovered that, unlike NGOs, local governments can provide their foreign-policy activism with money and legitimacy. As financially pinched as America's cities are, were they persuaded to allocate one percent of their budgets to promote world peace, they could expand the coffers of the entire U.S. peace movement more than ten-fold. Mayors may lack the clout of national ambassadors, but when venturing into foreign affairs they often receive red-carpet treatment, far better than most citizens or organizations. That Mayor Dianne Feinstein of San Francisco and seven other mayors convinced the Soviet Union in early 1986 to allow 36 people to emigrate after so many analogous private initiatives had failed can be attributed, in part, to the legitimacy of their offices.

In contrast to the Washington elitism governing much of the old peace movement, municipal foreign policies provide citizens with more opportunities to participate directly in international affairs. Through an expanding array of municipal foreign policies, Americans can further curtail unwise, unjust, and unpopular national military adventures and at the same time launch a wide array of alternative, nonmilitary policies.

In the 1950s and early 1960s, environmentalism was dismissed largely as a fringe movement populated by crazed tree huggers. But one by one, states and cities began to create their own environmental agencies dealing with land management, toxic waste disposal, water protection, and air quality. As strange as they might have seemed 25 years ago, Palo Alto's Department of Recycling and California's Energy Resources Development Commission are today regarded as perfectly normal instruments for local policymaking. Popular efforts to create green institutions made environmentalism a mainstream movement. It is now a multi-billion-dollar-per-year industry, employing hundreds of thousand of lawyers, scientists, economists, and policy analysts. These jobs, in turn, have opened up dozens of university programs dealing with environmental law, environmental science, and environmental economics.

All of this is possible with peace. If we start taking responsibility for promoting peace at the local level, if we begin creating strong local institutions for preventing and resolving conflicts, we can finally make peace a multi-billion-dollar-per-year industry, too. Young people interested in international affairs careers would no longer have to choose between working for the Foreign Service or multinational banks. Instead, they would be able to find thousands of exciting jobs in their hometowns across America. Peace would no longer be just an arcane discourse carried on by a small community of arms-controlaholics in Washington think tanks. Rather, it would become a matter of legitimate public debate, politicking, and policy-making for millions of people on Main Streets everywhere across America.

None of these changes will come quickly, easily, or cheaply. But giving ourselves permission to become active players in the nation's foreign policy is a critical first step. For with participation come education, experience, and wisdom. "Abolition of war," said General Douglas MacArthur in 1961, "is no longer an ethical question to be pondered solely by learned philosophers and ecclesiastics, but a hard core one for the decision of the masses whose survival is the issue."[101]

NOTES

1.   Francis Fukuyama, "The End of History?," *The National Interest*, no. 16, Summer 1988, p.18.

2.   Michael Doyle, "Kant Liberal Legacies, and Foreign Affairs," *Philosophy and Public Affairs*, 12:3-4, Summer and Fall 1983, pp. 205-35, 323-53. The exception that proves the rule is covert action. The United States, for example, helped overthrow Salvador Allende in Chile, an elected Marxist. But this underscores that wars waged by democracies against other democracies are so politically unsustainable that they can only be undertaken secretly. It also highlights why the elimination of clandestine military operations is necessary to perfect our own democracy.

3.   There's an argument, of course, that the process of democratization may unleash new conflicts within nations. The pro-democracy movement in China led to the massacre of thousands near Tiananmen Square in June 1989, and the unraveling of the Soviet Communist Party has caused conflicts among dozens of ethnic groups that have left hundreds dead. The counterargument, however, is that delaying democratization deepens popular frustrations and increases the probability of an even more disastrous political explosion down the road. A series of relatively small clashes in the Soviet Union and China that put these countries on a long-term evolutionary path to reform is certainly preferable to full-scale revolution.

4.   Bruce Russett, "Causes of Peace," in Carolyn M. Stephenson, ed., *Alternative Methods for International Security* (Lanham, MD: University Press of America, 1982), pp. 189-90.

5.   William Bundy, "A Portentous Year," *Foreign Affairs*, 62:3, America and the World, 1983, p. 503.

6.   Quoted in "Multiplicity of Relationships with Chinese," *Surviving Together*, October 1985, p. 6.

7.   Congress, for example, put sanctions on the Chinese government by pressuring President Bush to issue an executive order extending the visas of visiting Chinese students. This made it impossible for China to punish many students for their "subversive" activities abroad.

8.   Joseph V. Montville and William D. Davidson, "Foreign Policy According to

Freud," *Foreign Policy,* no. 45, Winter 1981-82, p. 155.

9. Gale Warner and Michael H. Shuman, *Citizen Diplomats: Pathfinders in Soviet-American Relations* (New York: Continuum, 1987), pp. 157-88.

10. Alex Pravda, "Costs/Benefits Point Soviets to the Door," *Los Angeles Times,* January 24, 1988, p. V-5.

11. Michael Doyle, "Kant, Liberal Legacies, and Foreign Affairs," pp. 211-12.

12. In New York State these barriers have prevented nearly a third of the voting-age population from registering. Martin Gottlieb and Dean Baquet, "Control of the Ballot Box: For Parties or the Public?," *New York Times,* October 21,1990, p. 1.

13. *Buckley v. Valeo,* 424 U.S. 1 (1976).

14. See the various papers of the Study Group on Electoral Democracy (Keets Road, Deerfield, MA 01342).

15. See: Hedrick Smith, *The Power Game* (New York: Ballantine, 1989); Philip M. Stern, *The Best Congress Money Can Buy* (New York: Pantheon, 1988); and Candice J. Newlson and David Magleby, *The Money Chase* (Washington, DC: Brookings Institute, 1990).

16. Francis Fox Piven and Richard A. Cloward, *Why Americans Don't Vote* (New York: Pantheon, 1988).

17. Sidney Verba and Norman H. Nie, *Participation in America: Political Democracy and Social Equality* (New York: Harper and Row,1972).

18. Michael Oreskes, "Poll Finds Americans Divided on Sanctions or Force in Gulf," *New York Times,* December 14, 1991, p. 1.

19. Michael Shuman, "What the Framers Really Said about Foreign Policy Powers," *Intergovernmental Perspective,* 16:2, Spring 1990, pp. 27-31.

20. *See, e.g., Lowry v. Reagan,* 676 F. Supp. 333 (D.D.C. 1987), in which the D.C. district court refused to entertain a lawsuit by 107 members of Congress that President Reagan's military actions in the Persian Gulf violated the War Powers Act.

21. One prominent example of official disinformation was the White House's efforts to destabilize the Libyan government by planting a story in the *Wall Street Journal* about an imminent U.S. attack on Libya. See Bob Woodward, *Veil* (New York: Pocket Books, 1987), pp. 548-52.

For an extensive discussion of the timidity of the American press, see: Mark Hertsgaard, *On Bended Knee: The Press and the Reagan Presidency* (New York: Farrar, Straus & Giroux, 1988); Noam Chomsky, "The Bounds of Thinkable Thought," *The Progressive*, October 1985, pp. 28-31; and various issues of the journal *Lies of Our Times*.

22. Daniel Yankelovich and John Doble, "The Public Mood: Nuclear Weapons and the U.S.S.R.," *Foreign Affairs*, 63:1, Fall 1984, p. 46.

23. Indeed, William Schneider argues that most of the American public is both noninterventionist and noninternationalist. "Public Opinion," in Joseph Nye, ed., *The Making of America's Soviet Policy* (New York: The Council on Foreign Relations, 1984), pp. 11-36.

24. This censorship power was previously held only by the Departments of Defense and State. Michael Schrage, "The Secret's Out: There's a New 'Sensitive' Security Classification," *Washington Post National Weekly Edition*, December 1, 1986, p. 32.

25. The Soviets have recently stated that they now have monitoring equipment capable of detecting nuclear weapons aboard surface ships or submarines from a distance. Peter van Ness, "Concealed Weapon," *The Nation*, March 12, 1988, p. 329.

26. Richard Falk, "Nuclear Weapons and the End of Democracy," *Praxis International*, 2:1, April 1982, pp. 6-7.

27. Testimony in the case of *Westmoreland v. CBS* firmly established a pattern of deception, even if the issue of General Westmoreland's personal culpability was never decisively resolved by the jury. Ronald Dworkin, "The Press on Trial," *New York Review of Books*, February 26, 1987, pp. 27-37.

28. John Markoff and Andrew Pollack, "Computer 'Hackers' Seen as Peril to Security of the Phone System," *New York Times*, July 22, 1988, p. 1 (Western Edition); John Markoff, "Top-Secret, and Vulnerable," *New York Times*, April 25, 1988, p. C1 (Western Edition); and Michael Shrage, "The Soviets Are Helping

Themselves to Our Computer Data Bases," *Washington Post National Weekly*, June 9, 1986, p. 31.

29. Neil Henderson, "For Sale: Aerial Close-Ups of Anything," *Washington Post National Weekly*, May 19, 1986, pp. 8-9; Eliott Marshall, "A Spy Satellite for the Press," *Science* 238:4832, December 4, 1987, pp. 1346-48. By the turn of the century, the International Space Year conference predicts, 17 countries will have scientific satellites orbiting Earth. Owen Thomas, "Nations Keep an Extra Eye on Each Other," *Christian Science Monitor*, September 26, 1988, p. 3. Because of the growing availability of high-resolution French and Soviet satellites, the United States recently removed constraints on its civilian satellites, which had been forbidden from resolving objects smaller than ten meters. "U.S. Lifts Bar on Satellite Photography," *San Francisco Chronicle*, January 21, 1988, p. A26. Greater resolutions are not really necessary to acquire important military information. In 1987 a Norwegian geoscientist used U.S. Landsat photographs with a thirty-meter resolution to find a secret Soviet airfield on the Kola Peninsula and hardened aircraft hangars. Owen Thomas, *op. cit.*, p. 4.

30. Robert Pear, "Congress Changes Spending Rules on Secret Programs for Pentagon," *New York Times*, October 31, 1990, p. 1.

31. Quoted in Anthony Lewis, "Reagan's Obsession with Nicaragua," *San Francisco Chronicle*, March 23, 1988, p. A14.

32. Eugene V. Rostow, "Repeal the War Powers Resolution," *Wall Street Journal*, June 27, 1984, p. 26.

33. Timothy Noah, "War Powers: An Act with No Action," *San Francisco Chronicle*, July 1, 1987.

34. J. Brian Atwood, "Sharing War Powers," *New York Times*, October 14, 1987, p. 35 (emphasis in original).

35. "Deployment Alarms Democrats," *Washington Post*, March 17, 1988, p. A30.

36. California Senator Alan Cranston notes, "Congress has proved reluctant to press for withdrawal of troops once deployed — however ill-advised the deployments might be." Alan Cranston, "Revitalize the War Powers Act," *The Washington Post National Weekly Edition*, November 2, 1987, p. 28.

37. Donald L. Robinson, "National Security Needs More than New Laws," *Los Angeles Times*, December 15, 1987, p. 13.

38. Helen Dewar, "War Powers Overhaul Proposed," *Washington Post*, May 20, 1988, pp. A1, A30.
The other "reform" proposed by this group — repealing automatic troop withdrawal after the sixty or ninety-day period has tolled — would be an unwarranted and dangerous concession that would further increase presidential power. Senate Majority Leader George Mitchell of Maine has complained that the current law "severely undercuts the president by encouraging our enemies to simply wait for U.S. law to remove the threat of further American military action" and by "prompting presidents to think in terms of short-term military action regardless of purpose." This misses the entire point of the War Powers Resolution: Presidents can deploy force for as long as they wish and for any purposes they wish providing they secure congressional approval first. Quoted in Peter Osterlund, "Senate Leaders Push War Powers Overhaul," *Christian Science Monitor*, May 20, 1988, p. 3.

39. Alan Cranston, *op. cit.*

40. *See Lowry v. Reagan, op. cit.*

41. Richard Falk, "Nuclear Weapons and the Renewal of Democracy," *Praxis International* 4:2, July 1984, p. 120.

42. Jeremy J. Stone, "Presidential First Use Is Unlawful," *Foreign Policy*, no. 56, Fall 1984, pp. 94-112.

43. Frank Church, "Covert Action: Swampland of American Foreign Policy," *Bulletin of the Atomic Scientists*, 32:2, February 1976, p. 11.

44. Stanley Hoffmann, "Under Cover or Out of Control?," *New York Times Book Review*, November 29, 1987, p. 3.

45. Frank Church, *op. cit.*, p. 11. Another argument for continuing covert actions, which President Reagan repeatedly used to secure congressional approval for covert aid to the Nicaraguan contras, is that covert actions provide the only intermediate option between diplomacy and military intervention.

46. Morton Halperin, "The Case against Covert Action," *The Nation*, March 21, 1987, p. 363. Gregory Treverton of the Council on Foreign Relations estimates that of the forty or so covert actions underway in the mid-1980s, at least half had been the subject of some press account." He further notes that "'leaking,' always present, has become routine in Washington; it has become almost acceptable. Officials sometimes leak information merely for the gratification of being pandered to by journalists more famous than they. More often, they leak to rally opposition to or, more rarely, support for a given policy. Administration after administration, regardless of its political persuasion, declares war on leakers. Those wars always fail. They fail for a simple reason: the ship of state is like no other, for it leaks from the top." Gregory F. Treverton, "Covert Action and Open Society," *Foreign Affairs*, 65:5, Summer 1987, pp. 1002-3.

47. Robert Merry, "Policy Makers Face a Trend: 'Covert' Actions Become Overt," *Wall Street Journal*, February 11, 1986, p. 38.

48. In August 1987, President Reagan tried to assure the Senate Select Committee on Intelligence that he would provide more timely, accurate, and comprehensive information on covert activities. "Text of Letter on Covert Operations," *New York Times*, August 8, 1987, p. 5 (Western Edition). At a minimum, these promises should be made binding on future presidents through amendments to the Intelligence Oversight Act. But it is important to remember that even the best reporting requirements do not put any restrictions on the president's activities.

49. Morton Halperin, *op. cit.*

50. Quoted in F.A.O. Schwarz, Jr., "Recalling Major Lessons of the Church Committee," *New York Times*, July 30, 1987, p. 25.

51. Quoted in Treverton, *op. cit.*, pp. 1012-13.

52. William V. Kennedy, "'No' to Covert Action," *Christian Science Monitor*, August 18, 1987, p. 12.

53. Robert M. Gates, "The CIA and American Foreign Policy," *Foreign Affairs*, 66:2, Winter 1987-88, p. 216.

54. Quoted in Tom Wicker, "The Price of Secrecy," *New York Times*, September 10, 1987, p. 25 (Western Edition). Robert McFarlane underscored a similar point in his testimony at the Iran-Contra hearings. With a secret policy, he said, "you

cannot get public and congressional support." Quoted in Joseph C. Harsch, "The Limits on Covert Activity," *Christian Science Monitor*, May 19, 1987, p. 14.

55. For a comprehensive review, *see* Michael H. Shuman, "Dateline Main Street: Local Foreign Policy," *Foreign Policy*, no. 65, Winter 1986-87, pp. 156-74.

56. The data that follow all appear in Michael H. Shuman, "Building Municipal Foreign Policies: An Action Handbook for Citizens and Local Elected Officials" and in various issues of the *Bulletin of Municipal Foreign Policy*. (Both are available from the Center for Innovative Diplomacy, 17931F Sky Park Circle, Irvine, CA 92714.)

57. See for example, Peter Spiro, "Taking Foreign Policy Away from the Feds," *The Washington Quarterly*, 11:1, Winter 1988, pp. 191-203, especially 202.

58. The Logan Act forbids any American from "directly or indirectly" corresponding with or meeting with "any foreign government...with intent to influence the measures or conduct of any foreign government... in relation to any disputes or controversies with the United States, or to defeat the measures of the United States." 18 U.S. Code, Section 953 (1976). Despite its sweeping language and despite frequent threats by officials to use it against various citizen diplomats, the act has never been enforced. Detlev F. Vagts, "The Logan Act: Paper Tiger or Sleeping Giant?" *American Journal of International Law*, vol. 60, 1966, pp. 268-302.

59. Michael H. Shuman, "Put Ollie in State Prison," *Bulletin of Municipal Foreign Policy*, 2:3, Summer 1988, p. 2-4.

60. Letter to Colonel Edward Carrington, January 16, 1787, in Adrienne Koch and William Peden, eds., *The Life and Selected Writings of Thomas Jefferson* (New York: Modern Library, 1944), p. 411.

61. In fact, fewer than a half-dozen Politburo members approved the Soviet invasion of Afghanistan in 1979.

62. This is the principal weakness of Gregory Fossedal's *The Democratic Imperative: Exporting the American Revolution* (New York: Basic Books, 1989).

63. Quoted in William Blum, *The CIA: A Forgotten History* (London: Zen Books, 1986), p. 235. Behind Kissinger's words stood a massive CIA covert operation that helped subvert and overthrow Allende's government. *Ibid.*, pp. 232-43.

64. Robert B. Cullen, "Soviet Jewry," *Foreign Affairs*, 65:2, Winter 1986-87, pp. 252-66.

65. Thomas F. O'Boyle, "To Radio Free Europe, Glasnost Is a Challenge to Be Better, Quicker," *Wall Street Journal*, March 25, 1988, p. 1.

66. John Spicer Nichols, "Wasting the Propaganda Dollar," *Foreign Policy*, no. 56, Fall 1984, pp. 129-40.

67. Irving Kristol, "Coping with an 'Evil Empire,'" *Wall Street Journal*, December 17, 1985, p. 26.

68. Linda Feldmann (paraphrasing Yale Richmond), "From Hand to Hand Flows . . .Trust or Manipulation," *Christian Science Monitor*, February 25, 1988, p. 5.

69. Ann Levin, "U.S., Soviet Scientists Progress in Nuclear Test-Monitoring Effort," *Christian Science Monitor*, November, 13 1986, p. 5; and Mary McGrory, "Verification Venture," *Washington Post*, July 10, 1986, p. A2.

70. Gale Warner and Michael H. Shuman, *op. cit.*, pp. 31-67.

71. Philip Taubman, "Gorbachev Has Come a Long Way, Too," *New York Times*, May 29, 1988, sec. 4, p. 1.

72. Franz Schurmann, "Fast Food Outlets Symbolize Capitalist Spirit at Communist Shrines," *East-West News*, December 3, 1987, p. 7.

73. Quoted in Flora Lewis, "Soviets Buy American," *New York Times*, May 10, 1989, p. A35.

74. "Cuddly Russia?" *The Economist*, February 14, 1987, pp. 13-14.

75. Kirk Johnson, "Soviets Allow U.S. Citizens to Send More Goods," *New York Times*, December 4, 1988, p. 23.

76. "All That's Glasnost Does Not Glitter," *U.S. News & World Report*, April 4, 1988, pp. 50-51; and Frank Tuttitia, *PC World* public relations staff, personal communication, October 1989.

77. Bill Keller, "For Soviet Alternative Press, Used Computer Is New Tool," *New*

York Times, January 12, 1988, p. 1; and Joel Bleifuss, "I.F. Stone Defends Glasnost," *In These Times*, June 22 - July 5, 1988, p. 4.

78. The AlphaGraphics Printshop on Gorky Street, for example, is the result of a joint Soviet-Canadian venture. Richard L. Wentworth, "Soviets Open to Deals with West," *Christian Science Monitor*, April 4, 1989, p. 9.

79. There are estimated to be only 33 million phones for 282 million Soviets, with 12 million on official waiting lists. Only half a million copies of the 1987 Moscow telephone book were printed for the city's three million subscribers. Antero Pietila, "New Moscow Phone Book Offers Directory Resistance," *San Francisco Examiner*, March 13, 1988, p. A 12.
    When East Germany analyzed why residents of Dresden were five times as likely to apply for permission to move than residents of other areas, it discovered that they were unhappy because they could not tune into television shows originating from West Germany. The government solved the migration problem, at least temporarily, by piping Western television into Dresden via cable. John Mueller, *Wall Street Journal*, May 23, 1989, p. A18.

80. Robert Pear, "U.S. Helping Polish Underground with Money and Communications," *New York Times*, July 10, 1988, p. 1.

81. Shirley Christian, "Group Is Channeling U.S. Funds to Parties Opposing Pinochet," *New York Times*, June 15, 1988, p. 1.

82. Roger Cohen, "Shift in U.S. Policy on Latin America Decreases Likelihood of Military Coups," *Wall Street Journal*, May 4, 1989, p. A10.

83. Robert Pear, "Poll Watching Becomes a Growth Industry," *New York Times*, May 7, 1989, sec. 4, p. 2.

84. *See, e.g.*, Douglas M. Johnston, Jr., and Paul J. Cook, Jr., "Beyond Sanctions," *Christian Science Monitor*, July 13, 1988, p. 12. One unsung success story of the global anti-apartheid movement occurred when it convinced the South African government to withdraw legislation that would have banned foreign contributions to domestic anti-apartheid groups. Lynda Schuster, "S. Africa Shelves Law Banning Foreign Aid to Opposition Groups," *Christian Science Monitor*, June 29, 1988, p. 9.

85. Many constitutions — most recently, those of the Philippines and Nicaragua

— are based in part on the U.S. Constitution. Says Stanford Law Professor John Henry Merryman, "Of all American influences in the world, our strongest is probably the Constitution." Quoted in Reese Erlich, "Exporting the Constitution," *California Lawyer*, August 1987, pp. 44-48.

86. By law, the American people have virtually no power to raise armies or use force abroad. *See* Michael H. Shuman, "Put Ollie in State Prison," *op. cit.*

87. *Budget of the United States Government, Fiscal Year 1988, Supplement* (Washington, DC: U.S. Government Printing Office, 1987), pp. 5-35.

88. Amory B. Lovins, L. Hunter Lovins, Terri Sabonis-Chafee, Bill Keepin, and Richard Heede, "Response to the Concept 21 Paper," (document on resources and the next 30 years). Presented by L. Hunter Lovins to the Army Concept 21 Conference, February 1988 (22 pages). Available from Rocky Mountain Institute.

89. Amory B. Lovins and Robert Sardinsky, *The State of the Art Lighting* (Snowmass, Co: Rocky Mountain Institute, March 1988), pp. 348.

90. The RDF was upgraded to a Unified Command in 1983. It is now called Central Command or USCENTCOMM.

91. Amory B. Lovins and L. Hunter Lovins, "Drill Rigs and Battleships Are the Answer! (But What Was the Question?)," chapter for Fereidun Fesharaki and Robert Reed, eds., *The Petroleum Market in the 1990s* (Boulder, CO: Westview Press, 1988).

92. Amory B. and L. Hunter Lovins, "Make Fuel Efficiency Our Gulf Strategy," *New York Times*, December 3, 1990, p. A19.

93. For example, the problem of radon gas accumulating in tightly constructed houses can be eliminated with heat-exchangers, now mass-produced at affordable prices by the Japanese.

94. For a complete treatment of this thesis, *see* Amory B. Lovins and L. Hunter Lovins, *Brittle Power: Energy Strategy for National Security* (Andover: Brick House, 1982)

95. Howard Geller, Jeffrey P. Harris, Mark D. Levine, and Arthur H. Rosenfeld, "The Role of Federal Research and Development in Advancing Energy Efficiency:

A $50 Billion Contribution to the U.S. Economy," *Annual Review of Energy*, vol. 12 (Palo Alto, CA: Annual Reviews Inc., 1987), pp. 357-95.

96. Amory B. Lovins and L. Hunter Lovins, "The Avoidable Oil Crisis," *Atlantic Monthly*, 260:6, December 1987, p. 29.

97. Mauro Suttora, "Trying to Keep the Red Cross Out," *World Press Review*, October 1988, pp. 29-30 (reprinted from the Italian newsmagazine Europeo).

98. For a discussion of the growth of environmental activism in Central America, *see* Tensie Whelan, "A Tree Falls in Central America," *Amicus Journal*, Fall 1988, pp. 28-38.

99. Robert M. Press, "Third-World Consumer Groups Chalk up Steady Successes," *Christian Science Monitor*, March 25, 1988, p. 11.

100. John Tagliabue, "Network of Dissenters Expanding in East Bloc," *New York Times*, March 22, 1988, p. 7 (Western Edition).

101. Major Vorin E. Whan Jr., ed., *A Soldier Speaks: Public Papers and Speeches of General of the Army Douglas MacArthur* (New York: Praeger, 1965), p. 316.

ECOLOGY

David Orr is co-founder of the Meadowcreek Project, an environmental education and research center in Fox, Arkansas. He is currently Professor of Environmental Studies at Oberlin College.

Orr's essay points out that the nation-state system exists within a larger system, the biosphere. In an increasingly interdependent world, nation-states that continue to assert their right to wage war will be incapable of solving complex problems that threaten the biosphere's very survival.

To avoid environmental doom, Orr recommends global cooperation — to stabilize population growth, to develop renewable energy resources, to preserve rainforests and biological diversity, to forgive Third World debt, and to strictly limit carbon-dioxide emissions and the use of ozone-depleting chlorofluorocarbons (CFCs).

Orr asks whether those who control the world's resources are prepared to make the sacrifices necessary to avert ecological peril. If they are not, he warns, the result may be a worldwide explosion of political upheavel and repression.

THE ECOLOGICAL FOUNDATIONS
OF NATIONAL SECURITY

David Orr

Throughout history, security has been regarded as the product of military strength. To be safe was to be well armed. Weakness only invited invasion, pillage, and destruction by aggressors. This may not always have been the case. Riane Eisler purports to show that war was not characteristic of human societies in Europe prior to 5000 B.C. Whatever the evidence reveals of our past and possibly of our future, history has been generally unkind to peaceful, pastoral societies. One by one they have been conquered or assimilated by their more aggressive neighbors. If the race is not to the swift nor the battle to the strong, you could not tell it from the record of civilization. History is a catalogue of human bloodshed and depravity dominated by the mighty.

The logic of a "war system" has been the accepted norm since the Treaty of Westphalia, signed in 1648. The treaty sanctioned the idea of self-help in a system of independent, sovereign nation-states. Security was defined implicitly as a function of military power. Threats originated from other nation-states whose interests ran counter to one's own. This system "worked" until 1914, when World War I began.

Threats to the well-being of citizens since the Treaty of Westphalia have increasingly originated from other sources, including citizens' own states. Moreover, the system of self-help created at Westphalia has proved incapable of meeting a growing array of problems that require cooperative solutions. Foremost among these are the precarious problems of providing security in the nuclear age and managing global commons (the atmosphere, the oceans, and critical habitats). Both of these problems now threaten the survival of humankind. They differ primarily in the speed with which they might render the planet uninhabitable, but not in their finality. There is simply no conceivable kind of self-help that can insulate a nation from the direct or indirect effects of nuclear war. Nor is there any purely national policy that can defend against pollution, acid rain, ozone depletion, or climate change.

Because of these changed circumstances, old measures of power tell us less and less about how secure people are from assaults on their well-being. In fact, many of these measures have become obsolete. For citizens in industrial countries, early death is much more likely to result from industrially created carcinogens and the careless use of technology (including automobile accidents) than from marauding armies. The most vital economies of the late twentieth century are those least burdened by military expenditures. Both the United States and the Soviet Union are sinking under the burden of debt, trade deficits, and the costs of militarization. Meanwhile, the well-being of the populations entrusted to the governments of the superpowers is being compromised by the very efforts designed to protect them. Military aircraft crash into civilian areas. Factories designed to build weapons, like those at Rocky Flats, Colorado, or Fernald, Ohio, leak radioactivity. The "opportunity costs" of military expenditures—that is, the expenditures foregone because of military expenditures — are even greater. The costs of military "preparedness" include unbuilt schools and hospitals, deteriorating infrastructure, declining democratic institutions, and wasted human potential. Why has military spending become so counterproductive?

First, as war has become more destructive it has become a less useful instrument of rational policy. The creation of atomic and hydrogen bombs marked a clear watershed in the history of human conflict, ensuring that war could no longer remain limited. The successful use of laser-guided weapons and "smart" bombs in the Persian Gulf War may have rehabilitated war, but it is simply too soon to know what the long-term effects of high-technology weaponry will be. It is worth noting that the costs of precision-guided munitions is low, that the technology is difficult to keep secret, and that it may ultimately enable our adversaries to launch missiles from cargo ships fifty miles off the coast of New York City. Future Saddam Husseins will be more careful to have terrorist networks in place before they act. Technologically advanced societies are filled with all kinds of tempting targets for terrorism — nuclear power plants, centralized energy-supply networks, concentrated population centers, vulnerable water and food systems. Moreover, as Hussein demonstrated by igniting the oil fields of Kuwait, a demented leader facing defeat can saddle both the victors and third parties with considerable environmental costs that may well exceed the gains of victory. Hussein managed to punish the West by fouling the Persian Gulf with oil spills and setting fire to half the Kuwaiti oil fields, causing acid rain to fall on surrounding areas and significant amounts of carbon dioxide to enter the atmosphere and speed the pace of global warming.[1] When all the bills are totaled, we may discover that a wiser course of action might have been a patient policy of economic sanctions along with new energy policies cutting our dependence on imported oil. The increasing destructiveness of weapons and the growing technological sophistication of every nation has effectively democratized the potential for terror. As a result, the nation-state, which originally justified its existence by its ability to defend national territory, can no longer provide security against adversaries, terrorists, or even technological accidents.

Second, economic life has changed with the creation of an integrated world economy. Industrial economies are more and more dependent on the international flow of capital, resources, and technologies. Prosperity increasingly rests on technological mastery, not on conquest. International competition demands continual improvement in productivity, consumer products, and other factors that contribute to economic power.

The same technologies that strengthen competitiveness, however, also can lower the quality of life and damage ecosystems. To balance its international accounts, for example, the United States exports grain. But for every bushel of grain produced, it loses the equivalent of two-to-three bushels of topsoil. Increasing labor productivity through the use of automated technologies such as robots creates a class of permanently unemployable people. Even "clean" industries like the manufacture of computers have caused significant environmental problems. We can no longer assume that economic growth, global interdependence, or technological change necessarily will improve people's lives or protect national security.

The term national security must now be broadened in recognition of the linkages among security, resources, and ecological stability. The reality of interdependence means that security is becoming planetary and can no longer be defined in purely national terms. Threats to particular nations remain, but they are now part of a larger fabric of forces and trends. The world in which sovereign nation-states controlled their own destiny, if it ever existed, is now past.

One of the biggest challenges now confronting the nation-state is its management of the flow of low entropy: materials, food, water, energy, and waste. Assaults on the well-being of citizens are increasingly coming from poisons in the air, water, and food. The future viability of a nation's economy now depends on its ability to manage the resource and ecological base on which the economy and all life forms depend.

The term "sustainable," first popularized by Lester Brown, has come to mean living within one's ecological means or "carrying capacity." But carrying capacity is a complex concept, measuring the levels of resource use, technology, and population against natural thresholds that are poorly understood. Advocates of sustainable development typically focus on the rate of population growth, the percentage of resource use that is nonrenewable, and the resulting burdens on the environment. These are straightforward enough. Questions arise when one asks about timing, rates of change, and orders of magnitude. Over what time period must a society become sustainable? What population size is sustainable at what levels of resource use? To what extent does sustainable development imply self-sufficiency? What is the relationship between sustainable development and equitable distribution? Advocates of sustainability differ on many of these questions. For some, the transition to a sustainable future implies a "paradigm shift" in values, institutions, and life-styles. For others, the transition is simply a matter of adjusting markets and prices or developing new technologies.

We may discover that the goal of sustainability, however necessary, is not to our liking. It may require sharp changes in many aspects of modern life to which we have grown accustomed, including mass consumption and easy mobility. Growth in western societies, for example, has been used as an all-purpose political solvent to avoid issues of distribution. If sustainability implies slower growth, no growth, or even economic contraction, how will the national wealth be divided? The rich have not often acquiesced gracefully in matters of equity, and it is certainly possible that efforts to promote sustainability will result in increased political repression.

Much in the way that medieval man placed his belief in religion, modern society has invested its faith in science and technology. Can these save us from ecological malfeasance? Any understanding of the crisis of sustainability must confront the Janus-like nature of scientific knowledge and technological innovation. Any solution to the crisis that does not confront the need to redirect technology will not work for long.

The transition to sustainability will lead to a very different kind of society. International politics from 1648 to the present have reflected the values and priorities of the dominant states. Domestically and internationally, the world of the twentieth century has unraveled on the altar of military power, technological change, and economic growth. The world of the twenty-first century and beyond, if sustainable, just, and peaceful, will require the creation of an entirely new system of security.

If the world were by some miracle to become sustainable, would it also be a world at peace? Not necessarily. Even if we eliminate the growing potential for interstate disputes over resources, land, water, and population, conflicts rooted in bigotry, sexism, pride, greed, arrogance, and pure human recalcitrance would remain. Given the human genius for conflict and malfeasance, the goal of sustainability should not be confused with utopia. Sustainability is now a necessary but insufficient condition for peace, and peace is now a necessary but insufficient condition for sustainability.

To paraphrase Charles Dickens, we live in the best of times and the worst of times. The dissolution of the Iron Curtain and the Cold War after forty-five years gives us a chance to build a durable system of peace. But time is short. We may have only a decade or two to reverse the trends of ozone depletion or global warming. And the Bush Administration has yet to show leadership in these matters remotely comparable to that which it displayed in opposing Saddam Hussein. To the contrary, the United States remains well behind other industrial nations in developing far-sighted policies to control global warming and to promote sustainable development at home and abroad.

A TALE OF TWO SYSTEMS

The Westphalian system was created when world population was 500 million, when the fastest speed attainable was by horse, and when the most destructive weapon was a naval gun that could hurl an eight-pound iron ball several hundred yards. This system made the territorial state the principal arbiter of issues of war and peace. For the next three hundred years, territory and territorial resources were the primary issues on the international agenda.

For reasons its founders could not have foreseen, the Westphalian system of nation-states no longer works. First, the system has failed to limit conflict; the twentieth century has been a period of unparalleled bloodshed.

Second, the state system now confronts the consequences of political events characterized by greater complexity and speed. The interaction of technological, economic, political, social, and military forces that produce change are poorly understood or undiagnosed altogether. Compared to the world of 1648, the sheer volume of events and interactions in the world system has risen by orders of magnitude, as have the adverse consequences of unanticipated change.

Third, the costs of resorting to violence or preparing to use violence have undermined the Westphalian system of military self-help. Since 1945, for example, military weapons have increased in cost 105 times while prices have increased only 6.5 times.[2] The direct costs of the Westphalian system, however, do not tell the full story. There are also "opportunity costs" exacted from society by military expenditures. Gold-plated military systems contrast markedly with declining cities, crumbling roads and bridges, and growing poverty. Militarization imposes more subtle costs as well. The veil of secrecy which is drawn around the process of weapons acquisition has allowed corruption of the most venal sort, as well as the monumental incompetence evident in large cost overruns.

Fourth, the Westphalian system has become ecologically implausible. War, the ultimate expression of sovereignty, has become too destructive for victor and vanquished alike. Any conceivable nuclear war, even a small one, would be utterly catastrophic, triggering "nuclear winter" and probably other ecological consequences which cannot be anticipated. Conventional wars have higher ecological costs, too. While environmental damage from the Persian Gulf war is not fully known, it clearly is substantial. It is also clear, as noted above, that terrorist actions targeted against nuclear power facilities, toxic waste dumps, population centers, and food and water supplies would change the balance sheet for even "small" wars.

The international system exists within a larger system, the biosphere, which operates independent of human volition. Until recently, statesmen could assume the stability of this larger system — and most remained ignorant of the biosphere's existence altogether. But assumptions of ecological stability that underlay the Westphalian system no longer hold. For example, hidden in the old logic of international politics are unstated beliefs that climate would remain stable, that resources for growth would be readily available, that the entire human population could be fed, housed, and clothed, that the biosphere would absorb all human wastes, that science and technology would be benign, that energy would be cheap and abundant, and that complexity would be managable. In other words, it was assumed, wrongly, that the ecological and biospheric foundations of our political, social, and economic systems were secure. But as our knowledge of the natural world expanded, we have learned not only to compose new materials and life forms, which the medieval alchemists only dreamed of creating, but also to expect that unfettered human creativity and procreativity can have tragic ecological and biological consequences. Knowledge of these consequences has regrettably developed more slowly than the reductionist knowledge necessary to tinker with nature. Gradually, we have discovered limits that must be the basis for any new peace system.

Limits of the Biosphere

Humans are now the dominant force on the planet, as powerful as the forces of previous geologic upheavals. Agriculture, energy use, and manufacturing lie at the heart of the impact of human beings on the globe. Since 1850, nine million square kilometers have been converted into permanent cropland. Energy use has risen by a factor of 80, disrupting natural geochemical cycles of carbon, nitrogen, and sulfur. Industrial production is up more than 10,000 percent. The area of forested land lost since 1700 is larger than Europe. Sediment loads in major rivers have increased by 300 percent, and in smaller rivers by as much as 800 percent.[3] Increased water use in the same period is roughly equal to the volume of Lake Huron. Methane in the atmosphere has doubled. Heavy metals and toxins can now be found everywhere in measurable quantities. Humans are causing a biological holocaust that is destroying life 10,000 times more rapidly than the natural rate of extinction.[4] Most of this change has occurred since 1945, and the pace is still accelerating.

Perhaps the most ominous trend is global warming, caused by the release of heat-trapping gases such as carbon dioxide from the combustion of fossil fuels and deforestation, methane from anaerobic decay, and chemicals released by industrial processes, including chlorofluorocarbons (CFCs), bromine, and halons. As a result, the earth has warmed by 0.5 to 0.7 degrees Celsius since 1860, and five of the warmest years on record occurred in the 1980s. Data on the rate of carbon dioxide accumulation show a rise beginning in 1987 from 1.5 parts per million to 2.4 parts per million.[5] One explanation for the increasing level of carbon dioxide in the atmosphere is the effect of warmer temperatures on the rates of plant decay and respiration. Planetary warming, which may well be irreversible, also will cause substantial changes in rainfall, flooding some areas and causing droughts in others.

Another instance of our exhausting the biosphere is the depletion of planetary ozone. The primary culprit, identified in the early 1970s, is a family of chemicals known as CFCs. Since their discovery in the 1930s, CFCs have been used widely in many industries as solvents, propellants, and cleaners, and in products ranging from computer chips to refrigerators. But they do not break down quickly, and once released they accumulate in the stratosphere where their decomposition releases chlorine which then destroys ozone. Each day we release some 2700 tons of CFCs to the atmosphere. The results have been one ozone "hole" over the South Pole that covers the Antarctic and extends as far as Australia, the beginnings of another hole over the North Pole, and a general thinning throughout the mid-latitudes. Even with an immediate ban on CFCs, stratospheric ozone is expected to decline sharply over the next thirty years.[6] Global warming and ozone depletion also may be linked; as the lower portion of the atmosphere warms, the upper layers cool and form ice crystals that destroy ozone.

Several conclusions are beyond contention. First, we are crossing, or will soon cross, thresholds affecting long-term climate stability. Second, we do not understand many of the critical causal linkages between complex ecosystems and human actions. Third, we do not have data about the "vital signs" of the planet comparable, to say, the Dow Jones Index. Finally, most research is still directed toward manipulation of the natural world, not toward understanding the results of our tinkerings or toward development of low-impact alternatives.

Population and Food Limits

World population reached one billion sometime around the year 1800, two billion after 1900, three billion in 1958, four billion in 1975, and five billion in 1987. The United Nations Population Division estimates that world population in the year 2025 will reach 8.5 billion. Given existing fertility rates and the age structure of the current population, we will add one billion people to the planet in each of the next three decades. Ninety-five percent of the growth will be in the poorest countries, which can least afford more mouths to feed.[7] While there is disagreement about the total population that the earth can support, three conclusions can be drawn from these numbers. First, population growth is exerting great pressure on ecosystems nearly everywhere. In developed nations environmental impacts are compounded many times over by high rates of resource consumption. In poor nations, the effects of growing population are evident in soil erosion, desertification, and deforestation. Second, perhaps 25 percent of the present population of the planet is malnourished.[8] While inadequate distribution and the decline in local subsistence farming are to blame, these figures cast doubt about how well we might do with a much larger population in the coming decades. Third, the race between population growth and food production will become more difficult as the effects of climate change, ozone depletion, and acid rain worsen.

The economist Thomas Malthus was among the first to recognize that population tends to increase exponentially while food supply grows arithmatically. If history proved Malthus wrong, as is commonly believed, it may have done so only partially and temporarily. Population has continued to increase exponentially. The food supply has increased as well, much more than Malthus could have known, primarily because of the greater availability of land for agriculture and cheap energy. But "Green Revolutions" work only with large inputs of fertilizer, pesticides, herbicides, and machinery, all of which depend on a stable supply of low-cost oil. U.S. agriculture, for example, uses about ten calories of fossil-fuel energy to put one calorie on the plate.[9] Conventional agriculture is becoming more and more dependent on chemical solutions for fertility and pest control, but insects are becoming increasingly resistant to pesticides.[10] World soil loss caused by poor farming practices is now estimated to be 24 billion tons per year.[11] These trends explain why the specter of famine once raised by Malthus continues to stalk many nations in Africa and Asia. At least one study has shown that as fossil energy supplies dwindle and prices for inputs rise, famine may visit developed countries as well.[12]

Climate change is now the joker in the deck. Projections made by the National Center for Atmospheric Research indicate that the grainbelt in the Midwest will become both hotter and drier, and that the prime growing area will shift northward to Canada.[13] Early studies on the effects of increasing ultraviolet radiation show that it suppresses biotic activity.[14] Crop productivity will also be reduced by acid rain and by air pollution, particularly in the form of ground-level ozone.

We have not escaped the trap Malthus described. In fact, we may have made it a much larger trap. Technology, dependent on fossil fuels, has increased our carrying capacity for a time. Whether this represents a permanent or temporary increase depends on a level of technological heroism that Malthus never could have imagined. We have only avoided starvation by using cheap energy and plentiful land, but these are fast disappearing. If feeding the world continues to depend on an energy input/output ratio of ten to one, Malthus will have the last groan. Additions to farmable land also will be much more difficult in the future. In fact, with global warming we will be losing land to rising oceans. In places like Bangladesh, flooding may well be catastrophic.

Energy Limits

The rate and volume of fossil-fuel use are two of the most distinctive features of the modern world. The ability to burn fuels at a time and rate of our choosing has facilitated vast increases in human population, the rise of large cities, and the growth of industry. Without fossil fuels, the world in its present form and scale simply could not have been created. The enormous increases we have seen in industrial and agricultural production are the result of our growing ability to substitute energy for labor. Yet we have been curiously slow to understand our dependence on energy supplies and our vulnerability to sudden cutoffs.

The low prices for energy in the late 1980s created a sense of unwarranted complacency. Now, however, the U.S. Department of Energy (DOE) projects sharp increases in the price of oil by the mid-1990s, perhaps reaching $30 a barrel. At the same time, DOE expects an increase in the demand for oil by developing countries of some 2.5 million barrels per day.[15] More ominously, a decade of increasing efficiency in the United States leveled out in 1986, and our appetite for all kinds of energy once again increased. The United States is now importing more oil than it produces, and this predicament could well worsen. [16] U.S. oil production peaked around 1970 and has been declining ever since. Despite huge outlays for exploration, proven U.S. reserves of oil have decreased from 32 billion barrels in 1977 to 27 billion barrels in 1989, and experts give no hope that this decline can be stopped.[17] Simply stated, we are running out of oil, and unless we find substitutes our dependency on foreign oil is bound to increase.

All U.S. energy sources now have a declining energy return on investment (EROI), which, according to Charles Hall, Cutler Cleveland, and Robert Kaufman, represents the ratio of the "gross amount of fuel extracted in the energy transformation process to the economic energy required to make that fuel available to society."[18] EROI, or net energy, is a much more important figure than total reserves available. It tells us how much energy it costs to deliver a given quantity of fuel. When it costs a barrel of oil to deliver a barrel of oil we have reached an EROI of 0. A close look at EROI measures reveals that fossil fuels have a declining return on investment. For example, one study of selected Louisiana oil fields indicates that the break-even point will be reached in the late 1990s. When that point is reached, the question of whether or not there is still oil in the ground will be moot. There will be no good reason to remove oil with an EROI of 0. From this perspective, efficiency gains in the use of energy may sooner or later be offset by the declining EROI of various energy suppliers.

While fossil fuels have shaped the modern world, our dependence on them now poses severe threats to a stable and sustainable future. Combustion of fossil fuels is the primary cause of global warming and acid rain. As we learned in the Persian Gulf

War, oil-importing economies are now hostage to the unstable politics of the Middle East. After world oil production peaks sometime in the first quarter of the next century, the decline of the fossil-fuel era may be traumatic, unless timely measures are taken to begin another era based on efficiency and renewable energy sources. These measures will not be cheap, only cheaper than the socioeconomic and ecological price to be paid if renewable sources of energy are not sought. The good news about energy is that efficiency improvements that are now technically feasible could substantially reduce consumption of all energy forms. A DOE study shows that U.S. energy consumption could be reduced by fifty percent with present technologies, and with a positive net impact on the economy.[19]

Nuclear power, at least in its present form, is not a viable alternative. The problem of energy scarcity has to do with a shortage of liquid fossil fuels that are used primarily in transportation and in heating, not a shortage of electricity. Moreover, aside from the well-known problems of the nuclear fuel cycle, including reactor safety, waste disposal, and weapons proliferation, nuclear energy also suffers from a low to negative EROI when *all* costs are counted, such as those of decommissioning plants. As for the argument that nuclear power is an answer to global warming, Gregory Kats and William Keepin have shown that even under conservative assumptions dollars spent on conservation in effect remove seven times more carbon than those spent on nuclear power. Nuclear power is simply not an answer to the global-warming crisis.[20]

From a policy perspective, we must chose among three broad courses of action: economic policies that rely on heroic technological breakthroughs to increase energy supplies in the face of declining rates of EROI; efficiency improvements that more than offset declining EROI; or national plans that prepare us for slower economic growth or even economic contraction. The crucial necessity is to ask of each course: Can this be done in time? At what cost? And what happens if the underlying assumptions turn out to be wrong?

The Westphalian system of political economy is now in conflict with the biosphere because each works in fundamentally different ways.

First, the biosphere functions by processes of evolution and ecology. The "machinery of nature" is a vast interconnected web of relationships, biogeochemical cycles, and energy flows. Its logic is evolutionary, adaptive, co-evolving. It is as dependent upon cooperation as on competition. Predator-prey relationships are seldom "zero-sum" games at the species level. James Lovelock, author of *Gaia*, argues that evolution legitimately applies to the planet more than to separate species. The passions that lead humans to genocide, mass warfare, and violent nationalism have no counterpart in nature. The war system, in contrast, is driven by the logic of power. The resort to force is most typically played as a zero-sum game — winner takes all. As the Westphalian order grew into the global war system, each nation worked assiduously to perfect its technology for destruction. In the words of Solly Zuckerman: "The momentum of the arms race is undoubtedly fueled by the technicians in governmental laboratories and in the industries which produce the armaments."[21] The technological revolution in warfare now exceeds the capacities of the biosphere and humans to manage it. The result is a widening "gap between mechanical intelligence and human intent," with weapons systems "passing out of human control."[22] Behind this technological momentum are worst-case fears institutionalized in defense bureaucracies and the dark side of human ingenuity. There is no apparent counterpart in natural systems for these dynamics; nature plays out its role in a more tentative and cautious way.

Second, natural evolution has occurred over millions of years, while the human-based political economy has been speeding up decade by decade for the past two centuries. Economic growth since 1945 has been more of an eruption than an evolution. Computers and instantaneous communication across the planet have changed the speed at which humans think, work, and live. The revolution in military technology now means that decisions about the fate of 2.5 billion years of evolution will be made in minutes, or seconds. There is a disjunction between the rhythms of nature measured in billions or millions of years, and technological time, measured in days, hours, minutes, seconds, and nanoseconds. As technological time is superimposed on older patterns of day and night and changing seasons, human behavior is increasingly disoriented in ways that suggest that speed has become an addiction.

Third, the evolution of ecosystems leads toward increasing diversity, ecological complexity, stability, and balance. Left to itself, nature evolves in ways that tend to create stable systems over long periods of time. As systems "mature," nutrient cycles become tighter and more energy goes into maintenance than into growth. Life at the planetary level, according to Lovelock, is an active agent in maintaining the climate and temperature conditions necessary for more life. As conditions move away from those suitable for life, biological organisms act to restore the balance. The purpose of human systems, in contrast, has become to grow as large as possible. Having eliminated most or all of their natural competitors, humans now face no limits other than those imposed by the planet or the perverse consequences of their own actions. Evolution has equipped humans with no instinct to know when enough is enough.

Fourth, natural systems are organized as a kind of loose hierarchy with a great deal of redundancy and diversity. Species fit together in a complex tangle of varying relationships, niches, and trophic levels, all governed by how efficiently they use available energy. The demise of any one life form has little effect on the rest of the system. Evolution has equipped ecosystems with spare parts, backup systems, and, at the genetic level, lots of information about what to do in emergencies. At the planetary level, Lovelock has made a convincing case that the feedback systems have been remarkably successful at maintaining atmospheric stability within fairly narrow limits for the past two billion years. The structure of human society, however, is increasingly homogeneous. What was once a great diversity of human cultures is being rapidly destroyed by modernization. Humans are now being lumped together into one great experiment. Gaia would have never wagered it all by attempting to replace the planet's diverse life forms with just rain forests or just deserts, for if there were any flaws in the logic, science, or adaptability underlying this great wager, the entire system would be in jeopardy. If the resources and energy on which Gaia depends run short, the system will collapse catastrophically. Cultural diversity, like diversity in natural systems, provided a margin for error. Not so long ago human societies constituted hundreds of experiments, each coping with different problems in different settings. The failure of any one did not pose significant problems for the others. The rise of a global civilization, whatever its benefits, has no such margin. Today, nations following the Westphalian logic simply assume that the human mind can create solutions faster than it can create problems.

THE AMBIGUITIES OF SUSTAINABILITY

A sustainable society, as commonly understood, would not undermine the resource base and biotic stocks on which future prosperity depends. To be sustainable means to live on income, not capital. The word "sustainable," however, conceals as much as it reveals. Hidden beneath its simplicity are assumptions about growth, technology, democracy, public participation, and human values. In 1987 the Brundtland Commission adopted sustainable development as the pivotal concept in its report, *Our Common Future*. As defined by the Brundtland Commission, development is sustainable if it "meets the needs of the present without compromising the ability of future generations to meet their own needs."[23]

This definition of sustainability, however, raises as many questions as it answers. It presumes that we know, or can discover, levels and thresholds of environmental carrying capacity — that is, how to determine what is sustainable and what is not. But a society could be sustainable with a number of different configurations of technology, people, and resources. The phrase also deflects consideration of the sustainability of political and economic institutions, which are often quite fragile. In effect, the commission hedged its bets between two versions of sustainable futures — *technological* sustainability and *ecological* sustainability. In the most general terms, the difference is whether perpetual technological innovations and proper pricing will be sufficient to remove limits to economic growth and with them any need for moral improvement or discipline, or whether instead we must learn to live within certain limits and reshape our economies, governments, and societies accordingly.

Advocates of technological sustainability believe that every problem has either a technological answer or a market solution. Resource scarcity, they claim, will be solved by materials substitution or genetic engineering. Energy shortages will be met by more efficiency improvements and, for some, by nuclear fusion. The World Commission on Environment and Development calls for a "new era of growth," by which is meant "more rapid economic growth in both industrial and developing countries, freer market access for the products of developing countries, lower interest rates, greater technology transfer, and significantly larger capital flows."[24] The commission plainly regards growth as the engine for sustainable development everywhere. Still, nagging questions remain.

First, since growth and environmental deterioration have occurred in tandem, how can the destruction of the ecological balance of the earth be stemmed with further growth? It is not easy to envision sustainable growth in the principal sectors of an industrial economy—energy, chemicals, automobiles, and extractive industries. Moreover, newer parts of the economy such as genetic engineering may spawn entirely new threats to the habitability of the planet. Growth will certainly lead to vast new concentrations of wealth, which will pose new challenges to democracy and development. Growth in the industrial world not only has failed to contribute to Third World development but also has widened the gap between the world's rich and poor. Why would future growth in the developed world lead to different results?

Second, advocates of technological sustainability are not clear on what it is that is being sustained: Are we seeking to maintain current growth with greater efficiency? The Brundtland Commission compounded the confusion by defining sustainable development in terms of economic growth. Sustainable growth, in Herman Daly's words, "implies an eventual impossibility" of unlimited growth in a finite system. Development implying qualitative change, however, and not just quantitative enlargement, might be sustainable. The distinction is fundamental and often overlooked. Since quantitative growth cannot be sustained in a universe governed by the laws of thermodynamics, we must confront issues of size and sufficiency. "We need something like a Plimsoll line," Daly writes, "to keep the economic scale within ecological carrying capacity."[25] But carrying capacity, defined as the total population times the resource-use level that a given ecosystem can maintain, cannot be determined with precision.[26]

A related ambiguity concerns the relationship between developed and less developed economies. For example, growth in the developed economies depends on a steady flow of energy, minerals, and agricultural goods from the less developed world. For theorists of sustainability these dependencies raise practical and ethical questions: Must any country's population and resource-use pattern stay within the limits of its own national carrying capacity? What level of imports, of which commodities, constitutes unsustainable development? The Japanese, for example, have preserved their forests at the expense of those in Alaska, Brazil, and Southeast Asia. In Daly's words: "A single country may substitute man-made for natural capital to a very high degree if it can import the products of natural capital from other countries which have retained their natural capital to a greater degree."[27] Either some nations must agree to remain undeveloped while others develop, or the structural disparity between developed economies and less developed economies must be reduced.

Advocates of technological sustainability often assume that unsustainable practices can be changed by "finding and using the (right) policy levers,"[28] adjusting prices to reflect true scarcity and real costs, and developing greater efficiency in the use of energy and resources. The policymakers, scientists, corporations, and international agencies that support technological sustainability, however, rarely mention citizen groups or grass-roots efforts around the world. They portray technological sustainability largely as a painless, rational process managed by experts who are pulling levers and pushing buttons while sitting coolly in the control room of a postmodern, computerized society. There is little evidence that its proponents understand democratic processes or comprehend the relevance or power of an active, engaged, and sometimes enraged citizenry.

A different approach to sustainability holds that we won't get off so easily. Wendell Berry, for example, writes: "We must achieve the character and acquire the skills to live much poorer than we do. We must waste less, we must do more for ourselves and each other."[29] This, however, has less to do with pulling "policy levers" than it does with making moral improvements in society. Ivan Illich regards "development" as a fundamental mistake:

> The concept implies the replacement of widespread unquestioned competence at subsistence activities by the use and consumption of commodities; the monopoly of wage labor over all other kinds of work; redefinition of needs in terms of goods and services mass-produced according to expert design; finally the rearrangement of the environment in such fashion that space, time, materials, and design favor production and consumption while they degrade or paralyze use-value oriented activities that satisfy needs directly.[30]

According to Wolfgang Sachs, advocates of technological sustainability "transform ecological politics from a call for new public virtues into a set of managerial strategies."[31] Without challenging the economic framework, they argue that one cannot question the "notion that the world's cultures converge in a steady march toward more material production."

Another group of advocates, known as eco-developers, propose a multifaceted agenda for ecological sustainability. Their position assumes that we live in a world of limits and that humans are limited, fallible creatures. Wendell Berry, for example, argues:

> We only do what humans can do, and our machines, however they may appear to enlarge our possibilities, are invariably infected with our limitations. . . . The mechanical means by which we propose to escape the human condition only extends it.[32]

Advocates of ecological sustainability stress two different kinds of limits: those on our ability to coordinate and comprehend things beyond some scale, and those inherent in our nature as moral creatures. Even if the first could be overcome by some nightmare of artificial intelligence, the second would infect the results. In other words, we cannot escape our "creaturehood."

Another component of ecological sustainability has to do with the political role of the citizen. Biologist Garrett Hardin argues that except for climate change or acid rain there are few genuinely global problems. Most "global problems" are, in fact, aggregations of national or local problems, for which the only effective solutions reside in the character and intelligence of people at the national or local level. Ecological sustainability, then, could restore civic virtue and develop ecological literacy and competence throughout the population.

Ecological sustainability is rooted as much in past practices, folkways, and traditions as it is in the creation of new knowledge. Michael Redclift, for example, writes that "if we want to know how ecological practices can be designed which are more compatible with social systems, we need to embrace the epistemologies of indigenous people, including their ways of organizing their knowledge of their environment."[33] One of the conceits of modern science is the belief that it can be applied everywhere in the same manner. Traditional knowledge, in contrast, as economist Richard Norgaard puts it, "is location specific and only arrived at through a unique co-evolution between specific social and ecological systems."[34] Traditional knowledge does not fit easily with what we call modern science. It is rooted in and functions as part of a local culture. It is a source of community cohesion and a framework that explains the origins of things (cosmology). It also provides the basis for preserving fertility, controlling pests, and conserving biological diversity and genetic variability. Knowledge is not separated from the complex task of living well in a specific place over a long period of time. The crisis of sustainability has occurred only when this union of knowledge, livelihood, and living has been broken and when knowledge is used for the single purpose of increasing productivity. It may be, as Redclift says, that a "more urgent question is whether 'we' [the "developed" nations] are prepared for the cultural adaptation that is required of us." The loss of traditional knowledge, Norgaard believes, is directly related to increased species extinction and the rise of a unified system of knowledge and economics controlling agriculture worldwide:

> [T]he patchwork quilt of traditional agro-economies consisted of social and ecological patches loosely linked together. The connections between beliefs, social organization, technology, and the ecological system were many and strong within each patch, for these things coevolved together. Between patches, however, linkages were few, weak, and frequently only random. The global agro-economy, on the other hand, is tightly connected through common technologies, and international crop, fertilizer and pesticide, and capital markets.[35]

In the present system, any failure of knowledge, technology, research, capital markets, or weather can prove highly destabilizing or fatal. Disruptions of any sort ripple throughout the system. Not so for traditional agroeconomic systems. A failure of one patch did not threaten others. Finally, Norgaard points out that the "global exchange economy" treats all parts of the world the same regardless of varying ecological conditions. Since "the diversity of the ecological system is intimately linked to the diversity of economic decisions people make," there is a steady reduction of biological diversity. Biological diversity is a factor in social risks, because "agroeconomic systems with many components have more options for tinkering and stumbling upon a stable combination or for learning and systematically selecting combinations with stabilizing negative feedbacks."[36]

Advocates of ecological sustainability regard nature not just as a set of limits but as a model for the design of housing, cities, neighborhoods, farms, technologies, and regional economies. Sustainability depends upon replicating the structures and functions of natural systems. Ecology, for example, is the basis for the work of John and Nancy Todd on the design of bioshelters (which recycle waste, heat and cool themselves, and grow a significant portion of the occupants' food needs) and solar aquatic systems (which purify waste water).

Amory and Hunter Lovins similarly draw on ecology to design resilient technological systems. Resilience implies the capacity to withstand external disturbances and internal malfunctions. Resilient systems absorb shocks more gracefully and are more forgiving of human error, malfeasance, or acts of God. Resilience does not imply a static condition, but rather a flexibility that permits a system "to survive unexpected stress; not that it achieve the greatest possible efficiency all the time, but that it achieve the deeper efficiency of avoiding failures so catastrophic that afterwards there is no function left to be efficient."[37] Like the process of evolution, designers of resilient systems tend to follow the old precepts such as: KISS (Keep It Simple, Stupid); if it ain't broke, don't fix it; don't put all your eggs in one basket; and if anything can go wrong, it will, so plan accordingly. Resilience implies small, locally adaptable, resource-conserving, culturally suitable, and technologically elegant solutions, which if they fail, will not jeopardize much else. Wes and Dana Jackson use the prairie as a model for farms that do not rely on tillage and chemical fertilizers. Ecologically and aesthetically, these farms would resemble the original prairie that once dominated the great plains. For the Jacksons, "the patterns and processes discernible in natural ecosystems still remain the most appropriate standard available to sustainable agriculture. . . . What is needed are countless elegant solutions keyed to particular places."[38]

The use of nature as a model and standard for farms, housing, cities, technologies, and economies rests on two propositions. First, the biosphere is a catalogue recorded over millions of years of what works and what doesn't, including life forms and biological processes. Second, ecosystems are the only systems capable of stability in a world governed by the laws of thermodynamics. The principle characteristics of ecosystems — energy efficiency, closed loops, redundancy, and decentralization — allow them to swim upstream against the force of entropy. Industrial systems, on the contrary, assume perpetual growth and progress, which can only increase entropy and decrease stability.

Among the most important questions raised by using nature as a model for human systems are those of scale and centralization. If ecology is our model, should society be more decentralized? Surface-to-volume ratios limit the size of biological organisms and physical structures. Are there similar principles of optimum size for cities, nations, corporations, and technologies? Leopold Kohr, E.F. Schumacher, and many others have supported decentralization and appropriate scale on two grounds. The first has to do with limits on the ability of human beings to understand and manage complex systems. Increasing scale increases the number of things that must be attended to and the number of interactions that can go wrong. Rising scale also increases the costs of carelessness. Preoccupation with quantity replaces the concern for quality: farms become agribusinesses; cities become megalopolitan regions; small shops become corporations; tools become complicated technologies; legitimate concerns for livelihood become obsessions with growth; and weapons become instruments of total destruction.

The second reason for decentralization is that centralization undermines the potential for ethical action and increases the potential for mischief. As scale increases, it becomes easier to separate costs and benefits, creating winners and losers who are mostly strangers to each other. The likelihood of ethical behavior decreases as the distance in time and space between beneficiaries and losers grows.

Scale also can make power unaccountable. Who is responsible for acid rain?

Carbon-dioxide-induced climate change? Species extinction? Chernobyl? In each case the costs are widely distributed in the form of environmental damage and health effects, but so is the blame. Responsibility is diffused among political leaders, utilities, corporations, government agencies, and the consuming public. At a gargantuan scale everyone is responsible — and no one can be held accountable.

As with all metaphors, we must ask where ecological sustainability applies and where it does not. Two categories are particularly problematic. Cities will always be something of an exception to the model of natural systems. Even under the best conditions, many large urban areas will import substantial amounts of food, energy, water, and materials, and they will export roughly equivalent amounts of sewage, garbage, pollution, and heat. Many municipal problems could be mitigated by better use of mass transit, solar energy, urban agriculture, reforestation, conservation laws (like bottle bills), and organic waste treatment. While significantly reducing environmental damage, these measures still will not produce "sustainable cities" such that the net environmental impact of urban concentrations is within the absorptive and healing capacities of the surrounding natural systems. The sheer concentration of large numbers of people will reduce environmental resilience, encroach on wildlife habitat, and impose significant resource costs elsewhere. Urban concentrations ultimately must be justified on the basis of their contributions to intellectual, economic, and cultural life, not their sustainability.

Another and increasingly problematic area is that of technology. The cumulative effects of technology extend human power over nature so that we can transcend the limits of gravity, space, time, biology, and mind. In the process we remove ourselves farther and farther from the natural conditions, both good and bad, that previously constrained human development. The goal of a sustainable society based on the model of natural systems is not antithetical to technology, but questions exist about what kinds of technology, at what scale, and for what purposes.

Technological sustainability and ecological sustainability represent fundamentally different approaches to the crisis. Yet they are complementary. The vital signs of a heart-attack victim must first be stabilized, and only then can follow the longer-term process of changing the problems of diet and lifestyle that really caused the trauma. Advocates of technological sustainability are correct to propose policy changes, particularly in the pricing of resources. And some technologies can improve the efficiency with which we use resources. Both can buy time. But time for what? This is a harder question about the fundamental direction of society, about the root causes of our problems, and about human potentials.

FRAGMENTS OF A STRATEGY

In thinking about strategies to reach a sustainable world we have three broad choices: relying on markets and economic self-interest; attempting to change values through education; and using public policy, government power, and regulation. Each of these offers important insights about how our society can ensure its survival.

Market Strategies

Adam Smith once described a strategy of change in these words:

> As every individual, therefore, endeavors as much as he can both to employ his capital in the support of domestic industry and so to direct that industry that its produce may be of the greatest value ... he intends only his own gain, and he is in this, as in many other cases, led by an invisible hand to promote an end which was no part of his intention. ... By pursuing his own interest he frequently promotes that of the society more effectually than when he really intends to promote it.[39]

As individuals pursue private interests they create wealth, part of which circulates in the larger society and becomes available for others. The advantages of these kinds of economic strategies are clear. They require no leap of consciousness, no Aquarian conspiracies, and no quick "paradigm shifts." They make no heroic assumptions about our moral possibilities. Does the same logic hold if sustainability, not economic expansion or private accumulation, is the goal? To what extent can rational economic self-interest be harnessed to control its earlier excesses?

Amory and Hunter Lovins maintain that there is a convergence between economically rational "least-cost" energy choices and longer term collective benefits. By purchasing the most efficient energy-consuming and energy-generating technologies, consumers and utilities can lower costs while conserving resources. It is cheaper and less risky to weatherize houses than it is to fight wars and to maintain a military presence in the Persian Gulf. Their research suggests that the same may hold true for other resources as well, such as water, food, and strategic minerals.

As a strategy of change, the least-cost approach promises five major benefits. First, it is aimed to take us as far down the road to greater energy and resource efficiency as possible. By all evidence this will be a long way. Second, by steadily wringing inefficiency out of the economy, the strategy buys us time that could be put to good use in rethinking long-term goals. Third, it harnesses the powerful engine of economic self-interest for the cause of lowering energy and resource use per dollar of GNP, and thereby it reduces environmental impacts. Fourth, by identifying win/win options, the strategy avoids unnecessary conflicts. Finally, the strategy avoids preaching altruism, which appeals only to a limited audience.

Since there can be no good case for waste, least-cost approaches to greater efficiency are, to a point, beyond reproach. But the driving force of rational self-interest also has built-in limitations. We have no choice but to be self-interested. Nevertheless, how people define their self-interest, or what economists call utility, is unclear. Utility is whatever people define as valuable. Even if we assume that people consistently seek out least-cost options, as theories of rational economic behavior predict, by definition they will not act if costs are high or rates of marginal return are low. The potential for good is limited to those cases where least-cost choices and ethics converge. But they may not converge as often as one might hope, and in some cases self-interested people might keep them from converging. Self-interested people will know that least cost is not the same as true cost. Food prices, for example, do not include the loss of topsoil, groundwater contamination, stream destruction, health costs to farmers and farm workers, or government subsidies for public water or transportation. Nor do we pay a depletion tax on nonrenewable resources or disposal costs for our trash and toxic wastes. If we did so, the true costs of many goods would be considerably higher. But our willingness to pay full costs, especially for no immediate gain, has very little to do with rational behavior as economists use the term, and has everything to do with ethical behavior that comes from a sense of responsibility and obligation. All of this underscores the persistent conflict between rationality applied to means (economics) and rationality applied to ends (ethics).

None of this is intended as an argument against economic rationality in the realm to which it legitimately applies. I would argue, however, that thoroughly rational economic behavior, which implies the willingness to analyze means *and* ends, ironically depends on an ethical perspective and a larger vision that transcends self-interest. Strategies that are based on the priority of economics over ethics will sooner or later founder on the shoals of human recalcitrance or technological malfeasance. When we have exhausted all those instances where ethics and economics converge and face more costly choices, it will matter a great deal whether or not we remember how to distinguish right from wrong and act accordingly.

Education as Strategy

Americans overwhelmingly agree that U.S. public education is a disaster, and many believe that higher education is not much better. It is probably true that we produce young adults who cannot read, write, or think. But there is a more serious shortcoming — our rising rates of ecological illiteracy and incompetence with respect to natural systems. Most critics of education worry that poorly educated students will be unable to compete successfully with the Japanese. I worry about a new generation who will not know, or care to know, that they are only a "cog in an ecological mechanism," as Aldo Leopold put it, whose well-being is ultimately dependent on their stewardship of nature. Most students now leave twelve or sixteen years of formal education without any such comprehension, let alone the competence to act on it. And why should it be otherwise? Few public schools or institutions of higher education have asked what planetary "finiteness" has to do with the way they define and transmit knowledge. This may be because good answers to these questions would upset comfortable educational priorities and research agendas.

Education in the fullest sense of the word will aim higher and will seek to produce persons with good character, broad knowledge, and commitment. A fully educated person, in J. Glenn Gray's words, is one who has "grasped the simple fact that his [or her] self is fully implicated in those beings around him, human and non-human, and who has learned to care deeply about them."[40] If we are to understand our implicatedness, as Gray argues, we must recognize that *all education is environmental education.* By what is included or excluded, emphasized or ignored, we teach that we are either a part of the larger fabric of life, or apart from it. We inculcate either attitudes of care and competence toward natural systems, or attitudes of carelessness and dependence. Above all, we teach that the experience of the natural world is an important element of good thinking in a world governed by the laws of ecology and thermodynamics, or we perpetuate the illusion that we alone stand above the laws of nature.

Comprehending the challenges of sustainability and peace cannot be done from the vantage point of any one academic discipline. It requires the broader perspectives of the liberal arts, including biology, physics, history, philosophy, religion, sociology, economics, and politics. Analysis of the vital signs of ecosystems or of world peace will require knowledge of mathematics, statistics, and computers. But art, poetry, literature, and music are elementary to the sense of humane celebration that will undergird a more life-centered culture. These disciplines need to be integrated in a way that overcomes disciplinary narrowness.[41] Whether through interdisciplinary courses or an integrated core curriculum, the goal should be the same — the development of young minds capable of thinking across artificial academic boundaries.

Beyond the linking of disciplines, a deeper connection must be made between practical experience and intellectual development. Gray argues for the inclusion of manual skills as a part of liberal education: "For unless the educated man learns to use his hands, unless he acquires the feel of an instrument exquisitely fitted for its function, he runs a danger of missing a whole area of his relation to the world." Liberal education, Gray writes, "can be pursued in the kitchen, the workshop, on the ranch or farm, in the casual acquaintanceships of every day as from the rarer friendships where we learn wholeness in response to others."[42] Alfred North Whitehead argued more explicitly that the relationship between good thinking and direct experience is "intimate and reciprocal." The lack of "productive activities," in his view, explains the "mediocrity" of the academy. What passes for higher learning has become more and more abstract, separating us from the natural and human environments. The danger is that we confuse abstractions with reality, committing what Whitehead called the "fallacy of misplaced concreteness."[43] Having done so we can only act simple-mindedly within complex systems with predictably disruptive results. Liberal education that includes carefully crafted experience is an antidote to the perils of specialization and excessive abstraction, and provides an essential foundation for a democratic citizenry.

Most colleges and universities, however, are designed to prevent ordinary experience from intruding into the educational process. As John Dewey once put it, "The school has been so set apart, so isolated from the ordinary conditions and motives of life that [it] is the one place in the world where it is most difficult to get experience — the mother of all discipline worth the name."[44] Dewey proposed developing the school and the local community as laboratories for education. To the extent that this can be done, a curriculum ceases to be abstract and distant. With few exceptions these proposals have been ignored. But from the perspective of sustainability, one can see that these ideas not only have educational merit but also offer a way for educational institutions to become leverage points for change.

One common criticism of using education as part of a political strategy is that the payoff is so far in the future. This year's graduate will not be in a position of responsibility to effect change for one or two decades, if then. This criticism, however, ignores the role of students in recent history, from the Vietnam protest movement to Tiananmen Square. The young have always been a potent source of change. The environmental movement and the peace movement have been largely built by persons in their twenties, who did not know that they lacked influence. They simply rolled up their sleeves and went to work.

If, as H.G. Wells once said, "we are in a race between education and catastrophe," then catastrophe is all but certain. Education has not yet come to the starting gate. The word *excellence* which administrators sprinkle through their university catalogues has become a buzzword denoting more of the same — high-tech research, computers in every nook and cranny, bioengineering, and big science. If we take human survival seriously, however, true excellence would lead to a more life-centered curriculum.

Politics and Change

The prospects for sustainability ultimately rest on political decisions about who eats and who goes hungry, who owns and who rents, who flies and who takes the bus. The politics of sustainability have to do with the siting of strip mines, power plants, and dumps — things no one wants. The politics of sustainability are about issues of fairness, risk, human rights, animal rights, and ecological rights. They are about how much we take from our descendants and what we leave behind. We need to create a politics of the earth to protect the biosphere, and we need to reinvent politics at the ecosystem level. Without pressure from an engaged citizenry, governments are too willing to settle for symbolic action that appears to solve problems while never doing so. And without competent citizens rooted in a place and willing to fight for it, "environmental protection" will come to mean trade-offs determined by experts and unaccountable elites. There is no reason to believe that any such nation, or world, would be either sustainable or democratic.

Paradoxically, Americans take environmental issues more seriously in 1990 than they did in 1970 or 1980, but they have not yet translated this interest into national political campaigns. Why? One answer is that these issues are complex and long term, while politics is about short-term issues like jobs and crime. Politicians who talk about complex issues and difficult choices do not win elections, or so we are told. Issues of environment and sustainability entail a radical critique of industrial societies, but Americans are conservative and pragmatic. In the words of Walter Truett Anderson:

> The whole style of American politics is nonecological. Ecology is a comprehension of systems, interdependencies, webs of relationship, connections extending over space and time—and the very essence of our politics is to zero in on single causes.[45]

In other words, the environment has not yet been incorporated into our political theories, political institutions, political language, and political symbols. To do so raises fundamental questions about power, economics, and citizen participation.

The first task of political reconstruction is to rediscover the proper role for various levels of government. National governments are too small to deal with pressing global issues of planetary warming, ozone depletion, rain-forest protection, and biological diversity. For these we need global institutions. Yet national governments are often too large and cumbersome to handle most other problems effectively.

Beyond the issues of appropriate size and authority of government institutions, beliefs about the causes of our problems and their solutions differ. Robert

Heilbroner and E.F. Schumacher could both agree that the ecological crisis is real while reaching opposite conclusions about the appropriate degree of centralization. For Heilbroner, "the centralization of power [is] the only means by which our threatened and dangerous civilization can make way for its successor."[46] William Ophuls cautions that "ecological scarcity" will create "overwhelming pressures toward political systems that are frankly authoritarian."[47] Garrett Hardin finds no solution other than "mutual coercion mutually agreed upon." Each assumes that the crisis can be managed only by the total centralization of government power. This is not a conclusion disagreeable to men of opposite bent like nuclear physicist Alvin Weinberg, who once proposed a "Faustian bargain" between scientists and society to "solve" the energy crisis.

Beneath such proposals are unstated beliefs about the causes of the crisis and about the capabilities of large institutions. From very different perspectives, Heilbroner, Weinberg, and others believe that an authoritarian state can manage nature and uphold its end of the Faustian bargain, while coping in perpetuity with its own increased size and complexity. This position, however, is not well supported by what we know about governments and large organizations.

Decentralists have a different response. They begin with the belief that the centralization of power is a cause of the earth's ecological crisis, not its cure. Once power is centralized, it is difficult to hold it accountable. Hence the transfer of power, authority, resources, talent, and capital from the countryside, neighborhoods, and communities to cities, corporations, and national governments have undermined responsibility, care, thrift, and social cohesion — qualities essential to sustainability. In contrast to Heilbroner and others, decentralists assume that people, given the chance, are capable of disciplined self-government. Democracy in this view has not failed; it has not been tried.

The reinvention of politics at the ecosystem level first requires clarity about what should be done locally and what should be done at higher levels, and why. In the transition to sustainability, the federal government must correct market distortions that undervalue biotic resources, ensure equity, establish environmental standards, disseminate information, and establish global environmental institutions. But many other essential aspects of society ought to be decentralized to increase social resilience, minimize environmental impacts, and achieve true economies of scale. Among these we can list agriculture, energy systems, property ownership, wealth, some aspects of governance, and certain technologies. Practically, this means ending subsidies and preferred tax treatment for agribusiness, large corporate enterprises, energy companies, utilities, and land speculators. On the other side, local communities, small towns, and neighborhoods that have suffered from decades of neglect must be rebuilt.

The reinvention of politics at the ecosystem level also requires the revitalization of regional economies that serve the interests of communities. This may require a community to disengage selectively from the global economy and to integrate carefully its own economy, culture, educational system, and institutions of governance with the ecology of the region. Another name for this process is bioregionalism. But bioregionalism is also a political strategy. In Kirkpatrick Sale's words:

> [Bioregionalism] asks nothing of the Federal government, and needs no national legislation, no government regulation, no Presidential dispensation . . . only Federal obliviousness to permit it. . . . [N]or does bioregionalism envision a takeover of the national government or a vast rearrangement of the national machinery . . . the task after all is to build power at the bottom not to take it from the top.[48]

This strategy has its roots in the nineteenth-century anarchism of Peter Kropotkin, and more recently in the thinking of Lewis Mumford, who concluded his magnum opus with the proposal that we withdraw from organized power to "quietly paralyze it."

In recent years there has been a proliferation of ideas in alternative economics, including the writings of Herman Daly and Hazel Henderson, the papers delivered at the Alternative Economic Summit, the works brought together by Paul Ekins, and the articles published in the *Human Economy Newsletter*. We are not without good ideas and workable bioregional alternatives to the economics of unlimited growth. In different ways, these authors propose to reward good work, provide basic needs for everyone, conserve biotic resources, expand barter and gift relationships, retain wealth in the community, subordinate economic to social relationships, and strengthen local cultures.

The emergence of bioregionalism also will require the development of different forms of technology. These have been characterized over the years by terms such as "convivial," "alternative," "appropriate," and "soft." They are generally small in scale, based on renewable energy, relatively inexpensive, widely dispersed, locally owned and controlled, and environmentally benign. The discussion of alternative technology, pro and con, has tended to focus too much on tools and too little on bioregionally appropriate designs and procedures that reduce the need for expensive and destructive technologies. Pliny Fiske in Austin, Texas, has developed a catalogue of cost-competitive materials available in each bioregion such as caliche and mesquite.[49] Similar inventories need to be done elsewhere to discourage the import of expensive, environmentally damaging materials. Similarly, the work of Chris Maser, Alan Savory, and Wes Jackson points to methods of forestry, land management, and agriculture adapted to specific bioregions and microregions that minimize the need for technology.[50] And Gary Nabhan's studies of the Papago

Indians of the Southwest reveal elegant possibilities for weaving local culture and ecologies together in the sparest environment.[51]

The transition to a sustainable world also will require the revitalization of the practice of citizenship. Benjamin Barber's proposals for creating "strong democracy"[52] are relevant here — they are roughly equivalent to rebuilding the crumbling foundation before trying to remodel the house. Despite our rhetoric about democracy, real democratic participation is declining. Whether from apathy or disgust, half of the eligible population in the United States does not vote. Opportunities for participation have declined with the rise of the mega-corporation and public bureaucracies. People are losing control over the basic conditions of their lives. What Tocqueville regarded as the seedbed of democracy, the civic association, the small town, the neighborhood, is in disarray. In John Dewey's words, "democracy must begin at home, and home is the neighborly community."[53] Restoration of the civic tradition depends on our ability to "rise above the language of individualism" to sustain a political conversation on the important issues of our time. The language of individualism, which is mainly about consumption and private interests, must give way to a renewed civic discourse on the responsible use of shared power.

Politics is the process by which we define the terms of our collective existence. Democratic politics is grounded in the faith that everyone is entitled to a voice, and that no one, whether by circumstances of wealth or of birth, is entitled to more. Representative democracy is an uneasy compromise between democracy and demography, with a touch of fear about mob rule. Strong democracy is premised on the belief that people can and do act responsibly given the opportunity, and that those opportunities can be nurtured in a mass society. Barber proposes twelve steps toward this end, including a national system of neighborhood assemblies, a civic communications cooperative, a national initiative and referendum process, electronic balloting, a lottery for local offices, universal citizens service, workplace democracy, and a new architecture of civic space.[54] He argues that strong democracy is the "only legitimate form of politics [and] constitutes the condition for the survival of all that is most dear to us."[55] To this I would add that strong democracy or some comparable program of civic renewal is a prerequisite for sustainability and real security as well.

Significant mischief in human affairs most often begins behind closed doors, and concentrated power enables a few to close doors to everyone else. The usual arguments for oligarchy of any kind rest on the premise that the public is incompetent to decide matters of public concern. Behind Oliver North's efforts to "create democracy" in Nicaragua was the belief that democracy does not work here and therefore must be subverted by whatever means necessary. The case for technocracy is similar. Issues, we are told, are so complex that only experts can make intelligent choices. In the full light of day, such arguments can be seen for what they are: self-serving chicanery by people who have little or no sense of the public interest, little understanding of the democratic process, and a great deal to gain by remaining aloof from both.

The steady erosion of democratic participation also affects the prospects for sustainability and, I think, for peace. Centralization of power has removed many resource decisions from the public arena. Disposition of large tracts of land and resources, including the use of common properties like air and water, are made as if they were private decisions with wholly private consequences. The concentration of power has led to the development of the technology necessary for large-scale resource manipulation and extraction—machinery that can level mountains, divert rivers, split atoms, and alter genes.

The crisis of sustainability has resulted largely from centralized power being exercised without effective public regulation, citizen complaints, or private morality. These constraints were eroded as the independent shopkeeper, the family farmer, and the small businessman became employees in enterprises over which they had no control. If dependence begets venality, as Jefferson once said, it also leads to demoralization and passivity in the face of wrongs. But frequently these wrongs occur incrementally in quiet crises and in remote areas where few can see what is happening. In either case the institutions, attitudes, and independence necessary to resist are weakened at the source. Orwellian nightmares are no longer idle fantasies in a world of genetic engineering, computers, fusion reactors, and star-wars technologies. Can anyone believe that sustainability will be taken seriously by persons so single-mindedly captivated by Faustian ideas of progress?

Civic renewal begins with the dispersion of power and the extension of the range of civic responsibilities decided by those affected. Participation is a way to acknowledge those effects and to elevate public discourse. In Jefferson's words, there is "no safe depository of the ultimate powers of the society but the people themselves; and if we think them not enlightened enough to exercise their control with a wholesome discretion, the remedy is not to take it from them, but to inform their discretion."[56] Informed public involvement is also a way to develop more prudent policy choices. Where an active citizenry is involved, we may expect greater equity in the distribution of costs and benefits. We might also expect their vigilance to counter elite interests. As Tocqueville, Dewey, and others have noted, civic education can only occur though participation in the neighborhood, community, and workplace. Civic education for the sustainable management of food, energy, water, materials, and waste can only occur if people have a part in these decisions and understand their consequences.

Strong democracy and civic renewal are necessary conditions for sustainability, but there is still a need for transformative leadership at all levels. The rebirth of environmental awareness across the planet has occurred without significant political leadership. Great figures capable of defining, clarifying, and motivating people toward a sustainable future have yet to appear at the national level. But they are beginning to appear at state, local, and neighborhood levels. Transformative leadership must first articulate what people feel in their bones and then translate this into a coherent agenda of reform.

PRINCIPLES FOR REAL SECURITY

The primary threats to human well-being increasingly come directly or indirectly from ecological malfeasance: overpopulation, pollution, energy inefficiency, species extinction, and industrial accidents. The best steps any nation can take to ensure its security are those leading toward the protection of biological diversity and the sustainable management of resources. The measures of sustainability may be more difficult to calculate than those of military power or economic growth, but they are the best indicators of national viability in the twenty-first century. Sustainable resource management and sound environmental policies promote security by reducing vulnerability to sudden change, lowering dependence on critical materials, increasing competitiveness, promoting social and political stability, safeguarding public health, and reducing risks of technological accidents. A society in the throes of overshoot, having exhausted its natural endowment, will be vulnerable to internal disruption and external intervention. Its leaders will be tempted to spend biological capital and incur risks that they otherwise would prefer to avoid. At some point such a society will simply cease to be a civilized and responsible member of the world community. Three principles can serve as guidelines against such outcomes — ecological responsibility, justice, and decentralized democracy.

Ecological Responsibility

In the course of recent history, equal rights have gradually been given to minorities, women, and children. These rights now should be extended to future generations, to other life forms, to natural systems, and to the earth itself. Doing so would acknowledge that our well-being is bound to that of an entire community of life and that a society lacking the wisdom to protect the interests of its children or those of its natural systems cannot in the end protect any of its own interests. This recognition of ecological interdependence should affect every transaction between humans and the natural world.

Being responsible ecologically also carries with it the possibility of learning from nature. Ecosystems provide the best model we have of systems capable of withstanding stress. They are decentralized; they have back-up systems, redundancy, and multiple pathways; and parts can fail without jeopardizing the whole. Resilient societies should mimic these attributes by having a dispersed structure with linkages that are numerous, short, loosely coupled, and simply designed.

Justice

Justice is a prerequisite for sustainability, particularly redistribution of wealth. In 1800 the ratio of per-capita income between the richest and poorest nations was three to one. At present this ratio is roughly 25 to one. Even in the United States the gap is widening. In 1975 the wealthiest one percent controlled 17 percent of the nation's wealth, but by 1985 the figure had grown to 35 percent. In the years between 1979 and 1987 the average income of the poorest fifth of the population declined by 6.1 percent while that of the top fifth rose by 11.1 percent.[57] Extreme income inequality diminishes the prospects for sustainability not only by weakening democracy but also by undermining civic competence, social morale, and local economies, each of which is integral to social stability and social longevity. The challenge of building secure and sustainable societies will require limits on inequity within and among societies.

Sustainable development must begin in the developed world. No amount of exhortation will convince Third World leaders to change until economic priorities in the First World reflect a similar commitment. Economic development is driven as much by comparison as by logic. Until sustainable development is no longer thought of as second-class development, it will not be widely accepted. But there are other reasons for First World action as well. The developed world is the major source of toxins, carbon dioxide, CFCs, acid rain, and radioactive waste. It is also the main source of economic pressure on Third World ecosystems. It extracts timber from rainforests, minerals from Africa, soybeans from Brazil, livestock from Central America. "The impacts of rich countries are so great," in the words of Paul and Anne Ehrlich, "that these nations should be called not developed, but overdeveloped."[58] Until this pressure is reduced, the devastation of the biosphere will continue.

Democracy and Decentralization

In the long sweep of history, democracy appears to be an artifact of abundance. Its emergence in Europe coincided with the growth of national economies and the discovery of a New World with vast new resources and land. Some believe that the long shadow of resource shortages may now force its contraction. Robert Heilbroner, for example, has written that "passage through the gauntlet ahead may be possible only under governments capable of rallying obedience far more effectively than would be possible in a democratic setting."[59] The problem, however, does not lie in the excesses of democracy but in its anemia. We suffer not from too much democracy but from too little. The environmental movement, for example, has been largely created by citizens opposing the abuse of power by various government agencies: the Corps of Engineers, Department of Interior, Bureau of Reclamation, Forest Service, Park Service, Department of Energy, Department of Defense, Department of Commerce, and even the Environmental Protection Agency. Without the freedoms of press, speech, and protest, and without the right to "vote the scoundrels out," the environment would have no effective protectors whatsoever. The same is true in Europe and now in the Soviet Union. An informed and active citizenry is always the best protector of nature.

GLOBAL POLICIES FOR REAL SECURITY

Six actions are called for immediately if we are to secure the sustainability of our nation and of our world. The first is to extend the Montreal Protocol on CFCs to a total worldwide ban on their manufacture and use.

A second policy challenge is posed by the trillion-dollar Third World debt, most of which cannot be repaid. Attempts to collect the debt will exact an increasingly serious environmental toll through the exhaustion of Third World timber, minerals, and food resources. Third World nations now pay $43 billion more in debt service than they receive in foreign assistance.[60] To meet their debt payments, many countries are now forced to trade future biological productivity and ecological stability, and nearly all find themselves unable to meet basic human needs. This is a set of choices that no government should have to face. Debt forgiveness will be far cheaper than the alternative political and ecological consequences.

Third, governments must address the threat of global warming. The Prime Minister of Norway has proposed the creation of a world atmosphere fund that would collect tax revenues from the use of fossil fuels and provide assistance with energy efficiency to poor countries. But carbon-dioxide emissions represent only half of the problem. The other half is caused by deforestation and the release of other heat-trapping gases such as methane, halons, and CFCs. In addition to a marked increase in energy efficiency worldwide, the manufacture of other greenhouse gases must be curtailed, and carbon must be trapped through reforestation and better agricultural methods. The Worldwatch Institute recommends the reforestation of 130 million hectares in the Third World and another 40 million in the industrial countries in order to reduce carbon-dioxide emissions by a quarter.[61]

A fourth global priority is to stabilize population growth as rapidly as possible. This means much greater funding for the United Nations Population Fund and for the International Planned Parenthood Federation. It also means a shift in the established policies of the Catholic Church that prohibit the use of birth control. And it means long-term plans to reduce the global population to a level that can be sustained in dignity. Population in the 1990s will increase by 90 million. In fact, the United Nations' population estimates were revised upward in the spring of 1989 to reflect new information about fertility rates, which have not dropped as rapidly as expected. In the meantime, soil-erosion rates worldwide are estimated to be 24 billion tons per year. The gap between these two curves, population demand and food supply, will grow in severity in coming decades at the same time as warming and ozone depletion reduce crop productivity.

A fifth priority is to preserve rain forests and biological diversity. At present rates we will have driven 15 to 20 percent of the life forms now living into extinction by the end of the century, a rate 10,000 times higher than "normal." We are in the midst of a biological holocaust, the vast extermination of irreplaceable life forms on the planet. The best way to preserve biological diversity is to preserve habitat, which also would slow rates of global warming and protect indigenous populations.

A final policy priority involves the creation of institutions that can protect the global commons: the atmosphere, the oceans, and critical habitats. The U.N. Trusteeship Council could become an environmental security council, assisted by a greatly expanded U.N. Environmental Program. With increased power, international institutions could restrict the power of national governments to make unilateral decisions that affect the global environment. The process of building international institutions to protect planetary commons will require the kind of vision and statesmanship that was necessary to meld thirteen independent states into a nation between 1776 and 1789.

U.S. POLICY CHANGES

Since the United States is the largest source of CFCs, carbon dioxide, solid waste, toxins, nitric oxides, and sulfur oxides, and has one of the least energy-efficient industrial economies, we are a large part of the problem. But our culpability also underscores how much we can do to facilitate a global transition to sustainability.

The keystone for this transition is an energy policy that maximizes efficiency through higher prices for fossil fuels. This would reduce emissions of carbon, sulfur, and nitrogen that cause global warming and acid rain; lower the nation's dependence on foreign oil suppliers; reduce the environmental costs of mining, transportation, and processing of fossil fuels; shrink the annual $400 billion bill we pay for energy; and raise the competitiveness of U.S. businesses, which now begin with a 5 percent cost disadvantage vis-a-vis Japanese companies because the latter are more energy efficient.

The potential for conservation is enormous. A 1986 Department of Energy study showed that existing technologies could reduce energy expenditures by half, saving $200 billion. We lose as much energy through our windows as flows through the Alaskan Pipeline. Refrigerators can be designed to use one-quarter the energy of current models. Efficient electric motors use forty percent less electricity then conventional ones. A compact flourescent light bulb is now available that uses thirteen watts to provide the same light as a sixty-watt incandescent bulb — and it can keep four-hundred pounds of carbon dioxide out of the atmosphere over its expected lifetime. Existing technology can reduce energy for commercial lighting by 75 percent. Present least-cost energy options applied worldwide in the transportation, residential, industrial, and commercial sectors between 1990 and 2010 could reduce carbon-dioxide emissions by three billion tons per year. No other policy can deliver so much or solve so many problems at once.

Can we afford energy efficiency? Data from a variety of sources indicate that the front-end costs of purchasing and installing most efficiency measures have remarkably short pay-back times. Their life-cycle costs are considerably lower than those of inefficient technologies. For example, one efficient light bulb will burn ten-thousand hours and use 160 kilowatt hours (kwh) of electricity. At New York City electric rates, 14 cents per kwh, the total cost for the bulb and its electricity comes to $39. Using incandescent lighting with lower costs, less efficiency, and lower life span to produce the same amount of light costs $94. Improvements in electrical efficiency average about two cents per kwh, while existing electric rates nationwide average 7.8 cents per kwh and the real costs of new electricity are considerably more. The same pattern holds for efficiency improvements across the range of fuels and uses. It is cheaper by far to improve efficiency than to increase supply.

The United States now uses more oil for transportation than we produce. New regulations will raise standards for efficiency to 27.5 miles per gallon (mpg), but experimental vehicles now get between 90 and 114 mpg. Simply raising the standard to 35 mpg would save 660,000 barrels of oil per day; over a thirty year period it would save as much as a 7.8-billion-barrel oil field. The policy measures that will move us toward fuel efficiency include both higher standards for auto efficiency and higher gasoline taxes. Before the Gulf War, U.S. consumers paid an average of 92 cents a gallon, while the Japanese paid $2.89, the French $2.95, and the West Germans $2.09. Higher gasoline prices would spur energy efficiency, improve our balance of payments, lower crop damage caused by ground-level ozone, and reduce air pollution, acid rain, and carbon-dioxide emissions.

If the government is to create a sustainable economy, it must correct market distortions to ensure that "prices tell the truth" about long-term scarcity and environmental costs. Markets frequently give misleading signals because subsidies and external costs are not counted, because oligopolies can fix prices, and because prices cannot always reflect future scarcity. Given more accurate prices, the market can be an efficient allocator of scarce resources. The government must ensure that prices in a sustainable economy reflect the real costs of consumption and production.

Full-cost pricing would leave the market substantially intact but also would include severance taxes on nonrenewable fuels to capture their environmental and social costs, as well as disposal taxes to meet real costs of cleanup. Such taxes must be high enough to encourage conservation and gradual enough to permit an orderly transition to renewable resources. Revenues from these taxes should be used to offset the costs of research on alternatives and to cushion the effects on low-income citizens. Consumers would make whatever decisions about energy use they wanted and could afford, but at least prices would reflect real costs. Sustainability requires a more accurate accounting that includes loss of natural and biotic capital and a system of price and tax incentives for their conservation and regeneration. It must reward good farming, good land husbandry, and good forestry; and it must penalize those who choose to waste precious resources.

Current forest policy provides one of the clearest examples of poor resource accounting. In Alaska's Tongass Forest, the U.S. Forest Service sells five-hundred year-old trees to the Japanese for pulpwood for "the price of a cheeseburger." [62] On the open market the same tree would command a price of $300. In some years the Forest Service has lost 98 cents for every dollar spent on timber sales in the region. Annual Forest Service subsidies run $40 million, but only a fraction of that amount returns to benefit local economies. This pattern is repeated throughout the 180 million acres of forest in the custody of the Forest Service, which now believes its business to harvest trees like corn.

The same pattern is evident elsewhere. According to Robert Repetto, the government has "typically sold off timber too cheaply" for "purposes that are intrinsically uneconomic." [63] Charles Peters of the Institute of Economic Botany has estimated that tropical rain forests are twice as valuable for providing fruits and latex as for supplying lumber. [64] The real value of forests, however, includes ecological and social values as well. Present methods of accounting do not include these values; rather they acknowledge only the short-term benefits of unsustainable practices.

The flow of materials in our society can be reduced by increasing product durability and giving priority to essential needs. In a 1977 study of the economies of developed countries, Dag Poleszynski estimated that 87 percent of energy consumed went into "less essential production." By this he meant the weapons, food-processing, packaging, cosmetics, and fashion industries. To these I would add political polling, advertising, and pet psychologists. Economists often defend the production of junk because it creates jobs and adds to the GNP, but a sustainable and humane economy will provide adequate work in the production of durable, useful, and high-quality products.

Finally, sustainability requires accountability. There is a long-standing pattern of the federal government providing subsidies for economic turkeys: for nuclear power instead of conservation and renewables; for virgin materials instead of recycled materials; for agribusiness instead of owner-operated family farms; for automobiles instead of trains, bicycles, and public transport. This pattern stems from the proximity of power and money to government officials. For the transition to sustainability, politicians must be held accountable. We must separate money from politics by publicly financing all federal and statewide elections and by outlawing all private contributions.

While we send young offenders to the penitentiary for vandalism, we do no such thing to the president of Exxon for having vandalized Prince William Sound and destroyed the livelihood of thousands of local people. The story is repeated hundreds of times daily. Heads of corporations guilty of environmental dereliction do not, as a rule, go to prison or even appear in court, while minor offenders are packed off in droves. This creates both disrespect for the law and great comfort to those who do not wish to be made accountable. Full accountability means that companies should have to pay the full costs of environmental restoration following damage of whatever sort.

Citizen action in the transition to sustainability will require right-to-know laws such as the Federal Community Right to Know Act, which requires manufacturers to detail chemical emissions. A similar bill, Proposition 65 in California, now requires companies to prove that their products are safe and to post warnings where such proof cannot be given. The Canadian government labels products that meet rigorous environmental standards. These measures enable an informed citizenry to use its buying power to reward and penalize companies on the basis of more complete information than is now available.

CONCLUSION

The recent conflict with Iraq illustrates the new security equation. First, traditional threats to security continue to exist in some parts of the world. Saddam Hussein is not likely to be the last to attempt conquest, although his humiliation may deter others for a time. Second, the factor which made Kuwait a tempting target for Hussein is oil and the dependence of industrial nations on it. Until that dependence is reduced through energy efficiency and renewable energy resources, the potential for trouble of one sort or another will grow. Third, even though Iraq was defeated, it was able to exact sizeable costs on its neighbors by releasing massive amounts of oil into the Persian Gulf and igniting oil wells that will burn an estimated ten-to-twenty percent of Kuwait's proven reserves. The effects on human health of those living downwind of these fires will be severe, and acid fallout hundreds of miles away will exact a long-term cost on forests and agricultural productivity. The combustion of an estimated 4.5 to five million barrels of oil per day may add a quarter of a billion tons of carbon dioxide per year to the atmosphere and speed the pace of global warming.[65]

When the euphoria over the war fades, as it will, a more sober analysis of the costs and benefits of the war will reveal several truths. This was a war over energy. If we are ever to halt global warming and insulate national security from sudden oil cutoffs, we must wean ourselves away from oil. But we are not yet in the mood to study the ironies of victory. While the Administration fought the war with dispatch, it has felt no comparable sense of urgency to fight for energy efficiency or the transition to a less destructive energy system. It will also soon become apparent that the ecological effects of the war are severe and long-term. While Hussein's troops were forced out of Kuwait quickly, the effects of his occupation will last for years, perhaps even decades. This is the yardstick which should be used to judge whether sanctions would have "worked." Patience and intelligent resolve — without violence — might have accomplished better results at a far lower cost.

What can be said for certain is that the war diverted our attention from problems which, in the broad scope of things, are far more important. I am referring to the growing burden of the national debt, crumbling infrastructure, decaying cities, poor schools, homelessness, poverty, crime, environmental deterioration, and climate change. The war, we are told, made us proud to be Americans again. This is false pride, purchased on the cheap without our having solved any of the major challenges before us. Sooner or later, we will have to address the use and misuse of the earth's air, water, soils, forests, minerals, and life forms. Until these realities become the keystone of national policies, real security will continue to elude us.

NOTES

1. Reports of environmental damage are still sketchy, but the evidence now suggests severe damage from: oil fires, oil released in the Gulf, and military operations that damaged desert flora. *See,* for example, Donatella Lorch, "Burning Wells Turn Kuwait into Land of Oily Blackness," *New York Times,* March 6, 1991, p. A1, and William Branigin, "Kuwait's Environmental, Economic Nightmare," *The Washington Post,* March 14, 1991, p. A1.

2. Ruth Leger Sivard, *World Military and Social Expenditures, 1987-1988* (Washington, DC: World Priorities, 1987), p. 15.

3. William C. Clark, "Managing Planet Earth," *Scientific American,* 261:3, September 1989, p. 50.

4. *Ibid.*

5. Richard Kerr, "Global Warming Continues in 1989," *Science,* 247:4942, February 2, 1990, p. 521.

6. Arjun Makhijani, *infra.*

7. Nathan Keyfitz, "The Growing Human Population," *Scientific American,* 261:3, September 1989, p. 119.

8. William C. Clark, *op. cit.,* p. 48.

9. John Steinhart and Carol Steinhart, "Energy Use in the U.S. Food System," *Science,* 184:4143, April 19, 1974, pp. 307-316. The ratio may now be slightly higher, perhaps 11:1.

10. Robert Repetto, "Population, Resources, Environment," *Population Bulletin,* July 1987, p. 22.

11. Lester Brown, "Re-examining the World Food Prospect," *State of the World: 1989* (New York: W.W. Norton, 1989), pp. 41-58; and Lester Brown and John Young, "Feeding the World in the Nineties," *State of the World: 1990* (New York: W.W. Norton, 1990), pp. 59-78.

12. John Gever *et al., Beyond Oil* (Cambridge: Ballinger, 1986), chapter 5.

13. For a summary of NCAR and other climate models, *see* Stephen Schneider, *Global Warming* (San Francisco: Sierra Club Books, 1989)

14. Jonathan Weiner, *The Next One Hundred Years* (New York: Bantam Books, 1990), pp. 158-9.

15. Jose Goldemberg *et al.*, *Energy for a Sustainable World* (Washington: World Resources Institute, 1987), p. 17.

16. Matthew L. Wald, "Oil Imports in January Toppled Output in U.S.," *New York Times*, February 16, 1989, p. D1.

17. Thomas C. Hayes, "U.S. Oil Discovery Off But Recovery Gains," *New York Times*, September 8, 1989, p. D2.

18. Charles Hall, Cutler Clevland, and Robert Kaufman, *Energy and Resource Quality* (New York: Wiley Interscience, 1986), p. 28.

19. Information from the office of the Honorable Claudine Schneider (R-Rhode Island), U.S. Congress, drawn from U.S. Department of Energy study done in 1986.

20. William Keepin and Gregory Kats, "Greenhouse Warming: Comparative Analysis of Nuclear and Efficiency Abatement Strategies," *Energy Policy*, 16:6, December 1988, pp. 538-561.

21. Solly Zuckerman, *Nuclear Illusion and Reality* (New York:Vintage Books, 1983), p. 103.

22. Daniel Deudney, *Whole Earth Security: A Geopolitics of Peace* (Washington, DC: Worldwatch Institute, 1983), pp. 39-40.

23. World Commission on Environment and Development, *Our Common Future* (New York: Oxford University Place, 1987), pp. 43, 89.

24. *Ibid.*, p. 89.

25. Herman Daly, "*Sustainable Development: From Concept and Theory Towards Operational Principles,*" Paper presented in Milan, Italy, March 1988. *See also* Herman Daly and John Cobb, *For the Common Good* (Boston: Beacon Press, 1990), pp. 71-76.

26. Herman Daly proposes three criteria to determine the optimal scale for economic development: the level of activity must be sustainable over the long term; human appropriation of global net primary productivity, which is now 25 percent (or 40 percent of terrestrial primary productivity), must not exceed an as yet undetermined level; and, from the work of Charles Perrings, "the economy be [must] small enough to avoid generating feedbacks from the ecosystem that are so novel and surprising as to render economic calculation impossible."

27. Herman Daly, *op. cit.*, p. 26.

28. Robert Repetto, *World Enough and Time* (New Haven: Yale University Press, 1986), p. 8.

29. Wendell Berry, "The Futility of Global Thinking," *Harpers*, September 1989, p. 19.

30. Ivan Illich, *Shadow Work* (New York: Marian Boyars, 1981), p. 15.

31. Wolfgang Sachs, "A Critique of Ecology," *NPQ*, Spring 1989, pp. 16-19.

32. Wendell Berry, *Home Economics* (San Francisco: North Point Press, 1987), p. 67

33. Micheal Redclift, *Sustainable Development: Exploring the Contradictions* (New York: Methuen,1987), p. 151.

34. *Ibid.*

35. Richard B. Norgaard, "Risk and its Management," Paper presented to the annual meeting of the Society of Economic Anthropolgy, April 1987.

36. *Ibid.*, p. 13.

37. Amory B. Lovins, L. Hunter Lovins, *Brittle Power: Energy Strategy for National Security* (Andover: Brick House, 1982), p. 191.

38. Wes Jackson, "The Necessary Marriage between Ecology and Agriculture," *Ecology*, 70:6, December 1989, pp. 1591-1593.

39. Adam Smith, *The Wealth of Nations* (New York: Modern Library, 1965), p.423.

40. J. Glenn Gray, *Rethinking American Education: A Philosophy of Teaching and Learning* (Middletown: Wesleyan University Press, 1984), p. 34.

41. Ernest Boyer, *College: The Undergraduate Experience in American Higher Education* (New York: Harper and Row, 1987), pp. 91-92.

42. J. Glenn Gray, *op.cit.*, p. 81.

43. Alfred North Whitehead, *The Aims of Education* (New York: Free Press, 1967), p. 50.

44. From John Dewey, *The School and Society*, reprinted in John McDermott, ed., *The Philosophy of John Dewey* (Chicago: University of Chicago Press, 1981), p. 246.

45. Walter Truett Anderson, "Beyond Environmentalism," in Anderson,ed., *Rethinking Liberalism* (New York: Avon Books, 1983).

46. Robert Heilbroner, *An Inquiry into the Human Prospect* (New York: W.W. Norton, 1980), p. 175.

47. William Ophuls, *Ecology and the Politics of Scarcity* (San Francisco: W. H. Freeman, 1977), p. 163. *See also* David Orr and Stuart Hill, "Leviathan, the Open Society, and the Crisis of Ecology," *Western Political Quarterly*, 31:4, December 1978, pp. 457-469.

48. Kirkpatrick Sale, *Dwellers in the Land* (San Francisco: Sierra Club Books, 1985), p. 170.

49. Pliny Fisk, *An Appropriate Technology Waking Atlas* (Austin: Center for Maximum Potential Building Systems).

50. *See*: Chris Maser, *The Redesigned Forest* (San Pedro: R & E Miles, 1988); Alan Savory, *Holistic Resource Management* (Washington: Island Press, 1988); and Wes Jackson, *New Roots for Agriculture* (Lincoln: University of Nebraska Press, 1985).

51. Gary Nabhan, *The Desert Smells like Rain* (San Francisco: North Point Press, 1984).

52. Benjamin Barber, *Strong Democracy* (Berkeley: University of California Press, 1984).

53. John Dewey, *The Public and its Problems* (Chicago: Swallow Press, 1954), p. 213.

54. Benjamin Barber, *op. cit.*.

55. *Ibid.*

56. Thomas Jefferson in a letter to William Charles Jarvis, September 28, 1820.

57. Martin Tolchin, "Rich Got Richer, Poorest Poorer in 1979-87," *New York Times*, March 23, 1989, p.A1.

58. Paul and Anne Ehrlich, *"How the Rich Can Save the Poor and Themselves: Lessons from Global Warming,"* Paper given in New Delhi, February 1989, p. 8.

59. Robert Heilbroner, *op. cit.,* p. 110.

60. Jim McNeill, "Strategies for Sustainable Economic Development," *Scientific American*, 261:3, September 1989, p. 157.

61. Worldwatch Institute, *State of the World: 1989* (New York: W. W. Norton, 1989), p.182.

62. Timothy Egan, "Logging in Lush Alaskan Forest Profits Companies and Costs U.S.," *New York Times*, May 29, 1989, p. 1.

63. Robert Repetto, *Public Policies and the Misuse of Forest Resources* (New York: Cambridge University Press, 1988), pp. 1-2.

64. "Rain Forests Worth More If Uncut, Study Says," *New York Times*, July 4, 1989, p. 18.

65. Author's estimate.

ECONOMICS

Arjun Makhijani is currently President of the Institute for Energy and Environmental Research in Takoma Park, Maryland. He received his Ph.D. in Engineering from the University of California at Berkeley.

Makhijani's essay analyzes how global capitalism, the dominant economic system in the world today, functions as a war system. His basic thesis is that war and violence are inherent in capitalism, because capitalism functions globally in a manner analogous to South African apartheid. The capitalist countries, which he defines as the members of the Organization of Economic Cooperation and Development and generally refers to as the "West" or the "North," play a dominant role similar to that of whites in South Africa, while the poor countries of the Third World, most of which are also a part of the capitalist system, play a role analogous to that of non-whites. Makhijani concludes by sketching an alternative economic system that could promote peace, justice, and environmental harmony and that people could begin to create individually and collectively.

GLOBAL APARTHEID AND THE POLITICAL ECONOMY OF WAR

Arjun Makhijani

How do we capture the overall structure of the capitalist system? Only a small and distorted portion of it can be expressed in the monetary terms that are the stuff of textbooks and economic statistics. Other important aspects of capitalism such as life expectancy, literacy, or infant mortality can only be found in quality-of-life indicators. Yet even these do not fully capture the context in which the system operates or reproduces itself.

The war system is as old as civilization. At its core has been an economic system controlled by an elite that exploits the majority of people and cares little for the health of the earth. This system generates oppression, exploitation, and vast inequalities. It safeguards the property and wealth that is produced from the exploited, the powerless, and the poor with violence and ever-present threats of violence. Ultimately, the system feeds on itself, reproducing more violence, greater inequalities, and more environmental destruction.

Violence pervades daily life in the war system. Social and economic divisions create conflict between one oppresed group and another. And oppression and exploitation are reproduced in ever smaller economic units, between religious sects, between racial groups, between castes — even within the heart of the family. Violence takes many forms, from domestic violence against women to assault rifles in the streets, up to the use of weapons of mass destruction.

The war system as it presently operates is dominated by capitalism. Socialism, whatever the ambitions of its adherents and whatever fears it inspired in the West, has never come close to dominating the world as an economic system. And even when socialist countries were militarily powerful, their global economic influence was small and never decisive. Today, the ideologues of capitalism are proclaiming victory. A senior officer in the U.S. State Department, Francis Fukuyama, recently dusted off his Marx and Hegel and gave them an often-quoted capitalist twist:

What we may in fact be witnessing is not just the passing of a particular period

---

The term Global-Apartheid comes from an essay of that title by Gernot Kohler, which Robert Irwin brought to my attention.

of postwar history, but the end point of mankind's ideological evolution and the emergence of Western liberal democracy as the final form of government. Borrowing the vocabulary of Hegel and Marx, it may be the end of history.[1]

Disregarding Marx's prediction that prolonged class struggle would be necessary before any such bliss would be visited upon humankind, Fukuyama brashly announced that "the egalitarianism of modern America represents the essential achievement of the classless society envisioned by Marx," and that all remaining inequalities were merely an aberrant "legacy of a pre-liberal past."[2] Fukuyama not only declared capitalism the victor in economic terms but he also equated political democracy with capitalism. But what are the criteria by which analysts such as Fukuyama evaluate centralized socialism and capitalism? How far-reaching is capitalism as an economic system? If it includes the United States, Japan, West Germany, and France, should it not also include countries like Mexico, Brazil, Indonesia, and Zaire, the countries that provide rich nations with resources, cheap labor, markets, and huge interest payments? Does not capitalism include exploited Third World children who toil twelve hours a day for twenty cents an hour to produce toys for export that they themselves cannot have? Does democracy really thrive in corporations in which workers have no freedom of speech about the conditions of their lives and work, except upon peril of losing their jobs? Does the system account for the helplessness of communities left destitute when corporations move away and plants are shut down? Can we understand the reality of Johannesburg separately from that of Soweto?

The reality of capitalism is more troublesome than its promoters allow. Given the extent of widespread economic misery, huge military expenditures, and appalling environmental destruction, today's most important questions do not relate to any narrow "contest" between state socialism and capitalism. Rather, they relate to how the "victorious" system really works: how poverty exists amidst plenty; how the instruments of war are used to create an order called peace; and how the environment and future generations are robbed for present profit and comfort.

The following are just some of the features of the capitalist system which give it a violent, bellicose character:

~ Just a week's worth of weapons spending in the world that capitalism has won could prevent the deaths of ten to fifteen million children each year from malnutrition and easily preventable diseases.

~ By placing such a high priority on present consumption, capitalism discounts the value of resources for future generations and accelerates pollution and irreversible environmental damage.

~ The capitalist economic system only values things which have a monetary price, and excludes a wide range of values, from nature and nurture, to the unpaid work of women.

~ For millions of young people in or entering the capitalist work force, there is little hope of finding meaningful jobs, leading many to turn to crime and transforming inner cities throughout the capitalist world into war-zones.

~ Capitalism disconnects the humanity of producers from that of consumers, and disconnects both from the environmental consequences of production.

~ Capitalism often subordinates product safety and quality to profit.

~ Physical and other barriers to the movement of workers, especially those of the Third World, proliferate, while the mobility of capital puts communities at the mercy of increasingly powerful corporations.

Violence results from each of these characteristics of capitalism, and violence is needed to maintain them. For instance, violence against women in the form of rape, wife-beating, or sexual harassment is bound up with the broader problem of women's economic oppression; were women not powerless in the marketplace and subjugated at home, they would have the independence and resources to resist or escape domestic violence. Similarly, violence is needed to allow a surfeit of goods and wastefulness to co-exist with deprivation and poverty. The production of shoddy goods or goods that soon become obsolete generates great profits but depends on the availability of cheap resources, a supply of low-wage workers, and a disregard for future generations. Most of this cheap labor, of course, is in the Third World, where it is kept in thrall by the threat and use of force.

Declarations of capitalism's victory and success, to say nothing about the "end of history, "are premature. Fukuyama's view from Foggy Bottom does not extend very far; indeed, the city of Washington, D.C., has a higher infant mortality rate than Shanghai does. A short distance from Fukuyama's office at the State Department, mothers stricken by hopelessness, poverty, and drugs are abandoning their children. Many other children nearby die for lack of social services and medical care. Meanwhile at the Pentagon, the same distance from Fukuyama's office in another direction, the military bureaucracy spends more than half a million dollars a minute preparing for war.

THE COLONIAL DYNAMIC OF CAPITALISM

Analysts tend to judge the successes of capitalism by looking at the conditions within the wealthy capitalist countries alone. But the reality of the capitalist economy has always been far more complex. From the Iberian quest for gold in the Americas, to the vast expansion of lands the Europeans occupied until the present century, the "lifeline" of capitalism has run outside the boundaries of Europe. Today, one often hears that this lifeline runs through the Persian Gulf, and this has just been reaffirmed by a major war over Kuwait. Contrary to both capitalist and Marxist theory, capitalism has never had a purely internal dynamic. The marginalization of vast areas of the world has been as integral to capitalism as the glitter and riches. Exploitation of large numbers of people in the Third World, as well as in the capitalist countries, has been a fundamental and inextricable part of the development of "liberal democracy," as the following examples attest.

The Volta Aluminum Company

Bauxite, the raw material for aluminum, is mined mainly in a few Third World countries. It is then refined into alumina, which is smelted into aluminum ingots by electrolysis, a very energy intensive process. One large aluminum ingot production plant is run by the Volta Aluminum Company (Valco), which is owned by two multinational corporations, Kaiser and Reynolds, and is located at Tema in Ghana, near the Akosombo dam.

Soon after Ghana won independence in 1961, the World Bank provided a loan to build the Akosombo dam, an engineering feat that was supposed to be the pride of Ghana and a symbol of its modernization. The dam also happened to be a project of great interest to Kaiser Aluminum and Reynolds, since most of its electricity was to be dedicated to the aluminum production plant owned by Valco.

When the dam was built, roughly two million acres of mostly forested Ghanaian land were flooded, creating Volta Lake. Large numbers of people were displaced, many of whom were not properly resettled. The lake divided the country North-to-South, making transportation difficult and costly. And soon river blindness and schistosomiasis, a debilitating parasitic disease, became endemic around Volta Lake.

But Valco hit the jackpot and got some of the cheapest electricity in the world. Its contract was guaranteed; the Ghanan government could not change the price and faced stiff financial penalties if it failed to deliver electricity to the aluminum plant. However, in a modern version of noblesse oblige, the company agreed to increase the payment rate from a quarter of a cent per kilowatt hour to half a cent.

Though Ghana's own electricity needs grew, it could not take more electricity from the dam. Instead, as a result of its long-term contract with Valco, the government had to build far more costly hydroelectric and fossil-fuel generating stations. The unfairness of this situation became stark in the early 1980s when Ghana was selling a huge amount of electricity to Valco for only $14 million, while paying $180 million to import an equivalent amount of energy in the form of oil (though the oil was used mainly for transport and not for electricity generation).

Repayment on loans taken to build the dam was also on the order of $10 million per year.

While Valco paid only half a cent per kilowatt hour for a steady supply of electric power, most other industries and Ghanaians paid four to sixteen times as much for unreliable and interruptible power. For example, in 1982 the mining sector and textile mills paid 0.7 cents, residential customers paid two to four cents, and light industries and small businesses paid five to eight cents per kilowatt hour. Normally, firm power is much more expensive than interruptible power. Moreover, during the same period, Kaiser, Reynolds, and other multinational corporations were paying much higher — and rising — prices for electricity to operate their aluminum plants in Europe, Japan, and the United States.

Valco reaped immense profits under these favorable conditions. Based on aluminum prices prevailing in 1982 and the assumption that the plant was functioning at eighty percent capacity, I have estimated that Valco's profits in Ghana after taxes and costs amounted to $125 million.[3] This is not the level of profit, however, which Valco actually reported. Valco calculated its profit based, not on straightforward economic considerations, but on a number of legal and accounting tricks that adjust prices in intra-firm transfers among Valco, Kaiser, and Reynolds to minimize tax obligations.

While Kaiser and Reynolds reaped large profits, the costs to Ghana were substantial. In 1981 Ghana received wages, taxes, and electricity amounting to about $50 million, but it spent $180 million that same year to import oil.[4] Ghana could have avoided these oil imports had it used only $14 million worth of its Valco sales for domestic energy use. Relative to aluminum production prices in Europe and Japan, Ghana lost revenue of roughly $50 million per year due to underpriced electricity.[5] Additional losses to the economy arose from supplying uninterrupted power to Valco at the expense of periodically disrupting the electricity supply to other domestic producers.

Along the way, Ghana fell into debt. To meet a shortage of foreign exchange, it cultivated cocoa on an ever wider scale, taking up large amounts of land. Gold, bauxite, and other extractive export-oriented industries were developed or expanded, which consumed more electricity. Oil consumption increased, as did foreign exchange bills, pollution, and greenhouse gas emissions.

If one tallies all the quantifiable costs, including production losses, disease costs, and underpaid electricity bills, annual losses to Ghana might well have amounted to several hundred million dollars. These costs, of course, exclude many significant items, such as the cost of skewing the nation's industrial structure to exports in order to pay for foreign exchange losses and additional debts. This lasted for about two decades. Then, in 1985, after three years of hard negotiations with Valco and the assistance of the U.N. Center on Transnational Corporations, Ghana was finally able to raise its tariff to about two cents a kilowatt hour.

The Japanese Timber Industry

The Volta story is not exceptional, as a brief look at the Japanese "economic miracle" reveals. It is true that hard work and inventiveness have contributed to Japan's leading economic standing in the world today. But there is much more to the tale than can be seen on the screen of a high-definition television.

Japan, situated on a chain of rather small, mountainous islands with 120 million people, has practically no natural resources. It imports most of its raw materials and much of its food. Moreover, fish, which Japan considers "domestically produced," is in reality the product of the systematic plundering of the world's oceans and the territorial waters of other countries.

Japan also uses up vast areas of land in other countries. Until the early 1970s lumber was Japan's second largest import after oil, and the largest amount of timber came from Southeast Asia. According to Jon Halliday and Gavan McCormack:

> In 1970, 42 million cubic meters of timber were imported...an increase of 16 per cent over the previous year's demand .... What is particularly important about lumber is [that] the pillaging of Southeast Asia's forests has [had] a devastating effect on the lives of millions of poor peasants throughout the area, and utterly negative, and often irreversible, effects on the whole ecology. One of the biggest uprisings in Taiwan in the early period of Japan's occupation there, was triggered off by Mitsui's devastation of huge forest areas on the island.[6]

A decade later, the situation had not changed. In 1979 Daniel Nelson noted that Japanese imports had been responsible for increases in timber production ranging from one hundred percent to six hundred percent in various parts of Asia, from Afghanistan to the Philippines.[7] Millions of acres of forest area have been destroyed in Southeast Asia over the past few decades. This destruction continues as Japanese corporations, joined by other multinational firms, tear down irreplaceable tropical forests to plant quick-growing trees for the production of disposable paper wipes and chopsticks. The rape of Asian forests is an integral part of the Japanese economic miracle.

Imperialism: A Pervasive Pattern

The brief portraits above are only a sampling from a long, ugly history of exploitation which continues to the present day. There are many other examples:
  ~ Three-and-a-half decades of misery in Guatemala were ushered in by the

greed of the United Fruit Company. In 1954 the CIA overthrew the democratically elected regime of Jacobo Guzman Arbenz after he had dared to expropriate fallow land belonging to the U.S.-based company for redistribution to the poor. The Guatemalan government actually had proposed compensation based on the company's own evaluation of the land for tax purposes, but the company deemed this offer inadequate. Instead, it turned to the U.S. government for "help," which came in the form of military and economic aid that propped up a succession of dictators, who have killed over 100,000 civilians and caused hundreds of thousands to flee.[8]

~ In 1953 the U.S. government played a central role in the overthrow of the elected Iranian president, Mohammed Mossadegh, who wanted to nationalize oil production facilities within the country. The United States and British governments replaced Mossadegh with the Shah, who brutally repressed opposition for nearly three decades.

~ Thousands of acres of Central American forest have been destroyed every year to create pasture land for beef exports, a tragedy that has been called the "hamburger connection." This destructive pattern, supported for many years by multinational banks, continues to be a major source of the environmental devastation in both Central and South America.

~ Vast areas of land in Africa have been destroyed every year by the mining and refining of copper, uranium, and other minerals that are destined primarily for export to the capitalist countries.

~ In Malaysia and other Southeast Asian countries eighty percent of the young women employed to solder gold wires onto high-tech electronic chips get eye diseases within a few years. They are laid off and disappear from the high-tech production process, and a fresh batch of young women with better than 20/20 vision replaces them. Today, even some of these production lines are being closed down as factory owners search for cheaper labor.[9]

A detailed and careful study of any of these stories would reveal relentless exhaustion and destruction both of human beings and the environment.[10] The riches which capitalism generates are not just the product of inventiveness and marvelously productive technology; they are also the product of plain, old-fashioned exploitation. From the wood veneer that makes many electronic goods look appealing, to toilet paper and high-tech electronics, production is being accompanied by the destruction of nature, land, and people that does not show up in the price of the finished goods. These costs appear as infant mortality, poverty, and ecological devastation in the Third World. They show their face in the form of human health problems, such as Minamata, the deadly mercury poisoning disease named after the city in Japan where it claimed so many lives. These destructive consequences persist long after the product is tossed into the garbage dump.

CORPORATIONS AND CAPITALIST THEORY

Annual sales of the largest multinational corporations total around $100 billion, exceeding the gross national products (GNP) of all but half-a-dozen Third World countries and the GNPs of many relatively wealthy capitalist nations as well. Moreover, banks and corporations have much more concentrated control over these sums of money than many nations do. They can generate revenue in hard currency, which generally is in short supply in Third World countries. Large portions of their holdings are liquid or can be converted to liquid assets. They can move capital around the world with the speed of an electric signal in a computer network. They can invest in or divest from communities and countries at a moment's notice. They are responsible for the extraction of vast quantities of the earth's natural resources. To a considerable degree they determine the prices of products around the world. Their policies are not restrained internally or guided by the well-being of the community or the environment. And they are institutions unabashedly devoted to the pursuit of profit.

Yet capitalist ideology maintains that there is no need to constrain corporations. One of Adam Smith's hypotheses is that an "invisible hand" guides the marketplace: if individuals work toward their own benefit, both private profit and communal well-being will inevitably follow. This premise remains a powerful strain in capitalist theory, often justifying government decisions not to intervene in corporate activities despite the practical failure of unfettered commerce to deliver widespread well-being.

Throughout the world technological decisions of great economic and environmental import are left to corporations. Even when corporations are not the technical innovators, their control of capital usually decides what innovations actually go to market. When there are environmental, health, or safety problems associated with industrial production, whether toxic dumps or ozone depletion, those corporations responsible practically never pay the full costs of cleanup, if indeed they pay anything at all. For instance, a $26 million plutonium production plant built by the Getty Oil corporation near Buffalo, New York, has left a billion-dollar radioactive mess for New York State and U.S. taxpayers to take care of.

The failure of national governments to regulate corporations demonstrates the close ties between capitalist governments and corporations, and is perhaps the single most important structural element of the war system. Governments regularly use their military, financial, and political power to protect corporate property and prerogatives. Capitalist states have hardly left anything up to the "invisible hand," and instead have actively supported corporate activities abroad, sometimes with military force. Government interest in corporate activities expresses itself in innumerable ways, from huge contracts for new weapons systems to subsidies for international arms deals. Over the last two hundred years, capitalist governments have used military force to prosecute colonial wars in Asia and Africa, to commit genocide of tribal peoples in North America and Australia, and to intervene in Latin America on numerous occasions. A principal purpose of these actions has been to support the pursuit of profit by home corporations.

The vast exploitation of resources and subsequent environmental destruction and impoverishment of the Third World would not have been possible without violence and the threat of violence. For instance, Japan's 1931 invasion of China, which marked the beginning of the Second World War as much as later events in Europe, was economic in origin. The Japanese attack on Pearl Harbor was rooted in a conflict over the control of colonial resources in Asia such as Indonesian oil. Similarly, German aggression in Eastern Europe and the Soviet Union was motivated in part by a desire to control more resources and cheap labor.

Despite their "free market" ideology, capitalist nation-states have played a central role in deploying the military forces that have been essential for capitalism to exist at all. More than any "invisible hand" guiding the marketplace, the military hand of the state has been central to the economic prosperity of capitalist countries. As the Second World War came to a close, the chairman of General Electric suggested the creation of a "permanent war economy" in which the government would protect domestic demand for goods made by U.S. corporations. Others also argued that the economic future of the United States depended on securing markets in Europe and the Third World. This required that the Soviets, with their antagonism toward capitalist multinational corporations, be kept out of both regions.

Explaining post-war policy to Congress in 1944, Dean Acheson firmly linked U.S. prosperity with access to foreign markets:

> When we look at the problem [of full employment] we may say that it is a problem of foreign markets . . . .[Y]ou could fix it so that everything produced here would be consumed here. That would completely change our Constitution, our relations to property, human liberty, our very conceptions of law . . . and nobody contemplates that. Therefore you must look to other markets and those markets are abroad.[11]

These considerations were at the heart of the U.S. containment strategy spelled out in National Security Council memorandum 68 (NSC-68), which guided post-war policy for capitalism:

Fostering a world environment in which the American system can flourish . . . embraces two subsidiary policies. One is a policy which we would probably pursue even if there were no Soviet threat. It is a policy of attempting to create a healthy international community. The other is a policy of 'containing' the Soviet system. These two policies are closely interrelated and interact on one another.[12]

The architects of U.S. post-war foreign policy viewed military power as an essential means by which to protect U.S. corporate interests abroad. Deterrence meant not merely preventing an equally armed Soviet Union from attacking the United States but also keeping the Soviet Union out of areas in which the United States or other capitalist powers exercised or hoped to exercise dominance. Soviet "influence" in both Europe and the Third World were to be eliminated with force. NSC-68 revealed that the U.S. definition of "deterrence," which prevailed until about the mid-1960s, meant threatening the Soviet Union with a "global war of annihilation" if it displaced U.S. dominance from any critical area of the world.[13] This contained the essence of the war system: a readiness to annihilate everything if one cannot secure resources and markets on one's own terms.

Subjugation at Home

The military power of the state also has been important to protect the interests of capitalist powers domestically. The extreme inequalities caused by capitalism inevitably create conflicts at home that must be quelled. The decision-making and financial power of corporations is usually great enough to purchase armed protection for their private interests. But capitalist governments also help corporations by using military force to break strikes or enforce the prerogatives of large property owners; rarely will they aid workers who have unjustly lost their jobs with the same alacrity. To be sure, the direct use of force has declined over the past century with the gains made by workers' struggles and enshrined in domestic labor laws, but one essential purpose of armed forces within most capitalist countries, whether local police or national military units, has been to protect the power and property of corporations and the wealthy. Generally, the poorer the majority of the population, the more frequently a government resorts to the use of force. Today, violence is used most frequently and directly on civilian populations in the Third World, where class and income differences between the poor and the affluent are enormous.

Military subjugation within Third World countries has changed somewhat since the end of direct colonial rule. Those areas which were the most relentlessly impoverished by capitalist practice were also the first to revolt. But rarely did these revolts improve the plight of landless rural workers, poor peasants, or the unemployed. Sometimes these revolts came in the form of socialist revolutions, which joined nationalist, Marxist, and Leninist ideas into an uneasy combination of theories, ideologies, and practice. Revolutions occurred generally when resistance movements confronted the wars, internal repression, and impoverishment produced by imperialism. In other cases, nationalist movements achieved independence when the local ruling classes (capitalists, bureaucrats, and landowners) gained political control from imperialists. But in these cases the economic connections to imperialism remained strong. Often imperialist rulers installed pliant regimes or puppet governments as they relinquished formal control to prevent nationalist or leftist governments from coming to power. The United States, for example, imposed governments at gun-point in many countries in Latin America in the twentieth century.

Though struggles for independence from colonial rule stemmed from a desire to reduce oppression, today the military hand of the state in Third World countries remains very strong. Since direct colonial rule ended, most Third World countries have embraced capitalism through the rise of powerful local elites, backed up by foreign military forces and multinational corporations. Whether these countries are governed by elected or unelected officials, repressive military institutions have united with local and foreign corporations that own property.

Nationalism and Racism

The military subjugation of the economically deprived, imposed by wealthy countries over destitute ones and by the rich over the poor within all countries, is an essential feature of the war system. However, the naked use of force is not the only means by which capitalism has been "marketed" nationally or internationally.

For many years capitalism was sold in the United States as anti-Communism, dressed up in the rhetoric of God and Country. The pitch was made easier by Stalin's violent repression, but long before the socialist countries even existed, similar capitalist policies of economic exploitation were clothed in the argument that European civilization was helping the backward peoples of the Third World. Exploitation was sold in Europe as the "White Man's burden." The use of force by some groups to oppress others was called "maintaining law and order," and it was bolstered by romantic images of conquest, scientific progress, and racial superiority. In the United States, both the genocide of Native Americans and the enslavement of Africans were rationalized by such arguments.

In most capitalist countries today, nationalism is a "respectable" ideology while racism is not, yet both are used to justify oppression in very similar ways. The connections are easy to see when comparing capitalism to apartheid.

The global reality of capitalism resembles South Africa in its racial divisions, its class structure, its violence, and its inequalities.[14] In South Africa the two main groups of whites — the English and the Boers — fought a very bitter and violent war, but then resolved that together they would establish dominance over the non-white people of South Africa. There was an analogous result in global capitalism after two bloody world wars. In exchange for markets, investment opportunities, and bases, the United States became the military guarantor of a continued flow of cheap resources and labor from the Third World to the wealthy capitalist countries. Despite tensions resulting from trade, financial, or other disputes, capitalist countries have enacted coordinated economic policies and similar rules for dominating the Third World. In the cases of both global capitalism and South Africa, differences among whites were largely set aside when dealing with non-whites.

The South African system of pass laws also has been constructed on an international scale through a coordinated system of passports, visas, and work permits, which has eased mobility for a privileged minority but made it difficult for everyone else. This reality is graphically illustrated by the difference between the heavily policed U.S.-Mexican border, which is designed to keep poor Latin Americans out of the United States, and the largely demilitarized U.S.-Canadian border, which fosters greater cooperation among the wealthier Americans and Canadians, whose wage levels are comparable. Similarly, the elimination of borders within Western Europe in 1992 will be accompanied by a hardening of the European Economic Community's border to immigrants from the Third World. European capital welcomes the Third World's cheap labor, markets, and resources, but not the Third World's people.

South Africa claims to have a "liberal democracy," but only for a minority of its population. Similarly, other capitalist countries embrace liberal democracy, but Third World peoples living within their territories are effectively precluded from full participation through a labyrinth of requirements for citizenship.

Other features of South Africa also match the aggregate picture of the capitalist world: about a quarter of both populations are white, three-quarters are nonwhite; income inequality is similarly skewed; the wealthy in both populations have an infant mortality rate of approximately ten per thousand births, while the poor have a rate ten times as high. And within each community there exist many kinds of divisions, including those of class and gender.

Furthermore, similarities between apartheid and Third World oppression can be found in the ideologies supporting the two systems. To rationalize exploitation, the ruling elite in both cases ascribe inferiority to the dominated peoples, setting in motion the dynamics of racism. Both race and nationality manifest themselves in the social interaction of the dominators and the dominated. "White" is defined by "Black" and "Black" by "White," but as soon as "Whites" have their own social setting, they take on diverse characteristics. A peasant in Brittany is a Breton when confronted with a Parisian, French when confronted with a German, European when confronted with a Russian, and White when confronted with a Moroccan, Algerian, or Senegalese. But while oppressed races and nationalities tend to internalize the attitudes of their oppressors, the reverse is not true of the oppressor races and nationalities. Thus, in an effort to escape their oppression, blacks seek to become more white and people in the Third World try to assimilate the culture and values of the dominant capitalist countries.

The passions associated with these identities are volatile and depend, in part, on an individual's judgment about the economic prospects of a particular group relative to that of his or her own. The working people of the dominant race generally identify with the elite of the same race, despite the long-term economic solidarity they should have with workers of other races. Exploited people can be quite prejudiced and are ready to commit acts of violence to protect the meager privileges they have because of their "superior" race. For example, overt racial prejudices are often strongly held and violently expressed by many white blue-collar workers in both the United States and Europe.

Of course, despite the similarities between the capitalist and apartheid systems, there are also significant differences. The overall analogy is useful, but important aspects of both oppressive systems need to be analyzed separately. Still, it is plain why violence occurs in both systems, for the principal motive underlying both systems is economic exploitation.

MONETARY IMPERIALISM

One of the most important elements of Third World oppression in the twentieth century has been the international monetary system. Since the end of World War II, Third World countries have faced a system dominated by the U.S. dollar, which has enabled the United States to deal with its internal problems by exporting them to other areas. When the United States and other economically powerful capitalist countries decide to print money, they create global inflation because their currencies, so-called "hard currencies," can be exchanged for goods all over the world. In contrast, when a typical Third World country prints money, it only creates local inflation because its currency is not easily convertible.

The United States began inflating the global economy in 1965 when it tried to wage both a war in Vietnam and a "War on Poverty" at home. This policy was expanded in the 1970s when the United States and other capitalist countries responded to OPEC's oil price increases by expanding their money supplies. As a result, capitalist countries shifted the burden of high oil prices to the Third World, where both oil-importing and oil-exporting countries had to pay higher prices for all their goods and services. Though the cumulative oil import bill of the OECD countries increased by $1.5 trillion between 1973 and 1982, as a group they showed balance of payments surpluses, not deficits.[15] Many Third World countries, in contrast, became seriously indebted during this period, in part because of inflation and in part because their elites corruptly transferred domestic capital into foreign bank accounts.

By 1973, the inflationary U.S. policies destroyed the international gold-exchange standard, under which the United States had promised to exchange dollars for gold at a fixed rate, and by the end of the 1970s, these policies almost caused the entire dollar-based international monetary system to collapse. Then in October 1979, President Carter called in a conservative banker, Paul Volcker, to institute tight monetary policies. Volcker increased interest rates, squeezed workers at home and abroad, reduced inflation, and increased the value of the dollar relative to other currencies. But high interest rates and a high dollar also increased the real value of Third World debt enormously. This meant that the people of the Third World had to pay far more than they originally contemplated in order to protect the international monetary system and to ensure that U.S. domestic growth would have low rates of inflation. As Beryl Sprinkel admitted, while serving as Under Secretary of the Treasury (he later became the Chairman of Reagan's Council of Economic Advisors): "[T]he debt crisis is, to a large extent, an indirect result of our success in curing inflation and revitalizing the American economy."[16]

Why didn't the indebted countries form a cartel, threaten to renounce the debt (and collapse the banks), and try for a better deal? One reason is that the capitalist countries controlling the trading and financial system probably would have resorted to economic blackmail. R.T. MacNamar, a Deputy Secretary in the Reagan Administration's Department of the Treasury, warned of the dire consequences of debt repudiation:

> The foreign assets of a country that repudiated its debt would be attacked by creditors throughout the world; its exports seized by creditors at each dock where they landed; its national airlines unable to operate; and its sources of desperately needed capital goods virtually eliminated. In many countries, even food imports would be curtailed, hardly a pleasant scenario.[18]

On another occasion, MacNamar was even more blunt: "Have you ever contemplated what would happen to the president of a country if the government couldn't get insulin for its disabled."[18]

There is at least one other powerful reason that the debtor nations never formed a cartel. Over the last several decades the rich in both the capitalist countries and the Third World have developed mutual interests. As Susan George has detailed, Third

World elites have stashed a good part of their countries' borrowings into private bank accounts in the United States, Switzerland, the Bahamas, and elsewhere.[19] When a Mexican policy-maker was asked why his country did not form a cartel and threaten the stability of the banks, he calmly replied, "Where do you think I have my money?" The corrupt relationships among the governments of Zaire, France, and the United States comprise another well known example.[20] Today, the outflow of capital from the Third World, and the criminal behavior it represents, continues. The transfer of capital from the Third World to the richer capitalist countries is not, however, all due to venality and greed. The instability of Third World currencies caused by repeated IMF-dictated devaluations drives the middle class and even the working class to transfer their holdings into dollars and other "hard" currencies. A vicious cycle is created in which capital flight and instability feed on each other until foreign-exchange considerations dominate every significant aspect of Third World economies. In countries such as Argentina, the severity of IMF-imposed "medicine" essentially destroyed the local monetary system. Now, even internal transactions occur in dollars. It is no longer possible for shopkeepers, farmers, or merchants to use local currencies with predictable value from day to day.

Capitalist manipulations of the international monetary system and the value of the Third World debt have been catastrophic for most indebted countries. Throughout the Third World, IMF "prescriptions" have aggravated the pain by increasing unemployment, poverty, and suffering. And despite all this, Third World debt has not declined; it has increased. In 1982, when the debt crisis became officially recognized, Third World debt totalled about $500 billion. By 1989 it was about $1.2 trillion. The patient receiving IMF medicine not only has suffered more; she is now a lot sicker.

Meanwhile, the multinational banks most endangered by risky Third World loans have had time to avert the danger of collapse by setting aside loan-loss reserves and diversifying portfolios. Most of these banks have made immense profits by loaning even more money to the Third World, which is paid right back as service on existing loans. Throughout the later 1980s, the Third World provided a net inflow of approximately $50 billion a year to the capitalist countries. Yet, the IMF has refused to reevaluate its theories or examine the fundamental defects in its prescriptions. Why should it? The patient may be suffering and sick, but the doctor is doing quite well, thank you.

PRELIMINARY CONSIDERATIONS FOR AN ALTERNATIVE ECONOMIC SYSTEM

The exploitation of capitalism, the authoritarianism of socialism, and the violence committed against human beings in the name of both systems have driven many people to seek an entirely new form of economics beyond capitalism and socialism. From the experiences of socialism, we need to learn how to redistribute income and wealth in a manner which alleviates poverty yet still manages to stimulate savings and the production of essential goods. Properly done, redistribution can increase the level of national savings and stimulate the economy. From the experiences of capitalism, we need to learn how the positive aspects of individual and community ownership can be incorporated into a more vigorous and universal democracy. We must learn how to disentangle redistribution from authoritarianism, and political democracy from imperialism and oppressor nationalism, and how to join these elements with economic democracy.

The scope of our vision, our concerns, and our actions must extend from the local to the global. Because the economy in which we live is global, and because the central institutions which control it—multinational corporations and banks—are also global, no vision which covers just a single country can begin to address the global need for economic justice. Three basic kinds of questions arise when we attempt to envision a peace-system economy:

1. What principles should underlie this system?
2. What kinds of economic institutions should manage the system?
3. What actions can individuals and communities take to transform the present economic structure into this desired new system?

One may ask the last question somewhat differently. The present order provides considerable short-term benefits to the one third of the population in the world that consumes over ninety percent of the resources. This minority has a stake in the present economic and military system. Why should it give up those benefits? What does it stand to gain? A part of the answer can be seen in the drama being played out in South Africa today. The conflicts which apartheid imposes are so intractable and have resulted in so much violence that the system has become untenable even for the white minority.

Francis Fukuyama may think the end of history is here. But the immense numbers of dispossessed and disinherited have only just begun to write it. The national struggles for formal political independence of a few decades ago are now moving toward a global struggle for an international system of economic justice and environmental sanity.

The Achilles Heel of the war system can be found in what it demands of its beneficiaries: that they remain prepared to give up everything, to go to war in an instant, and to risk nuclear holocaust. With two world wars and many lesser conflicts inflicting so much suffering in this century alone, many people are beginning to find that the human costs of maintaining the war system are unacceptable. Many are already organizing against it. They have found that strontium-90 in babies' teeth, the buildup of nuclear wastes, and the threat of instant annihilation are all unacceptable prices to pay for present comforts.

Within the capitalist countries there are basic problems which cannot be addressed unless steps are taken to improve the plight of the poor all over the world. Take, for example, the problems of drugs and inner-city violence that are widespread and are now spreading to Europe. Most coca leaves are grown in Peru and Bolivia, countries devastated by the debt crisis. Many poor farmers in these countries have decided that one of the few dependable ways to overcome at least some of their economic difficulties is to grow coca. As a result, Peru and Bolivia now depend on the sales of coca paste and cocaine for foreign exchange to pay off their foreign debts. The drug "war" in the United States is unlikely to be won without both improving conditions for the poor in the United States and relieving the economic crisis in the Third World.

The problems of unemployment in Third World and capitalist countries also are closely related. Corporations from the industrialized nations want cheap productive labor, but their workers want job security and decent wages. Consequently, many corporations have moved their factories to the Third World. This is one reason that wages, discounted for inflation, have not increased in the United States since 1973. Indeed, the purchasing power of wages for a substantial proportion of American workers has actually fallen. The immense differences of wages between countries, unrelated to differences in labor productivity, pull wages down. As long as wages do not rise in the Third World and companies can easily move their operations, low wages will continue to persist in the capitalist countries. Many workers in capitalist countries realize this and, consequently, are beginning to lobby for changes in the international labor system that would raise wages in all countries.

The beneficiaries of the current global economic system are beginning to appreciate the many hidden environmental and financial costs the system imposes. Elites in both Third World and capitalist countries must make substantial military expenditures, the end of the Cold War notwithstanding, to maintain the exploitative order, which carries high environmental, economic, and political costs. Under the guise of strengthening global security, the United States has continued to poison the land, air, and water by producing even more nuclear weapons. Entire agencies of the government, such as the Department of Energy, have routinely broken laws and created an immense economic burden for present and future generations in the form of "cleanup" costs.

Capitalism has other hidden costs as well. Goods manufactured as inexpensively as possible are cheaper to throw away than to repair, since the relative wages for repair work are far higher than those for assembly-line workers. Communities are beginning to realize that the conveniences of high levels of resource consumption wind up in the landfill and threaten the local environment. Not even the captains of industry can escape the need for an intact ozone layer to protect them from deadly ultraviolet radiation. Consequently, most corporations have now agreed to ban ozone-depleting CFCs.

The war system imposes human, environmental, and financial costs on everyone in the world. Obviously, those who have paid the most and have been pushed to the margin have the most to gain by breaking free. In the short-term, their demands are at odds with those who consume most of the world's resources. But considerable common ground exists between them. There is an urgent need to expand that common ground if we are to begin to heal the wounds of the permanent war that people have waged against the earth and its inhabitants.

SOME ELEMENTS OF ECONOMIC DEMOCRACY

The unfairness of "taxation without representation" inspired the revolt of the thirteen U.S. colonies against British rule. The scale of economic deprivation in the world today indicates a much greater failure of representation, but we have not even begun to attain economic democracy in which individuals and communities could exert some control over the economic decisions that affect their lives. One of the most glaring anti-democratic aspects of capitalism is how it extracts wealth from the labor of others and from the earth without the full representation of workers, communities, and future generations. This must be systematically changed.

Rampant starvation amidst plenty, widespread unemployment, unsafe working conditions, and environmental destruction are not the only problems afflicting the current economic system. The labor of half of humanity — namely women — is completely discounted as well. All these inequalities are indicative of an undemocratic system in which the economically weak have no representation in the marketplace. Economic weakness inevitably translates into political weakness. How can people without food, jobs, housing, or education, or people who experience so much violence in their daily lives become effective practitioners of democracy?

Without redistribution, without economic justice, without accountable economic institutions, there can be no real democracy and no real peace. Economic democracy and redistribution are needed at all levels — the family, the community, the nation, and the world.

Redistribution in favor of the poor has often been regarded as inimical to economic incentive, while redistribution in favor of the rich has been deemed pro-growth and pro-prosperity. The belief that the rising tide will lift all boats was the principal tenet of Reaganomics and inspired a series of tax breaks for the rich during the 1980s. This policy is still being promoted by the Bush Administration in its advocacy of lower taxes on capital gains. U.S. leverage in international financial institutions such as the IMF and the World Bank also has forced a number of other countries to accept the same premise. Yet the result in the United States and throughout the world has been quite predictable — the rich have grown richer, and the poor poorer.

Individual incentive and equality of wealth are, in fact, very much compatible. The redistribution of land in the People's Republic of China helped peasants become more economically productive. It also helped eliminate the worst aspects of poverty in China, fostered redistributive justice, and ended drug addiction and many other social ills within a few years after the revolution. The failure of other socialist revolutions to cultivate incentive is not a failure of redistribution, but rather a result of the squelching of local initiative by the state and the absence of democratic political processes.

Redistribution and economic incentive can and must be combined. What incentive to excel and innovate exists for people who earn fifty cents a day? Where are the incentives for peasants to invest and increase production when landlords, moneylenders, and corrupt government officials barely pay a subsistence wage? How can people be creative if they have no hope of meaningful employment at a decent salary? The creative energy of people can only be unleashed if equity and humanity inform the practical operation of the economy. The late Indian agricultural economist, Raj Krishna, used to say that if property is protected by government as a source of income, then labor must also be protected as a source of income. That protection implies guaranteed employment at minimum wages that pay an income above the poverty line for full-time work. Redistribution means more than progressive taxation. Just as fundamental is the question of who controls land, resources, and capital. Land redistribution created a modicum of popular control in China. The Japanese method of management has given workers some responsibility on the factory floor. Control, responsibility, and accountability by both communities and workers are all critical elements of economic democracy.

Redistribution does not mean abolishing riches. It means limiting riches and ending poverty. The example of Kerala, India, discussed below, shows how a strong commitment to redistribution can simultaneously enhance political democracy and improve economic conditions with very modest resources.

Economic justice also requires the establishment of democratic control over corporations and other economic institutions. As discussed below, however, control will be difficult or impossible at the local level alone unless basic changes also are made at the global level, including an overhaul of the international monetary system.

Restructuring the Large Corporation

Today, a multinational corporation can use and manipulate resources any-where on the planet while remaining largely unaccountable to the communities in which it does business. The corporation can open or close a factory, make a loan, shut down a mine, or relocate all its operations without any restraint, irrespective of the mark it leaves behind. As Charles Lindblom has observed:

> It has been a curious feature of democratic thought that it has not faced up to the private corporation as a peculiar organization in an ostensible democracy. Enormously large, rich in resources, the big corporations command more resources than do most government units. They can also, over a broad range, insist that governments meet their demands, even if these demands run counter to those of citizens . . . .and they exercise unusual veto powers . . . .The large private corporation fits oddly into democratic theory and practice. Indeed, it does not fit.[21]

Democratic thought has not addressed the problem of corporations, partly because the standard unit of analysis has been the political-economy of an indi-vidual country. Moreover, "free markets" are often confused with the notion of "freedom" in politics. In capitalist economic theory, "liberal" thought stands for the right of property owners and corporations to make profits in almost any manner they see fit, protected if necessary by the military power of the state. In "liberal" political theory, freedom connotes a democratic system in which just laws enshrine the rights for people with respect to their governments. But nowhere does the liberal concept of freedom establish rights for people with respect to corpora-tions.

Movement toward a peace system will require that communities and workers begin to exercise serious democratic control over corporations. It also requires that people begin to question the legitimacy of corporations dominating the global economic system. It is odd that a corporation has the legal status of a human being but cannot be sent to jail. When a firm goes out of business, large shareholders and chief executive officers can get richer by retaining fat fees from the corporate carcass, even as workers and communities become destitute. And all too often taxpayers bear the burden of cleaning up the mess. Corporate bankruptcy and national bailouts are both examples of taxation without representation and are assaults upon political democracy. The several-hundred-billion-dollar bailout of the U.S. savings-and-loan industry is perhaps the biggest example of this kind. The decisions of unelected executives of savings-and-loan banks caused the crisis, but once the financial system was threatened the political system poured hundreds of billions of dollars to pay for the cost of these poor decisions.

Internationally, there are few laws to stop or even regulate the most egregious corporate practices. The accident at Union Carbide's pesticide plant in Bhopal, India, for example, resulted in thousands of deaths and tens of thousands of injuries. It was the worst industrial disaster in history, yet there was no system by which the victims could force the corporation to account for its actions and secure just compensation.

Democratic control of corporations by communities and workers raises a number of difficult practical and conceptual issues. For example, what rights should communities have over property holders? How can a locality exercise legal power over an institution that may operate in hundreds of communities and dozens of countries? How can workers' interests in the economic health of a company be reconciled with the interests of different communities? And how can the short-term and long-term interests of communities be reconciled? In the short-term corporations provide communities with needed jobs and investment, but in the long-term communities must cope with the environmental and social impacts of corporate decisions.

Right now, the power of large corporations to mobilize huge amounts of capital, to market many types of goods, and to operate in dozens of countries simultaneously dwarfs the power of individual communities. For small communities with high unemployment and poverty, corporate power can be overwhelming. How can these large economic units be made amenable to democratic control?

Providing People with as Much Mobility as Capital

In capitalist theory, freely moving capital and goods are supposed to equalize wages among countries, while the mobility of people has been regarded as irrelevant. The reality is devastatingly different. Over the past two centuries, wage differences between capitalist and Third World countries have become immense, and these disparities have been institutionalized by the militarized boundaries between First and Third World countries.

The U.S.-Canadian border is relatively secure and open. The U.S.-Mexican border, in contrast, is highly militarized and separates high-wage earners from low-wage earners and high employment areas from low employment areas. Goods and capital can flow freely among all three nations, but Mexicans cannot easily move into the United States or Canada. The U.S.-Mexican border makes communities on both sides less secure. U.S. workers suffer when corporations close up shop and leave for Mexico's lower wages and more lax environmental regulations. At the same time, Mexican workers suffer because they have no power to bid up their wages to levels received by workers in the United States for the same work. This injustice causes Mexicans to emigrate to the United States to increase their wages and family income, often under ghastly and inhuman conditions.

Global corporations insist that the boundaries of countries should remain porous to goods and capital. Take, for example, the sentiments of a former chairman of IBM, Jacques Maisonrouge:

> For business purposes the boundaries that separate one nation from another are no more real than the equator. They are merely convenient demarcations of ethnic, linguistic and cultural entities. They do not define business requirements or consumer trends. Once management understands and accepts this world economy, its view of the marketplace and its planning necessarily expand. The world outside the home country is no longer viewed as a series of disconnected customers . . . but as an extension of a single market.[22]

To corporations trying to market products at low cost and high profit, ethnic, linguistic, and cultural matters are insignificant. To real people, however, these "demarcations" are among the most important ways that they define themselves and their lives. Besides the high economic costs of moving, people find it much more difficult to leave their communities than do corporations. For corporations, moving is sometimes little more than transferring electronic blips between their bank accounts.

Democratic control by communities and workers over corporations requires some limitations on the mobility of capital. These limitations need not, and should not, take the form of outright and total prohibitions. However, a minimum level of accountability and responsibility should be built into the operation of a corporation in any community. The degree of regulation should correspond to the scale and reach of a corporation's activities. Here are some examples of regulations that municipalities, national governments, and international institutions might impose on corporations:

- ~ Corporations should disclose information about all their operations in each community where they operate, including wage levels, worker health-and-safety conditions, past records of plant closures, and the nature of goods manufactured.
- ~ Companies should be liable for the accuracy and completeness of the information disclosed.
- ~ Top management should be held criminally liable for certain crimes committed by the corporation.
- ~ Freedom of speech for workers with regard to health and safety matters and with regard to environmental and financial accountability should be protected from employer reprisal.
- ~ Corporations should conduct a reasonable amount of research to

estimate health and environmental effects of their products prior to initiating sales, and they should be liable for a failure to do so.

~ International regulations should be established to protect labor rights, environmental standards, and worker safety and health, and there should be global liability for failure to obey these rules.

~ There should be global freedom-of-information rules enabling citizens to acquire information from corporations, similar to those of the Freedom of Information Act, which allows people in the United States to get information from the U.S. government.

~ International relief funds should be created for victims of accidents and environmental disasters.

No single community has enough power to establish and enforce these rules. Therefore, subjecting multinational corporations to the minimum requirements of social and environmental responsibility will require close cooperation by communities all over the world, both in high-wage and low-wage countries. One objective might be to establish an international agency to create and to enforce these rules. This agency, of course, should be governed by a democratic process in which nongovernmental organizations as well as governmental representatives could participate. We also need to reconsider the very institution of the large corporation. There is a strong case for global economic integration, but should an institution, organized for the profit of stockholders and run by a few managers, be the primary vehicle to achieve it? Can the policies suggested above suffice to change the nature of the corporation so that its productive functions continue without immense human costs?[23]

Considerable obstacles to establishing controls on corporations arise from the economic and military boundaries between capitalist and Third World countries. Because low-wage labor often is highly productive, many multinational corporations find it much cheaper to make goods in the Third World and then ship them to the areas of high consumption, such as the United States, Japan, or Europe. Therefore, when communities in the capitalist countries try to put restrictions on corporations, such as requiring front-end investments or strict adherence to environmental rules, a great incentive is created for multinational corporations simply to close up shop and move their operations elsewhere, especially to Third World countries with solid infrastructures and liberal rules for repatriating profits.

It is essential for communities in wealthy capitalist countries and the Third World, including the workers living in these communities, to team up in order to establish real restraints on capital mobility. Despite the tensions between wealthy and poor communities, all communities have substantial common interests in increasing wages, protecting jobs, and enhancing environmental quality. Fortunately, various kinds of international cooperation among communities and grassroots organizations are already occurring. For instance, labor unions in capitalist countries are now demanding that their employers maintain minimum standards for wages, worker safety, and public health in their Third World operations. Similarly, there are networks of tribal people, local organizers, and ecology groups in the Third World who have made common cause with environmentalist groups in capitalist countries to stop World Bank loans for projects that threaten massive destruction of the environment and local economies.

Elementary justice requires the loosening of borders between the dominant capitalist and Third World countries. People of European origin today occupy several times more land than they once did in Europe. To expand their access to land and resources, Europeans colonized and then exploited North America, Australia, New Zealand, considerable portions of Africa, and also the eastern parts of the Soviet Union. Bangladesh is poor today largely because British colonialism economically and physically devastated it with the help of local rulers.[24] To shut out almost all of the Third World's people from the European-dominated areas while still demanding control of the world's resources is to continue past injustices. Open borders cannot redress all injustices, nor do I advocate the mass movement of people from South to North; most people would rather not leave their homes and communities. However, the capitalist countries' current policies of excluding Third World people while insisting on access to Third World resources should be ended. Such hypocrisy is a fundamental feature of the war system. People who are shut out from riches and comforts derived at their expense ultimately will express their frustrations, perhaps through violence. Open borders may never occur as long as huge inequalities persist, but they constitute a long-term goal which, along with other goals for a peace system such as nuclear disarmament, provides vision and direction.

Boundaries between countries are only one kind of inequality, for there are significant borders within countries and within communities. From cities in the United States to villages in Pakistan or India, people are intensely divided today by income, ethnicity, caste, race, gender, and religion. Abolishing inequalities between and within countries is all part of the same process of achieving economic justice, and this process is at odds with corporate demands for unrestricted mobility of capital and resources.

National Self-Determination

Borders, of course, have positive value for those seeking self-determination. Socialist revolutions such as those in China and Cuba represented radical struggles to establish boundaries against imperialism. They restricted the mobility of foreign capital and at the same time redistributed land and created more private property. The justification for tight borders is lost, however, when they are used to facilitate internal exploitation and oppression, which was the case in the Soviet Union, in its former Eastern European satellites, and in much of the Third World.

Imperialism allowed the consolidation of nationalism in the rich capitalist countries, but nationalism has rarely been consolidated in the Third World. Those Third World areas that were exploited experienced sharpened internal divisions. Because of deliberate policies of the ruling classes, along with increased competition for diminishing resources and intensified class divisions, various combinations of class, ethnic, religious, and linguistic oppression now prevail within Third World countries. In many instances these conditions are producing demands for self-determination similar to those made during the earlier struggles for national independence from the European powers.

People in the Third World must cope with a multi-layered global system of exploitation. At each layer, the struggles against exploitation usually confine themselves to the most visible symbols and immediate instruments of oppression, whether a local military garrison, a landlord, or a dominant religious group. Sometimes these struggles represent the desires of local or incipient elites to control territory and government. In most independence struggles these strands have been mixed up. Establishing new borders against oppressive rule is part of the complex road to a peace system. People cannot begin to relate to one another freely and communities cannot become self-reliant unless they are free from linguistic, cultural, and economic oppression.

But at the same time borders can play only a limited and temporary role in ending exploitation. Borders are defensive measures, and they are justified only if issues such as class inequalities, the oppression of women, and environmental despoliation are being resolved. In areas where significant minorities live care must be taken to ensure that their rights are not endangered by the demands of national self-determination. The mixed results over the last few decades of independence movements and various kinds of governments in the Third World underscore that we must now ask questions more insistently about the long-term direction of various struggles: Are they truly committed to reducing conflicts and violence by increasing economic justice at all levels, from the family to the neighborhood, from the nation-state to the world? Self-determination can not become a license to oppress and exploit.

Local Self-Reliance

Another goal for a peace system is to reduce the scale of economic enterprises and make them more amenable to community control. A pioneer in peace studies,

Johan Galtung, has suggested that communities should strive to be self-reliant:

> [T]he basic rule of self-reliance is this: produce what you need using your own resources, internalizing the challenges this involves, growing with the challenges, neither giving the most challenging tasks (positive externalities) to somebody else on whom you become dependent, nor exporting negative externalities to somebody else to whom you do damage and who may become dependent on you.
>
> For instance, an obvious way of preventing pollution of rivers from riverside factories would be to force the management of the factory to drink downstream water . . . .Those who have made the beds should have an obligation to lie upon them.[25]

Self-reliant communities should become the fundamental building blocks for a peace system. Today, however, "community" in the sense of a non-exploitative and non-violent nurturing unit does not exist. Violence is rife in the home, in the streets, between religious groups, between races, and between landlords and landless tenants.

The reconstruction of communities first requires putting more power into the hands of local government. This does not necessarily mean local-government ownership. Patterns of ownership can be diverse, determined by local traditions and preferences, and they certainly can include private property. But communities must be able to shape the laws and policies that protect their own economic and environmental goals and that enable them to exercise democratic control over corporations.

Economic planning and control over investments is also essential. As Gar Alperovitz and Jeff Faux have noted for the United States:

> The fundamental answer to the increasingly short-term horizons in the private sector is a coherent full-production plan which reduces long-term investment uncertainty. Without firm guidelines to hold on to, public officials are vulnerable to the demands of any strong constituency that demands something they have the legal power to give. Only the existence of a specific plan gives government officials a way to defend themselves against the conflicting pressures of contending interests and constituencies. The more explicit the plan, moreover, the more an official is restrained from exercising arbitrary power . . . .Only an explicit plan, finally, provides the citizen with clear criteria to judge and discipline the bureaucracy.[26]

Today corporations can and do plan; indeed, they regard planning as essential. Now local governments must do likewise and develop economic plans that are as meaningful and comprehensive.

For local planning and investment to succeed, three weaknesses of local government prevalent in the United States and probably present in most other countries must be remedied:

~ The federal government has largely exhausted the tax base, making it politically difficult for state and local governments to raise revenues. This is one reason why so many state governments in the United States are in financial crisis today.

~ The use of vast amounts of tax resources for military spending has become an "industrial policy" affecting every community in the United States and has linked local jobs and property values to the continuation of huge levels of military spending.

~ Corporations can move in and out of communities and countries at will, which makes communities economically vulnerable to the power of corporations.

It will be difficult to free communities from the war system's daily violence until national policies lower federal tax burdens, cut the military budget, and control the behavior of corporations. Establishing non-oppressive communities also may require local democratic structures that extend to the global level. The tasks of building community locally and achieving economic justice globally are inseparable.

One broad principle for regulating international business is that the mobility of capital and commodities should not exceed the mobility of people. This responds to the reality that capital and goods mobility, without corresponding people mobility, allow vast areas of poverty and enormous wage differences unrelated to labor productivity, notwithstanding the lore of capitalism's textbooks. The intent is not to close borders or to stop trade, but rather to free people. Trade and the movement of goods are often beneficial, and economic intercourse among people helps overcome the kinds of prejudices and parochialism that can easily degenerate into exploitation and violence.

Galtung has proposed another principle for restructuring the trade system so that it is mutually supportive, not exploitative. He recommends that trade between countries "be carried out so that the net balance of costs and benefits, including externalities for the parties to the exchange, be as equal as possible."[27] To make this principle operational, production of any item entering into world trade must adhere to minimum international standards, as noted above.

Finally, there is the question of strategy. One basic reality of the war system is that exploiting classes have important connections with those outside the community on whom they rely for their local power. For example, landlords and moneylenders rely on the military power of the state to protect their properties and privileges. Dowry murders in India occur because the killers go scot free and there is practically no enforcement of anti-dowry laws. In the southern United States, local white supremacists relied on state police powers and a non-interventionist federal government to keep African-Americans in bondage long after the Civil War. An important corollary is that when oppressed groups rise up, they generally require support from outside the community to avoid being annihilated. Outside support was as necessary for African-Americans in the Mississippi Delta civil rights movement as it is now for tribal people in the Amazon forest fighting dams financed by the World Bank.

Restructuring the International Trade System

One argument used by the most powerful capitalist countries to justify their immense weapons arsenals is that they must maintain "freedom of the seas." This term has meant, of course, not only freedom of the seas, per se, but also free international trade. But these "freedoms" have long been an excuse for imperialist aggression, occupation of others' lands, and exploitation of the powerless. For centuries powerful countries have arrogated to themselves the authority to dictate what secure international trade shall mean and under what rules international trade shall be conducted. Abandoning this kind of coercion is an essential part of building a peace system.

Countries and communities that want to trade should be free to do so. But those countries and communities that do not want to trade, or that wish to impose restrictions upon it, also should be free to do so. This freedom of choice does not exist today. For example, the South African military has waged war on its neighboring "front-line" states — Angola, Botswana, Mozambique, Zambia, and Zimbabwe — to make these countries physically dependent on trade routes through South Africa.

In the long term we need a United Nations armed force to guarantee the security of international trade. This would remove the rationale of any single country or bloc of countries, whether it be the United States, Japan, Germany, or the European Economic Community, to maintain a huge navy and other armed forces. An international force under the auspices of the United Nations could be a transitional step to a world in which trade would not require armed force at all and in which people would be free to move as they wished. A number of steps are necessary for this force to be feasible and democratic. The veto power for the five nuclear-weapons states in the Security Council must be abolished and the ability of national military forces to wage large-scale attacks must be eliminated. The fact that the United Nations sanctioned the recent U.S.-led war against Iraq starkly demonstrates the current domination of nuclear-weapons powers, especially the United States, and reinforces the need to abolish the veto and democratize the United Nations.

Reforming The International Monetary System[28]

The last few decades of global exploitation may well be termed "monetary imperialism," because of the ways in which the capitalist monetary system has kept Third World wages far below the relative productivity of Third World workers. Economic theory asserts that if labor is sufficiently productive, wages can be higher and prices lower at the same time. This supposedly explains the relatively high wages and material consumption in capitalist countries. However, a comparison of the prices of goods at present exchange rates reveals that the same dollar can purchase more in Mexico, Bangladesh, or Brazil than it can in New York, Paris, or Tokyo. One explanation is the relative productivity of workers in capitalist countries. The average amount of investment and efficient equipment available to Mexican farmers and workers is far lower than in France, Japan, or the United States. Thus, they produce fewer goods per unit time. However, the differences between wages in capitalist countries and Third World wages at present exchange rates are much larger than the differences in productivity. This is because the currencies in various Third World countries are valued much lower than the productivity of their workers relative to the capitalist countries. This explains why the purchasing power of U.S. dollars, French francs, or Japanese yen in Mexico, Bangladesh, or Brazil exceeds that of local currencies.

The international monetary system does not base currency values, as it should, on the relative productivity of workers. Rather, currency exchange rates are set on the basis of balance-of-payments and capital-flow considerations. This creates negative impacts within Third World and capitalist countries. Widespread misery in Third World countries is related to the undervalued price of their labor and products relative to those of the wealthy capitalist countries. Under these circumstances, Third World countries face a structural disadvantage in their trade relations. The extent to which the goods and labor of Third World countries are undervalued can be gauged by calculating the amount of time people in capitalist countries work to import Third World resources and finished products. Less than five percent of the monetized labor time in the capitalist countries is necessary to pay for all Third World imports including oil, raw materials, agricultural products, and manufactured goods. It is not surprising that the Third World cannot purchase much from the industrialized capitalist countries or that the Third World has chronic balance-of-payments deficits.

For capitalist countries, low wages in the Third World mean that it is cheaper and more advantageous to shift manufacturing to the Third World, which as already noted, depresses wages within the United States and elsewhere. Undervaluing Third World natural resources also encourages a throw-away society in capitalist countries with grave environmental consequences across the globe.

To reverse these trends, the currencies of Third World countries need to be reevaluated to bring relative wages in line with relative productivity. Instead of basing currencies on a country's balance of payments, driven by the requisites of capital mobility, we should create a system which values currencies by the relative productivity of labor. An international monetary system with the following features could meet these requirements:

~ Currency exchange rates would be determined according to the relative prices of "baskets" of comparable consumer goods.
~ A world central bank would issue a new international currency with fixed purchasing power in every country according to the "baskets" of consumer goods.
~ And every country would maintain stocks of commodities of monetary value proportional to that of the country's foreign trade as a guarantee against balance-of-payment deficits.

Such a system would provide a stable, non-inflationary international currency with real commodity backing, without requiring management of each commodity's price. Countries would be free to pursue internal monetary and fiscal policies according to their internal needs and best wisdom. Their currencies would be automatically revalued or devalued accordingly, as the price of the "basket" of basic consumer goods went up or down locally.[29]

This system would mean substantial reevaluations of the currencies of Third World countries, especially for those nations with the lowest relative wages under the current system. The direct result would be to increase relative wages in the Third World. This, in turn, would have several significant effects:

~ Third World purchasing power for importing industrial goods and foodstuffs would increase.
~ Upward pressure on commodity prices would reduce the real burden of Third World debt repayment.
~ The cheap labor incentive for multinational corporations to invest in the Third World would be drastically reduced.
~ And capitalist and Third World countries could more easily lower trade barriers, since much of the incentive to be protectionist comes from the existence of arbitrary wage differences across boundaries.

The negative economic effects of this kind of restructuring would be the increased prices of many resources consumed by the North and reduced profits for many multinational corporations, banks, and other capitalists. But unlike the oil price increase in the 1970s and early 1980s, which was caused by a cartel arrangement and a price set much higher than cost, the price increases proposed here would come from higher relative wages in the Third World. As with the abolition of boundaries between countries, establishing an international monetary system in which countries and communities can relate to one another on equal terms should be viewed as a long-term goal.

There are also four short-term policies which could help reform the international monetary system.

~ First, that part of the Third World debt on which interest payments and fees have exceeded the original principal should be canceled, because the United States unfairly raised real interest rates on these loans after 1979 to maintain the dollar's world position.

~ Second, banks in all countries should disclose the identities of the holders of all foreign accounts in excess of $50,000, and obedience to this rule should be a minimum condition of allowing banks to participate in international transactions. Similar conditions should be imposed on foreign holdings of stocks, commodity futures, bonds, and other financial instruments. This will help expose, punish, and deter corrupt transactions that maintain dictators in power, support the Iran-contra types of secret weapons deals, aggravate the Third World debt crisis, and cause unexpected bank failures, such as those in the savings-and-loan industry in the United States.

~ Third, a tax should be levied on all foreign exchange transactions to reduce currency speculation.

~ Finally, depositors should be required to disclose income sources and expected areas of tax liability before a foreign bank deposits or purchases financial instruments exceeding $25,000. This would reduce illegal capital flight, tax evasion, and money laundering.

For too long, bank accounts in Switzerland, the Cayman Islands, and other "havens" have sheltered drug dealers, the Mobutus and the Marcoses, and the defrauders of the U.S. savings and loans. The rules proposed here restrain these unfair manipulations of people's hard-earned money while creating the necessary conditions for a transition to a new international monetary system.

RESTRUCTURING WITHIN COUNTRIES

Local inequities and exploitation, particularly those based on class, gender, or ethnicity must also be redressed in a peace system. For large numbers of people throughout the world, simple demands for jobs at decent wages, reliable and clean drinking water, affordable health care, and good education seem out of reach. Yet, there are quite enough resources in the world to provide everyone with jobs, water, health care, and education. The problem is unequal control over resources. It is not a lack of leaders' political will that prevents water, vaccinations, and vitamin A from reaching needy children, but rather the coercive presence of political, military, and economic power that is exercised to maintain the present order.

The class structure in most countries, especially Third World countries, is highly polarized. Third World elites are intimately connected to the global war system, and their privileges depend upon its maintenance. They derive a good portion of the money and weapons they use to repress their subjects from outside sources. In return, they provide the kind of "healthy" business environment for corporations which NSC-68 sought to establish after World War II.

To weaken the power of these elites, progressive forces in both capitalist and Third World countries should pursue six goals of economic justice:
   (1) guaranteed employment along with adequate job training and unemployment compensation;
   (2) minimum wages high enough to support a small family above locally defined poverty levels;
   (3) adequate day-care facilities;
   (4) security of people in their homes, whether they live in village huts or shanty cities;
   (5) guaranteed health care; and
   (6) minimum rules of accountability and responsibility for corporations operating wholly within single countries, similar to the rules governing multinational corporations.

Kerala

The experience of the state of Kerala on the southwestern coast of India demonstrates how progress towards these goals can be achieved, even in relatively poor areas. Kerala is the most densely populated state in India. Blessed with spices, coconut trees, and lovely lagoons, Kerala was the target of the early European traders and imperialists. Kerala also has a long tradition of militant struggle against exploitation. Its people gave the British imperialists a rough time for almost a century and a half. And in 1957 the people of Kerala elected a government led by the Communist Party of India — much to the displeasure of the Congress Party which dominated the country.

Over a period of two decades, leftist forces in and out of government organized nonviolent struggles for land, minimum wages, and other economic and social goals. These struggles took place in the context of a multi-party electoral system and they resulted in considerable redistribution of land, minimum wage laws, reduced caste prejudices, less discrimination against women, and even modest pensions for retired agricultural workers. Because these popular struggles were led by grassroots organizations in Kerala's towns and villages, the reforms have remained in place even though leftist parties have won and lost power in the state several times since 1957.

Real improvements in people's lives, measured in standards of human welfare, demonstrate the accomplishments of Kerala. The table on the following page shows life expectancy and infant mortality for Kerala, India, and the United States. It also shows per capita gross national product (GNP). Even though Kerala has a lower per-capita income than all of India, not to mention that of the United States, the human indicators of its well-being are closer to those of the United States, where the GNP is one hundred times higher and the level of material consumption is dramatically greater. In fact, overall conditions of life in Kerala are better than those prevailing in many U.S. inner cities. Kerala has the highest rates of literacy and newspaper readership in India. It has a vigorous "people's science movement," which has popularized scientific education. And it has a remarkably low infant mortality rate relative to the rest of India.

Table 1   **Quality of Life Indicators of Kerala Compared to India and the U.S.A. (1979-80)**

Countries:	Kerala	India	U.S.A.
GNP per capita (in U.S $)	182	290	17,458
Adult literacy (percent)	78	43	96
Life expectancy (years)	68	57	75
Infant mortality (per 1,000)	27	86	10
Birth rate (per 1,000)	22	32	16

Source: Richard Franke and Barbara Chasin, "Development Without Growth: The Kerala Experiment", Technology Review, April 1990, p. 45.

Kerala has shown that the worst consequences of poverty can be substantially reduced with radical reforms, coupled with grassroots empowerment, private property, and a multi-party electoral system. Moreover, this can be accomplished without shifting burdens elsewhere. It is also important to remember that despite long odds, communists with a practical dedication to democratic values and economic equity have been at the forefront of this achievement.

The difference in infant mortality between Kerala and the rest of India is one measure of the structural violence that can be eliminated with even a modicum of distributional justice. Kerala's low infant mortality rate is due to the fact that its health care resources, though scarce, are directed to the needs of the poor and stress prevention. The death rate of infants in the rest of India is three times higher. If India had Kerala's infant mortality rate, one-and-a-half million infant deaths could be prevented every year. No external aid or resources were needed to achieve this success — only a more equitable allocation of resources.

These successes occurred despite considerable difficulties. Coastal Kerala, where most of the state's people live, is one of the most densely populated areas in the world. Complete land reform has been blocked by rich property owners from Kerala and outside the state. Big industry and large-scale fishing enterprises have caused environmental damage to the land and to the state's oceanic resources, which has especially hurt the poor. And serious poverty, unemployment, inadequate housing, and other shortages persist.

Still, Kerala's commitment to redistributing land, setting minimum wages, ending poverty, and building grassroots democracy has created an important model of development. Kerala deserves close attention and international study not only by the countries of the Third World but also by those of Eastern Europe, by the Soviet Union, and by China, all of which are seeking to marry multi-party political systems with social justice and some private property ownership.

The gains in Kerala occurred where political forces committed to redistributive justice built grassroots organizations in the face of hostile political parties. Today, those gains have been consolidated and cannot be easily undone by other political parties, because power resides in the towns and villages of Kerala. No party would dare dismantle the land reform or minimum wage laws. The accomplishments of the people of Kerala are a beacon for the future.

Grassroots Internationalism

In the United States, as in other capitalist countries, it is necessary to prevent corporations or national governments from transferring problems elsewhere. One of the most hopeful developments in this regard has been the proliferation of people's efforts to link grassroots groups, non-governmental organizations, and local governments across national borders. In the United States, some of this movement came in response to the Reagan era. Throughout the 1980s conservative forces worked to strengthen large corporations, the Pentagon, the nuclear weapons establishment, and the rich, but at times they also promoted decentralization. During this period, public interest groups, city and state governments, environmental and peace activists, and unions implemented progressive local laws ranging from CFC-recycling statutes to assistance for "sister cities" in Nicaragua and South Africa.

Hundreds of churches in the United States defied the Immigration and Naturalization Service and provided sanctuary to people fleeing from the wars in Central America, which were financed and sponsored by the U.S. government. Despite the risks of imprisonment, despite considerable personal and financial expenses, they took a powerful stand against U.S. foreign policy. They did not ask whether the refugees were "economic" or "political" refugees, a false construct designed to discriminate against those fleeing from capitalist-supported authoritarian regimes such as El Salvador. These acts of solidarity and compassion created a basis for long-term cooperation between the people of the United States and those of Central America.

Or consider potters from the United States who helped build pottery cooperatives in Nicaragua in the midst of the Contra war against the Sandinista government. Potters for Peace and dozens of similar organizations helped Nicaraguans not only resist the U.S.-sponsored terrorism but also reconstruct their country. Ben Linder, a Portland engineer killed by the Contras while he helped to design a hydroelectric dam, worked in this spirit of resistance and creation. Similarly, an international effort helped Nicaraguans market their coffee in the United States despite the trade embargo imposed by the U.S. government.

Another example of a successful struggle within capitalist countries has been the effort to halt corporations from exporting hazardous wastes to the Third World. Networks of environmental groups made Third World dumping politically difficult and in 1989 helped pressure nations to sign an international agreement banning toxic waste disposal outside the country of origin unless it conforms to certain minimum standards. With this new global norm, local struggles against dumping can link up with and support similar struggles worldwide.

One economic innovation has been "alternative trade," by which people in the wealthy capitalist countries have attempted to eliminate the huge price mark-ups and profits that characterize most North-South trade. Some organizations now import goods directly from cooperatives in the Third World, where the workers are paid a guaranteed fraction of the final sales prices (large corporations often charge a final sales price several times higher than the wholesale price paid in the Third World).

There has also been the remarkable rise of the municipal-foreign-policy movement. Cities and communities across borders have become linked and actively have begun to assist each other with concrete problem-solving. For example, the city of St. Paul, Minnesota, has supported the struggle of the people of Lawaaikamp in South Africa to prevent authorities from bulldozing their homes. After the population dwindled from 5,000 to 1,200 under apartheid's pressure, the citizens of Lawaaikamp were finally able to fight back with support from the people of St. Paul. Visits, telephone calls, telegrams, letter campaigns, and lobbying by Minnesotan local officials, opinion-leaders, and citizens convinced the government of South Africa to allow the present inhabitants of Lawaaikamp to remain and the previous inhabitants to apply for resettlement.[30] Another example occurred in September 1990, when four hundred representatives of local governments from forty countries met at the United Nations to discuss how municipalities could cooperate to foster environmental protection and sustainable development worldwide.

The environmental movement presents still another hopeful example. In the 1970s, when scientists first hypothesized that chlorine emissions might damage the ozone layer, an international struggle began in the capitalist countries to phase out these chemicals. Gradually, however, it became clear that reducing the risk of severe ozone depletion would require the cooperation of all countries, including those in the Third World. This consensus, which began at the grassroots, led to an unprecedented treaty to phase out several ozone-depleting chemicals and to promote international cooperation to protect the earth's atmosphere.

Monetized and Non-Monetized Work

Annie Makhijani once said, "We should try to create a society in which it is never a tragedy to be pregnant."[31] Today, however, it is often a severe hardship to be a parent, maintain a home, look after sick members of one's family, and do any number of other labors which tend to be the domain of women. As Marilyn Waring, a feminist author and member of New Zealand's parliament suggests, national economic accounting must begin to include all the non-monetized work that is essential to our society.

Another shortfall of our current accounting system is that it usually excludes the non-monetized labor required to maintain the usefulness of goods. Thus, though it may take much longer to wash and iron a shirt over its lifetime than to produce it, economic accounting and product design do not systematically include shirt upkeep. Doing so would help us understand the subtle effects of the economy on our lives. When more women work in the monetized sector, for example, permanent press shirts proliferate. Manufacturers should provide estimates of both a product's expected lifetime and the amount of labor needed to maintain the product. Over the long haul, it may be that the construction techniques of the master carpenters who built Japanese temples, which have withstood earthquakes and the rigors of climate for centuries, are more valuable and productive than the modern designers who glue together pieces of plywood.

Of course, one need not monetize all aspects of social activity to recognize and "pay" for its social worth. Pensions and social security benefits should be made available to anyone who chooses to parent a child or care for the sick. Paid pregnancy and parenting leave could be made a social rather than corporate expenditure, as is done in France. Parenting work also can be indirectly recognized as part of the money economy by making the earnings of both parents "community" property that is split 50-50 in the event of divorce. This is already the case in some countries and some local jurisdictions such as California, but it would be a revolutionary concept in most of the Third World, that would provide women there with greater security.

Economic Culture

Perhaps the most insidious aspect of the war system is the profit-driven, individualistic character it breeds in its inhabitants. This ideology which lies at the heart of capitalism discounts the well-being of neighbors, other countries, and future generations.

The ethical justification for the rugged individualist in capitalism is that the "invisible hand" of the free market ultimately benefits everyone. This maxim, stated two hundred years ago by Adam Smith, is clearly deficient. Most people living under the rule of capitalism are desperately poor; indeed, vast numbers are so marginalized that they cannot even *enter* the marketplace. The environmental realities are equally dismal. And war and violence are widespread, with military expenditures far outpacing those for health, education, housing, and environmental clean-up.

To be sure, some aspects of capitalism are worthwhile. Capitalist theory is based on the idea that small-scale property is the foundation of economic growth. That notion, however, belongs to capitalist textbooks and mythology, not to the realm of history and fact. The capitalist system as it has been, and is, makes the small-scale enterprise dependent on large-scale corporations. Very often the latter destroys the former. If one includes local production in cottage industries around the world, one can see that the net result of two hundred years of capitalism has been, not to promote, but to destroy small private-property owners. There are far more landless people in India and Africa today than there were two hundred years ago. Family farms have been rapidly disappearing since the turn of the century.

Much of this history began with the English enclosure movement, when powerful landlords ousted poor peasants from their tenancy and from their common property rights to reap greater profits from an expanding wool trade. A system which truly emphasized small-scale initiative could in fact be highly beneficial, but this is not the natural course for capitalism.

Community property and individual property both can be compatible with the principle of local self-reliance. But property ownership must be overseen by an equitable global order with rules for corporations and trade that give communities real control over their economies. The rights of private property cannot override the rights of the people living today, or of future generations. To protect human rights, we must view property in the context of usufruct, that is, our need to employ land, capital, and technology to provide for ourselves, our children, our families, and our communities, while maintaining and enhancing the value of our resources for our descendants. Protecting the future gives meaning to the present.

Property ownership cannot and should not be divorced from the question of incentive. Capitalism has long operated under the assumption that there should be no limit to riches. The result has been fantastic riches for some, but also unfathomable exploitation, poverty, and misery for others. Incentives for all require redistribution and limits to riches.

Egyptian civilization, the feudal kingdoms of the Middle Ages, and the imperial epochs of Europe and Asia were all progenitors of modern economic culture. They all depended upon the relentless exploitation of land, resources, and people. In ancient Greece, a society often held up as a model democracy, neither women nor slaves were citizens, which meant that "consumerism" flourished only among a small minority.

In all these systems the existence of vast riches created two kinds of poverty: absolute poverty, in which people died for want of food, water and shelter; and relative poverty, in which wants multiplied because of the cultural example set by the rich and the advertising power of corporations. These two have not always been separate. Desires among the poor generated by the culture of consumerism often have taken precedence over basic needs for food, water, and shelter. In the competition for resources between vegetables and VCRs, the latter often win.

Capitalist culture, which was once limited to the ruling classes, kings, feudal lords, capitalist merchants, and slave-owners, has now come within reach of large numbers of people. A dramatic increase in human consumption and production has been made possible by three factors: the rapid spread of energy-intensive machinery; the exploitation of vast new areas of natural resources, including those underground and under the sea; and the expropriation of resources from the Third World. A culture of consumerism, characterized by permanent poverty despite increasing consumption, has now thoroughly entrenched itself in the capitalist countries. Consumerist culture also has seized the popular imagination of rich and poor in communist and Third World countries. The foundation of this culture is that it knows no limits to consumption. There is no notion of "enough."

Today, global environmental damage is often blamed on population growth in the Third World. However, as we have seen, if one-third of the people continue consuming more than ninety percent of the world's resources, most people in the world will continue to live in great poverty on small bits of land. The CEO of the Coca Cola Corporation is pleased that people in the United States drink more soft drinks than water. However, in terms of the quality of one's teeth and the condition of one's body, high soda consumption represents a step back from the time when one drank a few glasses of clean water every day. Consumerism creates desires for "high-definition television" with bigger and bigger screens, but we do not seem to notice that we are seeing lower quality programs. Today, a typical "middle class family" consumes more resources than Marie Antoinette did when she advised the poor to eat cake. Certainly the degree to which we have deprived future generations by despoiling the environment and endangering the atmosphere is much greater than that done by feudal lords and kings of centuries past.

The "population problem" frightens those who now gobble up the earth's resources, who fear the consequences of poor people consuming at a "desirable" standard that the wealthy have established through popular culture. But it is consumption by the world's rich, not by the poor, that threatens to exhaust the world's resources. In a sense, the wealthy are right to be afraid. With present levels of technology and a culture of limitless greed, the poor cannot become just like the wealthy without destroying the earth in the process. However, this is not a problem of population per se. With far fewer people, the same greed-driven structure would still despoil the earth. Today we see the spectacle of dissatisfied people with several enormous homes. In Beverly Hills a home of 6,000 square feet becomes too small and the owners move into one with 10,000 square feet, and then another home with 50,000 square feet and a bowling alley. The requirements of energy resources to heat and air-condition these modern palaces are so great that no conceivable production pattern could satisfy even a considerably smaller population with equal desires. We may say that there are two population problems: for the rich there are too many poor, and for the poor there are too many rich.

A peace system based on cooperation within and between communities and based on local self-reliance cannot be established securely unless we also establish the principle of "enough" as part of our economic culture. The ideology of limitless consumption goes hand and hand with that of limitless greed, limitless profit, and limitless riches. These beliefs have produced inequalities, nuclear weapons, militarized borders, and many other means of violence to protect the rich and privileged from the legitimate needs of the poor. Yet even for the rich and their children, limitless consumption is no guarantee for human happiness.

The culture of greed and exploitation also creates in the poor the idea that they must become rich. The few who escape poverty usually become loyal to the dominant economic culture and adopt its values. These structural conditions give the war system its resilience.

In global apartheid, the hungers, desires, tears, joys, and even the humanity of the dispossessed do not register as part of the economic system. The process by which we rid the world of economic depravity and excess is surely the same one by which we can help end the suffering of the children who die of want and of the parents who must bury them. That will be the process by which the "peace" of the war system will be replaced by a genuine peace in which neighborliness and friendship flourish.

NOTES

1. Francis Fukuyama, "The End of History? As Us Our Mad Century Closes, We Find the Universal State," *Washington Post*, July 30, 1989, p. Cl.

2. *Ibid*, p. C2.

3. Profits vary from year to year depending mainly on aluminum prices and total production.

4. Fui S. Tsikata, *Essays from the Ghana-Valco Renegotiations* (New York: U.N. Center on Transnational Corporations, 1986). The post-1982 data on Valco are drawn from this source, unless otherwise stated.

5. The calculation is based on the thermal input it would take to generate the same amount of energy at the rate of 11 million Joules per kilowatt hour (electrical). The energy in a barrel of oil costing about $32 per barrel amounts to 5.5 billion Joules. Most of Ghana's oil imports are for the transport sector, though some is used for electricity generation as well.

6. Jon Halliday and Gavan McCormack, *Japanese Imperialism Today* (Middlesex, England: Penguin Books, 1973), pp. 69-70.

7. Daniel Nelson, "Asia Must Plant More Trees," *Financial Times*, April 11, 1979, p. 39.

8. See Stephen Schlesinger and Stephen Kinzer, *Bitter Fruit: The Untold Story of the American Coup in Guatemala* (New York: Anchor Press/Doubleday, 1982).

9. Lourdis Beneria, "Gender and the Global Economy," in Arthur McEwan and William Tabb, eds., *Instability and Change in the World Economy* (New York: Monthly Review Press, 1989), p. 254.

10. There are many studies which bring out clearly the connections between imperialism and capitalism. I mention two: Eduardo Galeano, *Open Veins of Latin America* (New York: Monthly Review Press, 1973) and Walter Rodney, *How Europe Underdeveloped Africa* (Washington DC: Howard University Press, 1981) Rosa Luxemburg, *Accumulation of Capital* (London: Routledge and K Paul, 1951) also discussed some of the connections and tried to organize them into a theory of capitalist economy.

11. Dean Acheson, congressional testimony in 1944, quoted by William Appleman Williams in "Large Corporations and American Foreign Policy," in *Corporations and the Cold War* (New York: Monthly Review Press, 1969), pp. 95-6.

12. National Security Council Memorandum 68, as cited in Thomas Etzold and John L. Gaddis, *Containment: Documents on American Foreign Policy and Strategy 1945-50* (New York: Columbia University Press, 1979), p. 401.

13. *Ibid.*

14. The earliest publication which I have come across which explores the parallel between capitalism and South Africa is an essay by Gernot Kohler, "Global Apartheid," World Order Models Project, Working Paper No. 7, 1978.

15. Arjun Makhijani, "Oil Prices and the Crises of Debt and Unemployment," unpublished draft report prepared for the International Labour Office of the United Nations, 1983.

16. Beryl Sprinkel, congressional testimony of March 19, 1984, as reported in Stuart Auerbach, "Trade Deficit Surges in February," *The Washington Post*, March 30, 1984, p. F11.

17. R.T. MacNamar, quoted by Susan George, *A Fate Worse than Debt: the World Financial Crisis and the Poor* (New York: Grove Press, 1988), p. 67.

18. *Ibid.*, p. 68.

19. *Ibid.*

20. *Ibid.*, Chapter 7.

21. Quoted by Gar Alperovitz and Jeff Faux, *Rebuilding America: A Blueprint for the New Economy* (New York: Pantheon Books, 1984) p. 239.

22. Quoted by Richard J. Barnet and Ronald E. Muller, *Global Reach* (New York: Simon and Schuster, 1974), pp. 14-15.

23. This is a large discussion in and of itself, and like other subjects, I will only raise the question here and not pursue it. A useful starting point for that enquiry are two

publications of the Study of Democratic Institutions: Scott Buchanan, *The Corporation and the Republic* (Santa Barbara: Study of Democratic Institutions, 1958) and W.H. Ferry, *The Corporation and the Economy — Notes Followed by a Discussion* (Santa Barbara: Study of Democratic Institutions, 1959).

24. When the British conquered Bangladesh in the mid-eighteenth century, it was one of the world's centers for fine textile manufacturing. Indeed, the British protected the budding domestic textile industry in Lancashire by prohibiting the sale of Bangladesh textiles in England. A few decades after conquest, however, Bangladesh and nearby areas (present day India) lay in economic ruins, with perhaps a third of the population dead from famine and disease. As the proportion of industrial workers in England rose, the population in Bangladesh declined.

25. Johan Galtung, "Towards a New Economics: On the Theory and Practice of Self-Reliance," in Paul Ekins, ed., *The Living Economy* (London: Routledge, Kegan and Paul, 1986), p. 101.

26. Gar Alperovitz and Jeff Faux, *op. cit.*, pp. 254-5.

27. Johan Galtung, *op. cit.*, p. 102.

28. For a detailed discussion of this proposal see Arjun Makhijani and Robert S. Browne, "Restructuring the International Monetary System," *World Policy Journal*, 3:1, Winter 1985-86, pp. 59-82.

29. Johan Galtung, *op. cit.*, p. 102.

30. Richard Trubo, "Striking a Blow for Freedom," *Bulletin of Municipal Foreign Policy*, Spring 1990, pp. 28-9. Today, wholesale destruction of townships and settlements is not only a feature of South African apartheid; it is a routine feature of economic life for the poor in the Third World, especially in large cities. Class divisions in the Third World are so strong that razing neighborhoods is called "beautification." The destruction of people's homes is one of the most egregious indications of the lack of economic democracy.

31. Annie Makhijani, personal conversation, 1986.

COMMUNITY

Grace Boggs, a long-time activist and social critic, is currently the Newsletter Editor of SOSAD, Save Our Sons And Daughters. Sharon Howell is a member of the U.S. Green Party and Associate Professor of Communications at Oakland University.

As seasoned activists living in Detroit, Boggs and Howell reflect upon the state of community and political participation in their own neighborhoods. They show how the war system, amplified through the mass media, has distanced people from the consequences of violence. What is needed, they argue, is a coherent progressive movement, such as the anti-war or civil rights movements of the 1960s, which can etch the principles of nonviolence onto the public consciousness.

Despite the well-publicized poverty, crime, unemployment, and hopelessness in Detroit, Boggs and Howell describe how a new, vibrant sense of community is being created by local women who lost their children to inner-city violence. Calling into question the notions of manhood that turn children into killers, Detroit's mothers, sisters, and grandmothers are building a peace system by organizing protests, reclaiming their streets, and demanding a renewed respect for life.

CULTURE AND COMMUNICATION

Grace Boggs and Sharon Howell

For a brief moment in the late 1980s it seemed as if "peace" were at hand. Today, that moment seems very far away. Polls tell us that more than 90 percent of our citizens are celebrating the U.S. "victory" over Iraq. Yellow ribbons are everywhere. Military force is the unquestioned hallmark of American international power, and the "peace movement" seems discredited and insignificant.

Thinking about peace feels strangely out of step in a country gloating over winning a war. Yet there is perhaps no better moment to do so than now, when the war system has come out from the shadows and laid claim to center stage. Curtailed by defeat in Vietnam, frustrated in its efforts to defend an unending nuclear buildup, and humiliated by its inability to "rescue" American hostages in Iran, the war system and the cultural elements which support it finally have regained control of public life. Over the last ten years the war system has been rebuilding its power base, step by step: the invasions of Grenada and Panama, the bombing of Libya, the mining of Nicaraguan harbors, the escalation of "low intensity" warfare in El Salvador, and now the "Great Gulf War." All these events have brought war and the use of force back as legitimate means for solving global problems. Images celebrating destruction strut across our TV screens and headlines every day. They dominate the terms of public discourse, overwhelm dissent, and undermine the possibility of any sustained questioning of U.S. policy.

But behind all the media hype are the contradictions and challenges of a country having little left to offer the world but violence. Soon the parades end, the flags fade, the ribbons tatter, while the problems of day-to-day life worsen from inattention. Peace, not war, is the deepest longing of people. Peace, not war, requires time, energy, and imagination to be created and sustained. If the devastation of the people of Iraq shows anything, it is that those of us committed to creating a world based on harmony and mutual respect must take responsibility for looking squarely at the war system, for understanding how it has come to have such a hold on our national psyche, and for dismantling it. We, and we alone, must discover and nurture the pathways and processes of peacemaking.

The past decade has been a time not only of destruction but also of creation, imagination, and connection. Peace, after all, is not a final condition. It requires conscious, careful, and sustained effort. Peace is brought into being through choice, dialogue, reflection, and action. It does not just happen when the guns fall silent. Outside the view of the dominant culture and its media have been processes, actions, and ideas that are the beginning steps toward a culture that can nurture peace.

We are fortunate at this moment to be living in Detroit. Our streets are not cluttered with yellow bows and patriotic banners. As members of a city that is 72 percent African American, and that is made up primarily of women, children, and elders, we have been less swayed by the glibness of the war system and more aware of its hypocrisies and its mean-spiritedness. As Richard Joseph observed in a recent *New York Times* article:

> [M]ost African Americans cannot slip on blinders with practiced ease. Iraq's atrocities justified war while those of South Africa called for 'constructive engagement.' . . . It's easy to understand the skepticism of African Americans when George Bush of Willie Horton fame vetoes the 1990 Civil Rights Act and embraces Jesse Helms at the conclusion of a glaringly racist campaign, then declares that the war with Iraq is a case of 'right against wrong.' [1]

Even though many of our sons and daughters were on the "front lines," Detroiters have no illusions about why they were there. Most joined the army because it was safer for them to fight in a military operation, and offered better pay, than to try to survive in their own neighborhoods. While we were relieved about the limited loss of American lives, we now must face the harsh reality that during the month of the Gulf War more Americans were killed here at home by fellow Americans than died on the battlefield. How can it be that the only future we can think about for our children is that of leaving home, to be "safe" in the army?

With Detroit having one of the largest Iraqi and Arab populations in the non-Arab world, the death and pain of the Iraqi people was not so far away. What the American news cameras refused to show, we saw in the faces and lives of our neighbors. Iraqi-American families held memorial services for dead sons, their children talked of nightmares about the terror of bombings, mothers and fathers worried over loved ones and hometowns, and all of them suffered the indignity of being branded as "barbarians." Whatever the tensions that exist among various ethnic and racial groups in our city, the pain of the war has risen above them. Hand-written sheets covering doors and windows of Arab-American stores appeared every day saying simply, "Pray for Peace."

Hannah Arendt once argued that violence is the last death-grip of the state, and in Detroit it is clear how the war system is killing America. Over the past five years some 300 children have been shot annually, thirty to forty of them fatally. Driving through sections of the city, especially on the southeast and southwest sides near downtown, there are often more vacant lots than occupied buildings. Our schools are in chaos with almost half of our children entering seventh grade dropping out before graduation. There is no city hospital. Our infant mortality rate is higher than El Salvador's. The drug culture has taken over whole sections of the city, turning homes into prisons. The "American way of life" soldiers were supposed to be protecting has long been gone from the streets of Detroit.

Yet here in the midst of such devastation and hopelessness are the seeds of a new kind of peace, emerging through the development of a very different culture. In Detroit, as in other cities and towns, people not only are experiencing the death of the old ways of life but also are creating new ways of living, rooted in values that diverge from those of the dominant culture. Here, behind the hoopla heralding the return of gunboat diplomacy and high-tech war against the Third World, people are struggling to create a new culture capable of nurturance, patience, and compassion.

We are also fortunate in Detroit to have a rich history of political activism for peace and justice. Years of community struggles — for economic and social justice, for women's rights, for demilitarization — have given us a way to do more than just endure the massive destruction of our city. We, like thousands of Americans, have engaged in struggles to reconstruct it. Even during the Persian Gulf War, there was much about these efforts that gave us heart. Families with loved ones in the military refused to allow the army to be characterized as "volunteer" and focused public attention on the economic and social chaos that has made the military the only viable alternative for so many of our young people. Once the shooting and bombing in the Persian Gulf ended, these families were among the few voices demanding we avoid smug, self-congratulatory pronouncements that this war had "little cost" because it took so few American lives. As Donna Baker of the Military Family Support Network in Maine, whose son drove a tank in Operation Desert Storm, said:

> Just because this was a quick war with low casualties . . . the American people should not view war as the way to solve the problems of the world. I think we have to take a look at the destruction.[2]

Even though Congress acceded to the President's demand that we wage war, members of the Congressional Black Caucus stood firm. With one exception, they voted against the January 12th resolution to use military force against Iraq.[3] Throughout the war these black spokespersons continued to offer a critical perspective on the use of force and on U.S. foreign policy. As the troops came home, the voices of African-Americans raised pointed questions: Just what are our troops coming home to? How can it be that our troops are more likely to be killed here than in a war?

Women also exerted tremendous energy in organizing opposition and opening the imaginations of people to new forms of political action. Women of Arab, African, and European descent joined hands to lead silent protests honoring those who suffered in Iraq. They created "Walls of Women for Peace," held public wailings and flag washings to rid blood from the cloth, conducted vigils, circulated petitions, and wrote letters. The newly reshaped *Ms.* magazine published letters opposing intervention and provided a forum for activists and women in affected countries. Madre sponsored a Mother Courage Speaking Tour, which enabled women of all the countries involved in the war to speak in their own voices about the tragedy unleashed by U.S. military technology.

Grassroots opposition to the war sprouted in numerous other places. College campuses mobilized quickly with teach-ins and conferences. Computer networks such as PeaceNet offered not only up-to-date analysis and information but also ready-to-print letters to the editor and direct translations of Iraqi communiqués. Small, alternative publications chronicled resistance efforts around the country and around the world. Person-to-person diplomacy took on an urgent tone. Drawing on the experiences of witnesses for peace and of the practitioners of direct action, 167 people went to the Saudi-Kuwait border and set up a "peace camp." They stayed ten days into the bombing, until they were removed by Iraqi troops who could no longer guarantee their safety.[4] An international team of women went to Iraq and tried to negotiate a peace plan with Iraqi and Kuwaiti women.[5] A women's peace boat attempted to carry supplies into a Kuwait harbor, but was caught by U.S. navy men, who then harassed and beat the women on board.

All these alternative processes for peace-making were sources of strength and hope. But together these acts, however courageous and inspiring, were unable to provide a peaceful alternative to war. And once the ground war began, these critical voices became almost inaudible. A nation of peace-loving people had been transformed by the war system into a nation drunk on the blood of people it barely knew.

AMERICAN CULTURE AND THE WAR SYSTEM

Today our society has reached a precarious moment. The old division of the world between East and West is being replaced by the so-called "new world order." This new order, however, simply puts a new face upon the old war system. As Cynthia Enloe observed:

> [U]nder the old world order, East was pitted against West; in the new post 1989 order, North is pitted against a South personified by Saddam Hussein. Yet this allegedly "new" order remains stuck in the old presumptions that military power must be the principal tool with which to wield international influence.[6]

The "triumph" of U.S. military policy in Iraq is fundamentally the reassertion of an order imposed by force and maintained through force. But this order, a code word for the power and privilege of the United States, has been under siege for the last two decades both from abroad and at home. Profound challenges have been raised to the cultural assumptions that enable us to resort to force again and again while claiming the high moral ground.

The struggle against the war system came into sharp focus through the social movements of the 1960s and 1970s. The voices of new political actors introduced values that cut at the heart of the war system. The civil rights movement etched the principles of non-violence onto the public consciousness. The women's movement and the gay liberation movement raised our awareness of the entwining of manhood with the use of force. The anti-war and youth movements stripped away the hollow rhetoric of "just wars." Throughout the 1970s and 1980s struggles for disarmament wore away at the Pentagon's vision of a balance of terror, and grassroots resistance to U.S. involvement in Central America created close, personal ties between people of the North and people of the South. Native Americans, ecologists, new agers, and eco-feminists have all rejected long-held assumptions about our right to dominate the earth. These challenges by "outsiders" reject the values of the dominant culture. They have shaken the foundations of the war system and revealed powerful, new possibilities for peacemaking. As Vincent Harding has noted:

> I sense a time of tremendous opportunity, not an easy time, but a period of great possibilities ... [A]ll the hidden, driven, enslaved improvisers are thronging toward the stage, walking on it, creating the drama, reshaping the sets, reflecting the realities of the modern world. Of course, many of the old-line actors think that the show is still theirs, that they are at least in charge of saying which of the "newcomers" will be allowed to participate and how; they believe that their access to the levers of destruction gives them ultimate power to deny new creation. But they are wrong. The making of the United States — like the making of the modern world— is beginning again and the central question of our history is the question of our future: what kind of a nation do we want?[7]

Violence as Normal, Legitimate, and Essential

Under the war system violence has become a routine part of our culture. Recently the Senate Judiciary Committee released a report with the acknowledgment that "the United States is the most violent and self-destructive nation on Earth..." The report depicted "Americans killing, raping and robbing one another at a furious rate, surpassing every other country that keeps crime statistics." As one commentator reading this study observed:

> The nation's citizens committed a record number of killings in 1990—at least 23,300, or nearly three an hour — and a record number of rapes, robberies and assaults . . . .In 1990, the United States led the world with its murder, rape and robbery rates....When viewed from the national perspective these crime rates are sobering. When viewed from the international perspective, they are truly embarrassing. The report noted that the murder rate in the United States was more than twice that of Northern Ireland, which is torn by civil war; four times that of Italy, nine times England's and 11 times Japan's.[8]

The extent of violence in everyday life is obscured by its ordinariness. Violence rarely merits comment except when it takes the form of a particularly gruesome murder, or when it happens in a declared war zone. The daily terror experienced by women in the confines of their own homes, where one in three are battered and abused, or by children, three of whom die every day at the hands of their parents, underscores how much force rules our daily relationships. The dominant culture legitimates this violence by its silence.

Those struggling in our cities to eliminate violence are beginning to see that the violence practiced by our children is not far from that of a president who draws lines in the sand and prides himself on "kicking some ass." James Ricci, a local columnist in Detroit, has written:

> [V]iolence cannot be treated as a symptom of other problems, such as poverty and ignorance, but as a crisis unto itself. It is predicated on the grim reality that society condones the violent resolution of disputes, from the personal to the geopolitical . . . .[T]he punched-out wife, the belt-whipped toddler, the scuffling fourth-graders, the man shotgunned in a neighborhood quarrel, the ice-hearted drugland execution are interwoven fibers.[9]

Breaking the threads of violence in one sphere weakens the fabric in others. People professionally engaged in developing and teaching nonviolent conflict-resolution skills for businesses and communities were highly critical of Bush's plan for "peace" with Saddam Hussein. It was obvious shortly after Iraq's takeover of Kuwait that the Administration was deliberately choosing war. John Mack and Jeffrey Rubin, two of the nation's leading experts in conflict resolution, noted how our responses to Iraqi aggression seemed to demonstrate our desire to move toward violence:

We demonized and dehumanized our adversary . . . .
We denied our own contributions to the problem . . . .
We relied exclusively on the threatened use of force . . . .
We disregarded the other side's stated grievances and claims, while demanding unconditional surrender . . . .
We took no account of cultural differences . . . .
We offered a response that was disproportionate to the problem . . . .
We overcommitted ourselves to a course of action . . . .
We used public presentation of conditions . . . to intimidate the other side . . . .
We paid lip service to efforts at diplomatic solutions . . . .
We derogated the other side's conciliatory gestures . . . .
We insisted that the conflict be regarded as zero-sum . . . .[10]

It is precisely this legitimation of violence as a means of settling disputes which many are challenging today. Influenced by the principles of non-violent action brought into our culture by the civil rights, women's, and anti-war movements, elementary and high-school teachers across the country are preparing curricula on non-violent conflict resolution, university administrators are creating peace-studies programs, and communities are establishing local mediation boards, rape crisis centers, and shelters for battered women. Easy acceptance of violence is being challenged by public speeches, direct actions, op-eds, and movies. In a recent article in the newsletter of Save our Sons and Daughters (SOSAD), which is an organization of mothers in Detroit whose children have been killed by violence, the founder, Clemintine Barfield, writes:

> All too many people . . . have become immune to the violence around us. It has become to them 'just another event.' Yet the need is greater than ever for each of us to become a PEACEKEEPER in our schools and communities. Peace is not something that just comes automatically. It has to be struggled for through active cooperation for the benefit of all. That is why SOSAD is launching the PEACE-KEEPER PROJECT . . . .[W]e will teach young people to identify the situations that lead to conflict and violence and the methods they can use to resolve problems peacefully The youth trained in this Project will become leaders in the struggle to bring about peace in our communities. [11]

These new efforts encourage people to take direct responsibility for eliminating violence from their communities. Because these efforts have begun to wear away at the most essential premise of the war system, they have come under attack. Just as the calls for patience and sanctions against Iraq were denounced by voices of the war system, programs teaching children to solve problems with respect and care for one another are assaulted in school board meetings across the country for "interfering with family values." And rape crisis centers, domestic violence shelters, and conflict resolution programs are cut out of budgets so that the defense industry can continue to be profitable.

The Resurrection of Macho-man

The war system has reasserted itself not only by legitimating the use of force but also by restoring machismo to its "rightful place." In a culture where "manhood stands for aggression, winning at all costs, work over family, control over vulnerability," as Anna Quindlen observes, "war is inevitable."[12] The war system needs "men." Regardless of the gender of troops, those on the battlefront have to be masculine and tough.[13]

The stereotyped images of the male as aggressor and the women as nurturer gained credibility in the much-discussed Gender Gap between men who supported the Gulf War and women who opposed it. The women's movement, however, has called into question notions of manhood that justify turning our children into killers or cannon fodder. It has also argued that women's ways of knowing, thinking, and acting are essential to recreate civic life. As Elise Boulding notes:

> [W]omen offer a nonhierarchical, listening type of culture, and skills of dialogue and conflict resolution, to replace a culture based on the ability of the strong to dominate the weak. Generally, women operate with longer time horizons, are less reactive to crisis situations of the moment, and work harder to maintain relationships over the longer term, than men. They have more skills of empathy and therefore can see situations holistically. Because they have lived at the margins of the public sphere for so long, they are less emotionally invested in existing ways of doing things and can visualize alternative approaches to problems more easily.[14]

Of course, the entrance of women into public life has never been easy. Recent increases in the incidence of rape and wife abuse suggest that the response of the dominant culture has been to try to intimidate women into silence. The war system has steadfastly resisted any "feminization" of foreign policy. As Cynthia Enloe observes:

> The Gulf War . . . is being waged in the shadow of the sexual politics of another war. The Vietnam War has left a cultural legacy of gender guilt — the betrayed male vet. He has taken 15 years and a lot of celluloid and paper to create, but today he is a potent figure inspiring complex emotions. While there are at least 7,500

female American Vietnam veterans, it is the unappreciated, alienated male Vietnam vet whose image looms over the present war . . . .This war is about masculinity, just as all wars have been; but it is an historically and socially specific masculinity.[15]

The Denial of Consequences and the Fragmentation of Life

Finally, the war system depends upon cultural conventions that separate actions from results, the future from the present, ethics from politics, and our hearts from our heads. It is doubtful that we would tolerate the human, ecological, and spiritual costs of the war system if we really appreciated their magnitude. Even in today's United States, despite the violence in our streets, our hearts have not hardened to the point where we cannot respond to the crying of children or the suffering of others.

The war system, however, cannot tolerate compassion. It speaks a language devoid of emotion, context, and consequence. The patterns of thought it invokes depend upon images and metaphors that make it impossible to grapple with the real implications of our actions. George Lakoff, in an urgent message sent shortly before the United States began bombing Iraq, wrote:

> Metaphors can kill. The discourse over whether we should go to war . . . is a panorama of metaphor. Secretary of State Baker sees Saddam as "sitting on our economic lifeline." President Bush sees him as having a "stranglehold on our economy." General Schwartzkopf characterizes the occupation of Kuwait as a "rape" that is ongoing. The President says that the U.S. is in the Gulf to "protect freedom, protect our future and protect the innocent." The use of a metaphor....becomes pernicious when it hides realities in a harmful way ....Pain, dismemberment, death, starvation, and the death and injury of loved ones are not metaphorical. They are real and in a war they could afflict tens, perhaps hundreds of thousands, of real human beings, whether Iraqi, Kuwaiti or American.[16]

Our discourse on international relations is filled with these kinds of metaphors: "war as politics by other means," "strength as military might," "just wars," and "America as a hero." These phrases are not neutral. They provide a basis for thinking that deadens our capacity to respond to actual consequences.[17]

These metaphors contain a vocabulary intended to remove us from reality. In her groundbreaking study on the language used at the Pentagon, Carol Cohn reports:

> [Language] reveals a whole series of culturally grounded and culturally

acceptable mechanisms that make it possible to work in institutions that foster the proliferation of nuclear weapons, to plan mass incineration of millions of human beings for a living. Language that is abstract, sanitized, full of euphemisms; language that is sexy and fun to use; paradigms whose referent is weapons; imagery that domesticates and deflates the forces of mass destruction; imagery that reverses sentient and nonsentient matter, that conflates birth and death, destruction and creation — all these are part of what makes it possible to be radically removed from the reality of what one is talking about, and from the realities one is creating through the discourse.[18]

This language sets the framework of public discussion. It brings more than a new vocabulary with words like "collateral damage," "Scud," and "Patriot." It brings a mode of thinking, designed to break the connection between our actions and their consequences. The war system's voice speaks so loudly, argues Cohn, that "it will remain difficult for many other voices to be heard until that voice loses some of its power to define what we hear and how we name the world."[19] With the Gulf War we saw the ability of the state to amplify the voices of war through the mass media. This was possible because the media is, above all else, an instrument of the dominant culture, carrying its values and views of reality. The validity of the cultural premises challenged by "outsiders" is reasserted through all mainstream channels, from comic strips to the nightly news. All other perspectives are, by definition, biased.

The perspectives, language, myths, and priorities that flow through the lens of the dominant culture will never open our imaginations to new ways of thinking and acting. The voices of the war system define the boundaries of "mainstream culture," and they are primarily the voices of the government and the elite. John Conner, writing about TV shows on AIDS, has remarked, "Being taken seriously — never mind being treated sympathetically — is far more likely to happen if you're white or middle class or heterosexual, preferably all three."[20] The voices given emphasis in mainstream media are those that harmonize with the premises of the war system. For example, Peter Bruck cites a recent study by Fairness and Accuracy in Reporting (FAIR) of "Nightline," a program generally considered "progressive," showing that those who are critical of the cultural premises supporting the war system are rarely heard.

Nightline limits its range of guests overwhelmingly to white, male spokespeople of powerful institutions. Current or former government/military officials, professional 'experts' and corporate representatives make up 80% of Nightline quests. Public interest, labor and ethnic/racial leaders make up less than 6%. While no labor leader has appeared more than twice, Ted Koppel shook hands more than ten times with people like Henry Kissinger, Alexander Haig, Elliott

Abrams, Jerry Falwell or Lawrence Eagleburger. Not only are nine out of ten
guests male, men also speak longer than do women . . . .Nightline serves as an
electronic soap box from which white, male, elite, representatives of the status
quo can present their case, expound their political positions and legitimize their
actions.[21]

This "electronic soap box" gave up all pretense of "objectivity" during the Gulf
War. The war system explicitly "managed" the media. In her discussion of the
"Media's New War Role" in the *Christian Science Monitor*, Mary Mander observes
that war today is conducted in the presence of "civilian audiences" rather than
civilian populations:

Just as General Pershing was the first military officer in the West to realize that
modern warfare was, above all, a management affair, military commanders in the
Gulf demonstrated with remarkable unity of purpose and professional commitment an understanding of the media as an essential component of the successful
conduct of the War.[22]

Today the voices of the war system speak to us directly, overshadowing journalistic
convention. The "press" has ceased to play an interpretive role, let alone a critical
one. As Mander comments:

At televised press conferences, the military had direct access to the people — and
at the same time was able to undermine the credibility of journalistic interpreta-
tions. It was a stunning reversal of roles from Vietnam, where the press called
military credibility into question.[23]

When former U.S. Attorney General Ramsey Clark returned from Iraq with
video documentation of the devastation caused by U.S. bombings, all major
networks refused to air it, despite the fact that the video was the only uncensored
footage available from inside Baghdad. NBC executives said that they were not
"going to prostitute" themselves by showing coverage produced by people who
have a history of aligning themselves with "causes." This prompted columnist Marc
Gunther to write:

These are strong words, and revealing too. After all, NBC willingly let its
reporters work under strict Pentagon controls throughout the war. They trav-
eled with government escorts and reported the official, approved story of the
war. Now contrast that with NBC's fear of being associated with Clark and his
unpopular, anti-war views. That's risky. Worse, it's "prostitution." That's

network thinking for you. Transmitting government-approved news is objectivity. Transmitting a minority viewpoint is bias.[24]

It is hardly surprising that the voice of the war system drowns out the grounds for ethical discourse. The words coming out of the mouths of the generals in their daily briefings — about "surgical strikes," "collateral damage," and "the need to restore freedom" — become the framework for our thinking. The actual massacre of a hundred thousand Iraqi men, women and children is set aside by the celebration of "light" U.S. casualties. In the curious language and logic of the war system, Iraqis are responsible for their own deaths. General Neal justified the slaughter and suffering created by the U.S. bombing of Basra by saying, "It was a military town in the true sense of the word." Thus, in the turn of a phrase, an entire town is reduced to the status of a military target.[25]

The media is clearly an instrument of war, and public opinion is its target. Television is the weapon of choice. The Gulf War revealed the power of TV over all other media to shape and control public discourse. TV proved decisive for the dominant culture to manufacture consent and marginalize dissent. Images overpowered analysis, history, discussion, and dialogue. This was a war watched by more Americans than any other single event in our history. Ratings skyrocketed as millions were captivated by live reports from newscasters watching the bombs bursting in air and smart missiles going neatly down chimneys.

What was the effect of this instant, constant coverage? According to a University of Massachusetts study, the more people watched television, the less they actually knew about the war and the more they tended to support it. Heavy television viewers were more likely to support the war but were remarkably ignorant of key facts:

> Fully 23 percent of all viewers thought that Kuwait was a democracy. Only 31 percent knew that Israel is occupying land in the Middle East. Only 15 percent could identify the intifada as the Palestinian uprising in the Israeli-occupied territories. Even more surprising is that 65 percent of viewers thought the Bush Administration had warned Saddam Hussein before Aug. 2 that the U.S. would intervene with military force if he invaded Kuwait.[26]

The visual images of television, with their overpowering sense of completeness, provided the interpretive framework within which most Americans evaluated this war. Television, by its very nature, distorts the ability of viewers to make ethical judgments in a complex world. The lives of those of us in urban and suburban America are becoming increasingly characterized by "sensory deprivation" as our sense of ourselves and our world is mediated though the mass media and high-tech gadgets. Our experiences of "inner reality" and the "outer world" have become narrowed to fit the demands of communications technologies. The soundbite, the photo opportunity, the chosen images are all that matter. In this way the voices of the war system drown out all others.

The media rig our capacity to judge by invoking those sensibilities most likely to call for peace and then twisting them into justifications for war. The longing to stand for something decent since Vietnam, Watergate, and Iran-Contra led to the comparison of Hussein with Hitler. Our natural compassion for children was cynically played upon to demonize the Iraqis by showing a three-year-old Israeli girl hospitalized after the explosion of a Scud missile. She, not the charred bodies in Iraq, became the image of the "victims of war." Concern for human rights was exploited by the media as they gave graphic accounts of Iraqi torture while maintaining the image of Uncle Sam conducting a clean, sanitary war. Most striking about the American war system is not that it appeals to baseness. Rather, it appeals to the best in us — decency, compassion, fairness, and justice. As Lars-Erik Nelson said in his critique of Bush's repeated invocation of an Amnesty International report (which has since been retracted) that Iraqi soldiers had caused the death of Kuwaiti babies by removing them from hospital incubators: "[Americans] might not understand the need to fight for oil or restore the homeless Emir, but you can understand Iraqis murdering babies."[28]

The Media and Community

The voices of the war system resonate so loudly because the community ties and relationships that once held Americans together and enabled them to make ethical judgments and undertake collective action have weakened. People as isolated individuals feel powerless in the face of large, impersonal forces over which they have no control. The war system holds cultural power because the state has become the only home of the individual. With the disappearance of intermediate community structures, individuals are adrift, prey to the manipulation of images and symbols.

Gradually, the individual has been stripped of all ties to people and place, and now he or she confronts the state alone. The individual has been turned from citizen to subject, actor to victim, witness to spectator. Commenting on this transformation a lifetime before the Persian Gulf War, C. Wright Mills wrote:

> In the expanded world of mechanically vivified communication the individual becomes the spectator of everything but the human witness of nothing....The atrocities of our time are done by men as "functions" of social machinery — men possessed by an abstracted view that hides from them the human beings who are

their victims as well as their own humanity. They are inhuman acts because they are impersonal. They are not sadistic but merely businesslike; they are not aggressive but merely efficient; they are not emotional at all but technically clean-cut...[29]

The deterioration of our humanity is the result of changes in our social structure that go far beyond the media and other channels of communication. The loss of community is more than the loss of a nostalgic dream. It is the loss of the context that supplied meaning and balance to daily life, that provided the boundaries for discussion and debate, that connected our actions and their impacts in the world.

Certainly, the media play a role in furthering the policies of the state and have tremendous power to influence our understanding of reality. And certainly there are many ways to reform the media so that they can better report the complex realities of our society. But peacemaking also requires a much more fundamental change. It is too easy to scapegoat the media as though they were a single entity, totally under the control of government. As Edgar Allen Beem wrote about the Persian Gulf War:

The press, of course, took grief from all sides — the flag-wavers complaining that war coverage endangered national security and the safety of U.S. troops in the Gulf, the anti-war activists charging that the muzzled media was just doing play-by-play for the Pentagon and abandoning its responsibility to question authority.[30]

In the absence of community, the capacity of the media as an instrument of peacemaking, regardless of its content, is severely limited. In a recent column proclaiming "Not Our War, Not Our Soldiers," George Bradford argued:

[P]atriotism is an expression of the defeat of community and the triumph of the state. As authentic community is progressively eroded by anonymous economic and technological forces, the innate desire for community is harnessed by the mass media to reassemble millions of atomized individuals into a pseudo-community of passion for the state and its wars. The state and its spectacle now beckon with outstretched arms to provide the only shelter from a heartless, alienated existence. Home is now the state.[31]

Or as the *New York Times* put it more directly when explaining its support for the war, "People want something to believe in ....They want some part of their life to have meaning."[32]

To develop a public discourse reconnecting our actions with consequences, and to experience our humanity in relation to other human beings no matter how distant, we need to rebuild and re-create community. In Eastern Europe pressure "from below" initiated the most profound steps for global peace in this century: the end of the Cold War; the beginning of electoral democracy (with all its contradictions) in a half-dozen European nations; and genuine steps toward disarming the most militarized continent in the world. Writing in the *Nation*, Mary Kaldor notes:

> If we are to keep alive a peaceful vision of the post-cold war world, then what is important is to confront the cold war culture — to work for changes in attitudes, new forms of self-organization, the development of democratic relationships. One of the key concepts of the democratic movements was the rediscovery of civil society — the notion that change comes about through the development of autonomous citizens' groups, movements or initiatives that can articulate public discontent, organize social activities and negotiate with governments.[33]

People have been most able to stand for peace within those communities and networks where human bonds and public principle were alive and well. Fran Shor, a sociologist at Wayne State University, has commented:

> Where there were massive anti-war protests—San Francisco, Seattle, Minneapolis—there existed deep-rooted structures of cultures of resistance, from the gay/lesbian communities to extensive alternative institutions, such as various kinds of co-ops. Thus, if we are to challenge the "New World Order," we have to expand the communal basis of that resistance.[34]

The war system can only succeed if civic life and society fail. And it is here that we can see why the war system thrives in America. Americans may be triumphant about a victory halfway around the globe, but they are also unsettled about the costs of the war system: that they must equip their houses with alarm systems and bars; that they must fear their neighbors more than distant enemies; that they must drive on roads and bridges crumbling from neglect; that they face unemployment and sickness in a deteriorating economy; that they must drink water and breathe air that are increasingly poisoned. By addressing these problems squarely, we can begin to build a grassroots movement that holds the essence of a culture grounded in peace rather than war.

The pathways to peace cannot be found simply by resisting the war system; the war system is able to marginalize resistance whenever it is divorced from reconstruction of our social, economic, and political processes. As Fran Shor comments:

Expanding the communal basis of opposition to the "New World Order" requires more than a re-affirmation of the Great Refusal. Moreover, while vital reforms are certainly necessary in institutional and everyday life in the United States, radicals need to create the kind of public space and public discourse that promotes a fundamental reconstruction of society and a meaningful transfiguration of our lives. Thus, talk of economic conversion falls far short of the kind of social conversion that encompasses the changes required.[35]

Throughout the Persian Gulf War, the peace movement was marginalized because it did not address the disintegration taking place in American society. The anti-Vietnam movement, in contrast, was effective because it came out of the civil rights and black power movements — movements that were addressing the most urgent problems of American society at that time. Many of the young people who opposed the Vietnam War had marched in Selma, had struggled for Free Speech in Berkeley, and had done community organizing in Newark, New Jersey. Young people also took to the streets because the draft gave them a personal stake in the struggle. But the anti-Gulf war movement emerged in a vacuum. The peace movement had been virtually dead with the end of the Cold War. And even though African Americans were invited to speak at anti-war demonstrations, the movement essentially came from people who had not been engaged in collective struggle and who had no organic ties with the inner cities where most people of color and poor people live. Despite fairly broad support (half of the country wanted to rely on sanctions prior to the war), the anti-war movement lacked domestic roots.

Our initial task to create a new, more peaceful culture must be to draw the connections between war and domestic problems in a holistic way — and to begin rebuilding cities like Detroit. We must show how the war system depends upon our sacrificing urgent domestic needs for foreign adventures. We must help Americans understand that a culture that tolerates violence in the home can easily perpetuate destruction abroad, and that a culture that separates consequences from decision-making can easily commit mass murder.

THE KEY ROLE OF COMMUNITY

The paths for cultivating peace begin in very different places than those usually looked to by mainstream society. We should look to those around us who have refused to become part of the dominant culture, to those whose memories still hold images of ways of living that are life affirming, to those who have resisted accepting how things are. Those whose lives are least regarded — women, working people, poor people, African Americans, Native Americans, the elderly, lesbians, gay men, Third World peoples — all are engaged in struggles that offer hope for a vibrant future. And it is in these struggles that the fundamental assumptions of the war system are being challenged.

In Detroit we see the elements of this new culture taking shape all around us. Even though the city is often represented by the mass media with images of Devil's Night and abandoned houses, or in phrases like "the murder capital" that turn tragedy into snappy copy, those willing to look beneath the surface in Detroit can find a number of encouraging signs of creative activism.

The first important sign of hope grew from the pain of children killed by violence. In the mid-1980s these homicides reached epidemic proportions. People talked openly of black youth as an "endangered species." No one felt safe, and no one had any idea how to stop the madness. Then a small group of women came together under the leadership of Clementine Barfield, who had lost one of her own sons in a shooting. These mothers refused to see themselves as victims and transformed their grief into action. Patiently talking to each family that had lost a child to violence that year, they organized a city-wide memorial service. Over a thousand people came to stand and pray with the grieving families, to say that all of us were affected by these losses, to pledge an end to the violence. The organizers called themselves Save Our Sons and Daughters (SOSAD), and they have since become an insistent voice for positive change in Detroit. SOSAD struggles against the silence that has allowed violence to become normal. It reminds Detroiters that a secure future for our children begins with the courage to examine the values that lead our children to kill over expensive gym shoes and gold chains.

Accompanying random violence in Detroit has been the drug culture. Whole neighborhoods are being held prisoner by the crack house down the street. Afraid of being robbed or shot, people lock themselves in their homes. The much publicized "War on Drugs" is a joke. Police are as frightened as the average citizen of the well-armed dealers. After seeing many homes and families crumble under the lure of fast money, two neighborhoods began to fight back. In the neighborhood around Sharon Street, a predominantly white, working-class section of the city, block-club members began to publicly challenge crackhouse operators, first with signs on posts and trees telling them to get out, and then with street marches and pickets. Led by two women, the club realized that it wasn't enough to drive dealers out of their neighborhood, since they would only start all over again in another neighborhood. They put out a city-wide call to drive the crack dealers out of every neighborhood.

At the same time the REACH Community began organizing marches to demonstrate that people were not going to give up their homes and streets to drugs. Under the leadership of Dorothy Garner, an African-American woman who had moved from the South to Detroit in the 1950s, friends and neighbors marched every month. Coming together with other community groups, they formed We the

People Reclaim Our Streets (WE-Pros), a city-wide network of neighborhood groups. In weekly marches, WE-Pro members chant: "We love our neighborhood, pack up your crack and don't come back," or "Hey, Drug Dealer, better run and hide, 'cause people are uniting on the other side." These small bands of mostly older Detroiters are breaking the cycle of fear that has paralyzed so many people. With nothing more than pots and spoons and an occasional drum, they have ventured out week after week to nearly deserted streets challenging the drug dealers to join with them to rebuild the city.

These community efforts are part of a larger vision taking shape in Detroit, a vision that judges the health of the city by looking at the kind of life our children experience outside their front door, not by tallying the amount of money made through "downtown development." For more and more Detroiters, the city begins in each neighborhood and on each block. If these are strong and healthy, then so will be the city as a whole. The dominant culture, however, wants to build major projects with considerable tax breaks and public money — even if they wind up destroying neighborhoods. Detroit has had almost three decades of such megaprojects, from major office buildings, hotels, and auto plants, to the much-ballyhooed "People Mover." It is now clear to almost everyone that these schemes only drain the community and the taxpayer.

In the summer of 1990 Mayor Coleman Young announced his agreement to sell the Ford Auditorium, the only civic hall in the city, to Comerica Bank for $17 million, payable in 25 years at low interest. Comerica, for its part, would knock down the auditorium, accept $8 million in public money, and build a "World Class" bank building. After the deal was announced, City Council members who are rarely noticed were deluged with calls registering opposition. Public hearings were jammed with citizens from all walks of life. Young women and men who had graduated from high school in the auditorium, church groups who had held community fashion shows there to raise money for local projects, members of the symphony who had played there, architects, restaurant owners, mothers — all united their voices in opposition. "Civic Pride, not Corporate Greed" became their slogan. Opponents of the deal petitioned to have the fate of the auditorium decided by a city-wide referendum on the issue of re-zoning a "public center" for commercial development, and ultimately Detroiters voted "No." A local business columnist for the *Free Press*, John Gallagher, wrote, "It was vigorous public debate that turned the trick . . . .This placed this major development decision right where it belonged: on the public agenda, not the private one."

None of these groups opposing violence, drug dealers, or neighborhood destruction through commercial development can claim any great victories. Each has a long and difficult struggle ahead. But the people in these movements give new meaning to the word "citizenship." Moving from victim to actor, from fear to courage, from despair to vision, these citizens are part of a new movement. This is a movement in which town meetings where citizens talk and politicians listen are more important than press conferences; a movement in which trees are planted in memory of children who have died so that neighbors and family members can embrace life and hope, not death; a movement in which neighbors long isolated from one another by fear can march against the crack houses and inspire high school kids to hold their own marches. And while we know Detroit best, we also know that we are not unique. The outlines of these stories are familiar to most people who live in America's cities today.

Throughout the world citizens groups are taking direct action. In Eastern Europe, for example, these actions were a critical force for liberation. Activism, wherever and whenever it occurs, is the cornerstone of peacemaking. As Czechoslovakian President Vaclav Havel has observed, it is efforts by citizens that "make a real political force out of a phenomenon so ridiculed by the technicians of power — the phenomenon of the human conscience."

The best way to reverse the inclination of our culture toward violence is to engage citizens in the reconstruction of community life. Violence, whether wielded by individuals or by nations, is a natural response to powerlessness, frustration, and alienation. The reconstruction of communities restores power to citizens and enables them to break the cycle of violence. Reconstruction means shifting our touchstones for judgment away from global abstractions to the local problems of daily life. It means embracing new forms of political participation, so that we all can become citizens instead of clients and consumers. It implies implementing new structures of accountability so we can reconnect those who make decisions with those who bear the consequences. And it involves developing language and images that enable us to think and talk about peace, compassion, and justice.

NEW VOICES, NEW VISIONS

Carol Cohn has observed that the task for peacemakers is "to create compelling alternative visions of possible futures, to recognize and develop alternative conceptions of rationality, to create rich and imaginative alternative voices — diverse voices whose conversations with each other will invent those futures."[36] We must magnify the voices of citizens engaged in the creation and recreation of community life, the voices of those who have resisted dehumanization, division, and destruction, the voices of those who embrace nonviolence.

Among the most significant voices for reconstruction are those of women in whose lives the failure of the dominant culture is most painfully felt. In the face of gang violence and the shooting of their children, there are mothers, sisters, and grandmothers who are proudly walking the streets again and demanding a respect for life. On sacred lands, as the government tries to take mountains, forests, and seashores for mining and development, women are leading resistance movements. In communities where so many of our young people have little hope of productive lives, women are creating programs to recruit young people for community service and to help them learn about social responsibility. Rejecting the fragmentation and isolation that is so natural in our culture, eco-feminists are insisting upon a new understanding of the web of life and the connections that bind us to one another and to the earth. Women are leading the movements for disarmament, environmental protection, and international justice by revealing the connections between violence at home and violence abroad. They are finding ways to move beyond bureaucracy and ideology to person-to-person diplomacy and direct action. In countless ways women who have for so long been taught to take care of our children are beginning to take care of the problems facing future generations.

A new kind of talk is being generated by women and finding its way into our public spheres. It is the talk that says listening to one another's stories is essential for life, that relationships are more important than ideologies, that questions are more fruitful than answers, that it is no crime to make mistakes as long as we learn from them. This talk, ignored by the dominant culture and abhorred by the war system, is desperately needed. By taking the talk of women seriously, we can formulate new means of communication that will help all voices to be heard.

After centuries of efforts to devalue, suppress, and destroy the multitude of cultures on the planet, the war system can no longer sustain itself in the face of growing diversity. In the years ahead, the old, tired, white, male, heterosexual, self-absorbed, middle-class perspective may no longer be able to continue its dominance. America has always been a nation that embraced people from the cultures of the world, and in this last quarter century we have become a home to people whose eyes and hearts have been shaped by struggles in the Third World. These new Americans bring with them an understanding of the real costs of the war system. And they offer a rich assortment of languages, perceptions, and images that can help us create a more tolerant peace system.

Each day that we rely upon the old institutions and the old methods of thinking only exacerbates our problems. We now have an unprecedented opportunity to call upon the voices of all those struggling to reclaim their communities and to restore our relations to one another and to the earth. By creating a living democracy, rooted in the daily lives of all people, we can find hope — that people of very different origins, holding very different beliefs, can find ways to create harmony amidst diversity.

NOTES

1. Richard Joseph, "Injustice Taints the 'Just War'," *New York Times*, March 2, 1991, p. 17.

2. Edgar Allen Beam, "Even the Wars We Win Are Terrible Defeats for Humanity," *Maine Times*, March 8, 1991, p. 22.

3. Richard Joseph, *op. cit.*

4. "The Peace Team in the Desert," *Green Letter*, Spring 1991, p. 9.

5. Margarita Papandreou, "When I Become One of Them," *Ms.*, March/April 1991, pp. 12-13.

6. Cynthia Enloe, "Tie a Yellow Ribbon 'Round the New World Order," *Village Voice*, February 19, 1991, p. 37.

7. Vincent Harding, *There Is a River: The Black Struggle for Freedom in America* (New York: Vintage Books, 1983), pp. xxv-xxvi.

8. Tim Weiner, "U.S. Called the World's Most Violent Nation," *Detroit Free Press*, March 13, 1991, p. 6A.

9. James Ricci, "TV May Be the Best Weapon against Gunfire in the Streets," *Detroit Free Press*, March 24, 1991, p. 1H.

10. John E. Mack and Jeffrey Rubin, "Is This Any Way to Wage Peace?" *Los Angeles Times*, January 31, 1991, p. 7B.

11. Clementine Barfield, "Learn to Be a Peacekeeper," *Save Our Sons and Daughters Newsletter*, April 3, 1991, p. 1.

12. Anna Quindlen, "Regrets Only," *New York Times*, February 7, 1991. p. A19.

13. Cynthia Enloe, *op. cit.*

14. Elise Boulding, *Building a Global Civic Culture* (Syracuse: Syracuse University Press, 1990), p. 136.

15. Cynthia Enloe, *op. cit.*

16. George Lakoff, "Metaphor and War in the Persian Gulf," Part I, unpublished PeaceNet computer transmission, December 31, 1990, p. 2.

17. *Ibid.*

18. Carol Cohn, "Sex and Death and the Rational World of Defense Intellectuals," in Daniela Gioseffi, ed., *Women on War: Essential Voices for the Nuclear Age* (New York: Simon & Schuster, 1988), p. 97.

19. *Ibid.*, p. 99.

20. John J. O'Conner, "3 Shows About AIDS (Straight AIDS, That Is)," *New York Times*, April 11, 1991, p. B7.

21. FAIR, "Are You on the Nightline Guestlist? An Analysis of 40 Months of Nightline Programming." (New York: Fairness and Accuracy in Reporting, 1989).

22. Mary Mander, "Media's New War Role," *The Christian Science Monitor*, March 15, 1991, p. 19.

23. *Ibid.*

24. Marc Gunther, , "NBC Snubs Reporter's Exclusive War Footage," *Detroit Free Press*, March 13, 1991, p. 4E.

25. George Bradford, "These Are Not Our Troops; This Is Not Our Country," *Fifth Estate*, Spring 1991, p. 5.

26. Christopher Cook, "Uncensored Tape Shows Devastated Iraq," *Detroit Free Press*, March 13, 1991, pp. 1, 11A.

27. Elise Boulding, *op. cit.*, pp. 77-89.

28. Lars-Erik Nelson, "Bush's Outrage at the Invasion of Kuwait Was Built on a Lie," *Detroit Free Press*, May 1, 1991, p. 11A.

29. George Bradford, *op. cit.*, pp. 1-7, 26.

30. Edgar Allen Beem, *op. cit.*

31. George Bradford, *op. cit.*

32. Peter Applebome, "Sense of Pride Outweighs Fears of War," *New York Times*, February 24, 1991, Sec. 4, p. 1.

33. Mary Kaldor, "Taking the Democratic Way," *The Nation*, April 22, 1991, p. 518.

34. Fran Shor, "Kicking Old Habits: Challenging George Bush's 'New World Order'," Wayne State University Teach-In. (Unpublished speech), April 6, 1991.

35. *Ibid.*

36. Carol Cohn, *op. cit.*, p. 99.

EPILOGUE

W.H. Ferry

The allied doctrines of Progress, Technological Wizardry, and Bigger Is Better present numbing obstacles to would-be peace system architects. In opposition, there is a growing number willing to dig at these foundation stones of the war system. As usual, a poet puts the matter most clearly:

> The wealthiest man among us is the best.
> No grandeur now in nature or in book
> Delights us. Rapine, avarice, expense,
> this is Idolatry; and these we adore.
> Plain living and high thinking are no more;
> The homely beauty of the good old cause
> Is gone.

> Tennyson, England, 1802

Our nation's history, and destiny, are entwined in such impulses. Greed reigns. Nonetheless the question has to be asked, Is a peace system imaginable? The answer is Yes. The Exploratory Project on the Conditions of Peace, and others, indicate where the planning has to begin. Can and will a peace system be constructed? The lumber is there, the main outlines fairly apparent, the appropriate technology waiting to be summoned. Most of the major components are set forth in the book you are holding.

But the answer is also No. At this moment there is little public will or appetite for a peace system. Popular imagination does not embrace the possibilities of another way of composing our national life. Debate about such a transformation has barely begun; one of the principal purposes of this volume is to furnish some of the argument for those favoring a peace system. The general lines of this position are clear. Advocates argue for the primacy of human welfare, for benign technologies, for defense of embattled air, water, soil, and other natural resources, for community as against anonymity, for cooperation, for nonviolent methods of dealing with conflict.

Peace isn't easy to think about. Peace is placid, unexciting, conciliatory. Peace is easygoing, soft, shadowy, undemanding, benevolent, pale.

War is easy to think about: imperious, concrete, enterprising, muscular, patriotic, high-handed, heroic.

Such words underpin a war system that is the central economic and cultural fact of our lives. It is plainly the source of jobs, profits, and mighty technical achievements. The war system enters out lives through so many doors that its presence, to say nothing of its dominance, is virtually unnoticed. The country is bound together by the system's omnivorous requirements. Simply put, the war system and the American way of life are one and the same phenomenon.

Megacorporations and financial institutions are the essential elements of the war system. It has outposts in every state and continent and envoys throughout the world. So incalculable a force irks even Presidents occasionally. Congress chafes at the excess of the system but rebels against it only idly and sporadically. Its wildest absurdities are tolerated — witness, for example, the system's insistence on the Strategic Defense Initiative, SDI.

Any possible justification for this multibillion-dollar enterprise disappeared with the end of the Cold War, but it will apparently be with us indefinitely. To describe the process that authorizes SDI is to relate the war system in operation. Despite its inconceivable cost, SDI has many adherents. It is emblematic of public fascination with high technology, with the instruments and armaments of modern war that nurture the war system. The system reaches the sea bottom, the depths of space, and the remotest of islands. Its ultimate promise is that, should the nation's interest deem it so, it will blow up much of the world.

One shudders at such millennial prospects and asks Why? The system answers with the Technological Imperative, "If it can be done it must be done." This underlies the perception that the foreign policy of this country — indeed of all major powers — is largely made in its laboratories. Accelerating technology is the decisive element, assuring steadily increasing competence in the arts of slaughter. This is invariably described as progress. There are always new techniques to be discovered. Some years ago Herman Kahn, a departed saint of the war system's pantheon, declared, with approval, that somewhere scientists were trying to figure out a way of blowing up the entire world.

But there remain grounds for hope, if not optimism, that a peace system will emerge. The case for a continuation of a war system — essentially the doctrine of Power first, War if need be — is fading. The public is beginning to understand that this may readily turn out to be a recipe for national suicide. The case for a peace system — the view that people and persuasion come first — may turn out to have a great deal more public acceptance than now appears. It is not utopian but sensible to wish and work for such an outcome.

Fiat lux.

APPENDIX A

Essays Commissioned by the Citizen's Peace Treaty Project:

1. Lourdes Beneria, "*Gender and the Global Economy.*"

2. Peter Bruck, "*The Role of the Mass Media and the Promoting of Peace.*"

3. Shiela Collins, "*The Culture of Western Bureaucratic Capitalism: Contributions to the War System and Implications for the Peace System.*"

4. Jonathan Dean, "*The Vienna Force Reduction Talks: Some Unresolved Issues.*"

5. Lloyd Dumas, "*Economics and Alternative Security: Toward a Peacekeeping International Economy.*"

6. Riane Eisler, "*From Domination to Partnership: The Foundations for Global Peace.*"

7. Howard Frederick, "*Communication, Peace, and International Law.*"

8. Sean Gervasi and Jennifer Smith, "*A View of the Living Economy.*"

9. Michael T. Klare, "*The United States, the Soviet Union, and the International Arms Trade.*"

10. Sharachchandra M. Lele, "*A Framework for Sustainability and Its Application in Visualizing a Peace Society.*"

11. Vincent Mosco, "*Communication and Information Technology for War and Peace.*"

12. Colleen Roach, "*Information and Culture in War and Peace.*"

13. Juliet Schor, "*On the Definition of the Boundaries of an Economic System.*"

14. Richard E. Sclove, "*Democracy, Technology, and International Security: Exploring the Linkages.*"

15. Mark Sommer, "*Rescuing the Reform Process: A Marshall Plan for a Reunited Europe.*"

APPENDIX B

Other Publications and Papers Commissioned by EXPRO

Publications

Robert A. Irwin, *Building a Peace System* (Washington, DC: EXPRO Press, 1988).

Mark Sommer, *Beyond the Bomb* (Washington, DC: EXPRO Press, 1985).

Papers

EXPRO Paper #1: "*Steps Toward a Peaceful World.*"

EXPRO Paper #2: Kirkpatrick Sale, "*Centrifugal Force.*"

EXPRO Paper #3: Robert Irwin, "*Coercion, Force, and Nonviolent Sanctions.*"

EXPRO Paper #4: Kermit Johnson, "*What Is Peace? Judeo-Christian Insights.*"

EXPRO Paper #5: George Rathjens, "*First Thought on Problems Facing EXPRO.*"

EXPRO Paper #6: Mark Sommer, "*Ten Strategies in Search of a Movement.*"

EXPRO Paper #7: Carolyn Stephenson, "*A Research Agenda.*"

EXPRO Paper #8: Robert Johansen, "*Toward National Security without Nuclear Deterrence.*"